The Death *of* Meriwether Lewis

To Don,
Let's solve the
mystery!
Kira Gale
1-23-2010

Meriwether Lewis—
Of courage undaunted,
possessing a firmness
& perseverance of purpose
which nothing but impossibilities
could divert from its direction.

Thomas Jefferson

The Death *of* Meriwether Lewis

A Historic Crime Scene Investigation

James E. Starrs & Kira Gale

River Junction Press LLC, Omaha NE
2009

River Junction Press LLC
Omaha, Nebraska 68104
www.death of meriwetherlewis.com

First Edition   First Printing

Library of Congress Cataloging in Publication Data

Starrs, James E.
  The death of Meriwether Lewis : a historic crime scene investigation /
James E. Starrs & Kira Gale.

  p. : ill., maps ; cm.

  Includes bibliographical references and index.
  ISBN: 978-0-9649315-4-1

1. Lewis, Meriwether, 1774-1809--Death and burial. 2. Meriwether Lewis
National Monument (Tenn.) 3. Historic sites--Tennessee. 4. Explorers-
-West (U.S.)--Biography. 5. Death--Causes--Case studies. 6. Lewis and
Clark Expedition (1804-1806) I. Gale, Kira. II. Title.

F592.7.L42 S82 2009
917.804/2

Contents

Part Three: The Case for Murder

FOREWORD

by

Thomas C. McSwain, Jr.

Colonel (Retired), USAF

Great, Great, Great, Great Nephew of Meriwether Lewis

President, Locust Hill Graveyard Foundation

What really happened on the night of October 10th and the early morning of October 11th, 1809 at Grinder's Stand along the Natchez Trace? Did Meriwether Lewis die by his own hand or that of an assassin? If by an assassin, for what reason was he killed? Was he, as some have asserted, suffering from alcohol and drug abuse, syphilis, or malaria? Was he the victim of a conspiracy led by General James Wilkinson or some other nefarious contemporary character? What is the truth about these matters and why does it matter now as we approach the 200th anniversary of his death?

Finding the truth matters because Meriwether Lewis was one of our fledgling Nation's greatest early explorers and heroes. He was an army officer; the private secretary to President Thomas Jefferson; leader along with William Clark of the Lewis and Clark Expedition; and after the expedition, the presidentially appointed governor of the expansive Louisiana Territory. As John D. W. Guice indicated in the preface to *By his Own hand? The Mysterious Death of Meriwether Lewis*, finding the truth matters to scholars and historians who are concerned about the integrity of their profession and it matters to Americans who expect accuracy in our nation's history.

Finding the truth also matters to our family who are the collateral descendants of Meriwether Lewis. Although President Jefferson did not question reports of suicide as the cause of Uncle Meriwether's death, our progenitor, Lucy Marks, mother of Meriwether Lewis, purportedly did not believe that Uncle Meriwether died by suicide. This view has been held by many in our family down through the generations. So, as in the words of Voltaire, we believe that,

> "We owe respect to the living;
> to the dead we owe only truth."

We may never know the answers to all of the questions surrounding the life and death of Meriwether Lewis that have been the subject of seemingly ceaseless debates for almost 200 years. However, exhumation and scientific investigation of his remains using forensic and other scientific procedures now available should provide the truth and answers to many of the questions about his life and the manner of his death. In addition, from our family's viewpoint, such an exhumation would enable us to provide Uncle Meriwether with a Christian burial, which the circumstances of his sudden and unexpected death on the Natchez Trace deprived him.

A coroner's jury which is presented and discussed in this book was convened during 1996 into the matter of the death of Meriwether Lewis in Lewis County, Tennessee, the present day jurisdiction in which Meriwether Lewis died. The jury issued a unanimous verdict on June 4, 1996 stating that exhumation and scientific examination of the remains of Meriwether Lewis from his burial site at Meriwether Lewis Park, Natchez Trace Parkway, which is managed by the National Park Service is necessary for closure in this matter. The Coroner of Lewis County accepted this verdict, ruling it so to be.

The Lewis Family through its Locust Hill Graveyard Foundation comprised of friends and collateral descendants of Meriwether Lewis and Professor James E. Starrs along with the help of attorneys at Crowell and Moring, an international law firm in Washington, DC, have sought for eleven years, beginning with an application to the National Park Service on June 18, 1997, for the opportunity to exhume the remains for scientific study, under the Archaeological Resources Protection Act (ARPA). In response to our long standing request, The Assistant Secretary of the Interior of the United States, The

Honorable Lyle Laverty, performed an independent review, and on January 11, 2008 determined that our proposed exhumation of the remains for this purpose is appropriate and in the public interest. (See letter, Appendix B.)

Having gained this approval and as 2008 nears its end, we have been diligently engaged in working through the permit process under ARPA and shepherding an Environmental Assessment required by the National Environmental Policy Act. With luck the necessary permit required to enable this scientific investigation into the life and death of Meriwether Lewis including exhumation of his remains for forensic analysis will be in hand by publication of this book in 2009, paving the way for this book's sequel on its results a year or so thereafter.

With firm resolve and undaunted determination our family will continue to press for completion of this scientific investigation into the life and death of Meriwether Lewis and re-interment with a Christian burial at Meriwether Lewis Park, Natchez Trace Parkway near Hohenwald in Lewis County, Tennessee.

PREFACE &
ACKNOWLEDGEMENTS

by

Kira Gale

This book is divided into three parts. Part One is the official transcript of a Coroner's Inquest into the death of Meriwether Lewis held in Lewis County, Tennessee in 1996. Part Two contains documents pertaining to his death and illustrations, and Part Three is an account of the last three years of his life after the expedition, and my own theories as to who murdered him and why.

The 200 year old mystery of Meriwether Lewis's death has intrigued both me and my co-author, Jim Starrs, for many years. In his Introduction to the Coroner's Inquest, Professor Starrs explains his role in organizing the hearings. When I learned of the existence of a transcript, I contacted Professor Starrs and suggested we do a book together.

I am the author of *Lewis and Clark Road Trips: Exploring the Trail Across America,* which features over 800 destinations along the Lewis and Clark Trail. Research for the guide book, published in 2006, gave me a broad general understanding of the expedition, but I knew I needed to do a great deal more research for this book.

Vardis Fisher's book, *Suicide or Murder? The Strange Death of Meriwether Lewis,* had convinced me that the stories of his death by suicide just didn't add up—what I needed to do was to study the numerous conspiracies of the time period, particularly the Burr-Wilkinson Conspiracy to invade Mexico, which was happening when the Lewis and Clark Expedition was returning to St. Louis in 1806.

This conspiracy has intrigued historians ever since. I also need to study national, international and territorial politics, as

Meriwether Lewis became the second Governor of Louisiana Territory a few months after he returned, replacing General James Wilkinson, who was the first governor of the territory and co-conspirator with Aaron Burr. Since Meriwether Lewis's first assignment as governor of the territory was to root out suspected "Burrites" I knew I had to start there. After a year of research, I found what I think is a plausible motive for his assassination, which I discuss in "The Case for Murder."

In 1996 the Coroner's Inquest Jury called for an exhumation of his remains to determine the cause of death. Lewis family members submitted a request for exhumation to the National Park Service in January, 2009, and as this book goes to press the permit process is underway.

Acknowledgements

The first acknowledgements must go to the witnesses who traveled to Hohenwald, Tennessee, paying their own way, to testify at the Coroner's Inquest on June 3-4, 1996. Thanks also go to the members of the local community who participated in the Inquest and the Lewis family descendants. They made this book possible. Special thanks go to Jerry Richards for continuing to stay with this project and donating his services to examine the new documentary evidence.

Members of the Mouth of the Platte Lewis and Clark Study Group, which meets weekly at the Western Historic Trails Center in Council Bluffs, Iowa, were the original inspiration for the book. Evelyn Orr discovered a copy of the Coroner's Inquest transcript at the Lewis and Clark Trail Heritage Foundation Library & Archives in Great Falls, Montana. Dr. Jay Buckley of Brigham Young University deserves special thanks for his help in this matter. Dr. Carl Camp and Don Shippey contributed their services as copy editors. From beginning to end, my husband, Henry, has helped with this project.

Interlibrary Loan at the University of Nebraska-Omaha Library has been of great aid in tracking down materials. The

Grace Lewis Miller Archives at the Jefferson National Expansion Memorial in St Louis are the source of many important facts and interpretations. Materials were also obtained from the Jonathan Williams Collection, Lilly Library, University of Indiana; the Meriwether Lewis Memorial Papers at the Tennessee State Library and Archives; the Missouri History Museum in St. Louis; the Dawson Phelps Collection at the University of Southern Mississippi; and the James Wilkinson Collections at the Newberry Library and the Chicago History Museum. Many other collections supplied material, but major photocopy was supplied by these institutions.

And last—but not least—are the resources of Google, Wikipedia, Amazon.com, and ABEbooks.com. It is an extraordinary time to be a researcher. I encourage you to explore history for yourself by searching for whatever interests you using the Google search function. Many old history books, letters, genealogical records and congressional records have been posted on the internet; and Wikipedia has become the universal history resource. ABEbooks offers second hand, out of print books from book sellers around the world. The more you learn, the more interesting it becomes.

Join us for the bicentennial commemoration of Meriwether Lewis's death. The Lewis and Clark Trail Heritage Foundation will hold its annual meeting October 3-7, 2009 at Olive Branch, Mississippi (suburban Memphis, Tennessee) with a visit to the Meriwether Lewis National Monument and Gravesite at Hohenwald, Tennessee. The re-enactors who toured the country in 2003-2006 will be there. It promises to be very interesting meeting and you are invited to attend. The group welcomes new comers.

Visit www.deathofmeriwetherlewis.com and join the mailing list to receive my monthly email newsletter, *Proceeding On*, to stay in touch and keep up with the latest Lewis and Clark news. You may contact me at kira@lewisandclarktravel.com.

Part One

The Coroner's Inquest

Note:
The reader is advised that this testimony was taken in less than perfect acoustical circumstances. The witnesses have reviewed their testimony and made a few corrections for clarity, but the testimony remains as it was first presented, as the "spoken word" and as the court reporter recorded it.

An Introduction to an Inquest
on the death of Meriwether Lewis

by
James E. Starrs,
Professor Emeritus
The George Washington University

"Behind the corpse in the reservoir, behind the ghost on the links,
Behind the lady who dances and the man who madly drinks,
Under the look of fatigue, the attack of migraine and the sigh
There is always another story, there is more than meets the eye."

W.H. Auden, "At Last the Secret is Out"

"Down, down, down into the darkness of the grave
Gently they go, the beautiful, the tender, the kind;
Quietly they go, the intelligent, the witty, the brave.
I know. But I do not approve. And I am not resigned."

Edna St. Vincent Millay, "Dirge without Music"

The dead can have no voice, I have sometimes learned to my regret, unless they are fairly given the chance to speak. I tremble
at the thought and the knowledge that the dead can be denied this
"last right" by the cold, calculated or curious attitudes of those who
control the decision to grant such a last rite.

Some deaths are so electrified as legend that the truth may be
known, if at all, only with the modern methods of science, and
where the legend outruns the truth, then, as in Jesse James, an exhumation may well be in order so that the truth will surpass and
even dispel the legend. Meriwether Lewis' death is a prime example
of the necessity to right the imbalance between far-fetched legend
and inestimable truth.

My involvement in the issues surrounding the death of Meriwether Lewis occurred quite serendipitously in the early 1990s
when my wife, Barbara, and I were returning home from a Florida
family wedding. We had been traveling by car on the Natchez Trace
Parkway from Tupelo, Mississippi northward toward Nashville. As

my wife's urgent insistence we stopped many, many times at the sites of historical markers along the roadway, she being a dedicated and quite learned amateur historian.

One of our intermittent stops was at the "Pioneer Cemetery" where a rustic cabin stood uncontrolled and open to all passers-by and there were surely few of those in this somber, lonely woodland location. A short walk away but in sight of the cabin was the monument. As we stood looking up at this graffiti-desecrated monument my wife remarked quite non-committally that this was a death I should investigate with the instruments of science. As we sat leaning our backs against the base of the monument with Jefferson's words to Meriwether Lewis inscribed above us

> "His courage was undaunted: His firmness and perseverance yielded to nothing but impossibilities ..."

Barbara gave me a lesson in basic facts underlying the controversial death of Meriwether Lewis. Her informed description added to my sum total of the man as I knew him from the abbreviated *Journals of Lewis and Clark* by Bernard de Voto (1953). I still have that much paged paper edition which Barbara read to our children in the late 1960s as we journeyed via a VW bus across the country following as best we could on roads near the land and water route of the Lewis and Clark expedition, known as the Corps of Discovery. At that time like so many Americans I knew of the expedition but not what happened afterwards, certainly not of the deaths of its leaders, Lewis and Clark. My wife's detailing the facts of Meriwether Lewis' death set me on my own journey of exploration seeking the answers to the tragedy and the dilemma of Meriwether Lewis' death. That journey has continued to this day and which I am resigned to continue unflaggingly in the future.

An examination of the circumstances and documents associated with Lewis' death provide clear evidence that no one has proof beyond a reasonable doubt as to the actual manner of his death, whether it resulted from suicide or homicide. The only evidence that remains to clarify this issue are the bones of Meriwether Lewis, buried some 70 miles south of Nashville, Tennessee, a strong outfielder's throw from the Natchez Trace. A broken shaft monument (symbolizing a life cut off in its prime) marks the place where his remains rest.

It is correct to say that my research turned me into a Meriwether Lewis devotee. It was a warming experience to investigate the death of a great man. Here was no Jesse James, no Albert DeSalvo, and certainly no Alfred Packer. Now for the first time in my career as an exhumer I had a notable and historic person of immense stature whose death, come what may from my work, demanded my unfettered attention. He had become my investigative passion, little realizing the hurdles that would be planted even higher in my path towards the true facts of his death.

Apart from a visit to his Tennessee grave and my seeking to determine the soil constituents there to estimate the condition of his remains, the first order of my business was to obtain consents to an exhumation, for all sides and both far and wide. Locating living descendants of Meriwether Lewis was simply a matter of visiting the Hohenwald, Tennessee public library where the names of prominent descendants were recorded. Unlike the stone-faced attitude at the Fall River Historical Society, the librarian in Hohenwald, Pattie Choate, was delighted to provide me with names and addresses. The name that she singled out as the one I should contact first was William M. Anderson, M.D. of Williamsburg, Virginia.

Upon returning to my office from my Tennessee trip I immediately telephoned Dr. Anderson who immediately and enthusiastically agreed to join forces with me to accomplish the objectives of an exhumation. From Dr. Anderson I was led to Jane Sale Henley, also a descendant of Jane Lewis Anderson, Meriwether Lewis's sister. Jane later became the President of the very influential Lewis & Clark Trail Heritage Foundation, which courtesy of its former president, Arlen Large, passed a resolution in support of an exhumation of Meriwether Lewis.

At this point the consents from the Lewis descendants were proceeding smoothly without any objections being received. Ultimately and to date I have received signed formal consents to an exhumation from 170 persons claiming to be descendants of Meriwether Lewis, all in various collateral lines of descent, there being no known direct descendants of Meriwether Lewis. More official consents were received from the Lewis County Board of Commissioners due to the gentle lobbying efforts of a Hohenwald attorney, Tony Turnbow. The Lewis County Historical Society also passed a resolution signed by, of all names, its president, Philip Griner. And Terry Bunch, the Lewis County Executive weighed in with a strong letter in support for me and the exhumation I proposed. All of these consents were unequivocal and unconditional and as firm as firm could be.

Still not satisfied that my groundwork would convince the National Park Service to grant permission to exhume, I sought out the Lewis County District Attorney General Joseph Baugh who was readily available and very game to assist me. Our discussions led us to agree that Joe Baugh would, in his official capacity representing the law enforcement needs of Lewis County, direct the holding of a Coroner's Inquest into the death of Meriwether Lewis in 1809, since there was no record of a previous inquest and the death could reasonably be deemed to be suspicious.

In 1809, in the state of Tennessee there was no appointed or elected medical examiner, either locally or with state-wide jurisdiction. As a result an inquest in 1996 for a death in 1809 would not appear to be out of order, even though exceptional in its delayed timing. Even though the office and functions of the coroner in the twenty states where an inquest is statutorily authorized are diverse, still the basic format follows that of the common law. In Tennessee an inquest is permitted only upon the filing of an affidavit by "two (2) or more reliable persons" alleging "good reason to believe that (a person) died by unlawful violence at the hands of some other person." (T.C.A. 38-5-101). This prerequisite eliminates the opportunity to hold an inquest in the case of an out-and-out suicide. However, the affidavit submitted by me and three others, namely Professor Walter F. Rowe, Ph.D, Nancy K. Raber, and Patrick D. Zickler, filed March 25, 1996 deliberately left unstated the possibility of Lewis' death having been a suicide (felo de se).

The inquest, in Hohenwald, the Lewis County seat, was held for two days, on June 3rd and 4th, 1996 with Richard Tate, the local Coroner and co-owner of McDonald's Funeral Home in Hohenwald, presiding over the receipt of testimony and the deliberations of eight jurors from the community, including one who was a medical doctor. After the National Park Service declined my invitation to take part in the proceedings (although their Tupelo representative Gary Mason was in attendance as a spectator), I obtained the consent of twelve experts in a variety of disciplines to appear and testify.

Among them was Dr. William Bass, a forensic anthropologist of considerable national and international recognition, as well as three historians, Arlen Large, Dr. John Guice, and Ruth Frick, one geophysicist Dr. George Stephens, one psychologist Dr. Thomas Streed, two pathologists Drs. Jerry Francisco and Martin Fackler, a firearms expert Lucien Haag (who demonstrated for the jury the firing of a 1799 .69 caliber North & Cheney flintlock), an epidemiologist Dr. Reimert Ravenholt and two document examiners Dr. Duayne Dillon and Gerald Richards who spoke to the issue of what Meriwether Lewis' handwriting could tell us of his state of mind when the documents were drafted; if they were drafted or signed by him as well as the authenticity of the Major Russell "statement" portraying Lewis' death as a suicide by knives as well as by firearms.

The testimony of all of the experts was presented through the questioning of Joe Baugh and Paul Phillips, another of Tennessee's elected District Attorney Generals, and through the queries of the experts from the members of the Coroner's Jury. It was a most impressive array of talent and a most telling presentation by all and sundry. The result, as announced by Coroner Richard Tate was a unanimous verdict signifying that "there is very little tangible evidence for this jury to base a credible ruling as to the matter of suicide." The sworn testimony of the experts appearing as witnesses is reproduced in this volume. As a result it was stated "because of the importance of the person in question to the history of Lewis County, we feel exhumation is necessary for closure."

BEFORE THE CORONER AND JURY
OF LEWIS COUNTY AT HOHENWALD, TENNESSEE

CORONER'S INQUEST:
DEATH OF MERIWETHER LEWIS

TRANSCRIPT OF THE PROCEEDINGS
TAKEN ON JUNE 3-4, 1996

APPEARANCES

CORONER
OF LEWIS COUNTY: Mr. Richard Tate

CORONER'S JURY:

Ms. Carolyn Hensley

Mr. David Brewer

Ms. Sandra Dearth

Ms. Kathy Carter

Mr. Robert Burklow

Dr. R. W. Bouldin

Mr. Vincent Flynn

Mr. Tony Turnbow

FOR THE STATE:

Mr. Joseph Baugh
District Attorney General
Franklin, Tennessee

Mr. William Paul Phillips
District Attorney General
Huntsville, Tennessee

INDEX

DAY ONE: JUNE 3, 1996

TESTIMONY OF GERALD B. (JERRY) RICHARDS
Direct Examination by General Baugh

TESTIMONY OF MARTIN FACKLER
Direct Examination by General Baugh

TESTIMONY OF LUCIEN HAAG
Examination by Mr. Turnbow

DAY TWO: JUNE 4, 1996

TESTIMONY OF DUAYNE DILLON, D. CRIM.
Examination by General Baugh
Examination by Mr. Coroner
Examination by Mr. Turnbow
Examination by Mr. Coroner

TESTIMONY OF REIMERT T. RAVENHOLT, M. D.
Examination by General Baugh
Examination by Mr. Burklow
Examination by Mr. Turnbow
Examination by Mr. Bouldin
Examination by Mr. Flynn
Testimony by Dr. Ravenholt
Examination by General Baugh

TESTIMONY OF WILLIAM M. BASS III, M. D.
Examination by General Phillips
Examination by Mr. Coroner
Examination by Mr. Turnbow

EXHIBITS

CORONER'S INQUEST:
THE DEATH OF MERIWETHER LEWIS

Day One: June 3, 1996

GENERAL BAUGH:

As far as questions, Mr. Tate, the coroner, has suggested and I agree that at the end of each witness's testimony, he will receive written questions, so if you have a question that you want to give to the witness, then you will please write that question out, pass it to Sheriff Kilpatrick or one of the officers and they will pass it up to Mr. Tate and he'll read those over and ask what questions he thinks are appropriate. He'll also take questions from the members of the coroner's jury on anything that they might have, questions of the witnesses.

We'll probably take a break around 10:30 and then break for noon also. However long the breaks are, he can make it any length he wants, if you have left the room to do whatever you need to do, get a coca-cola or talk to somebody, please be back on time because this building as you can tell it has the acoustics of a National Guard Armory, strangely enough, and it can be disquieting or disturbing to have people coming in and out and to have noise going on during the time of the break.

As you can tell also these lights are going to light this fairly well. We would ask if you are going to make flash pictures or use other lights, other than these constant lights that are here, that you do that at the breaks, don't do it during the testimony or questioning of any of the witnesses involved.

This gentleman is going to be introduced to you, Mr. Paul Phillips. He's the District Attorney from the Eighth Judicial District. He's going to carry on part of the questioning. If you are here and you wish to present something to the coroner's jury, we would request that you make that known to one of us and we will talk to you and then discuss what you want to present with the coroner and he will make the ultimate decision about whether that is presented in the form of live testimony.

This is an official proceeding and you may present by means of sworn affidavit, with exhibits any kind of testimony you wish. The coroner's jury is an inquisitional function and it deals with the elements of the panel. We simply ask that you get that done today or tomorrow. We anticipate that we'll go to approximately 5:00 today and furthermore, I anticipate we'll go until approximately noon or over tomorrow, but probably not past afternoon in tomorrow.

Anybody have any questions?

Thank you very much. We really appreciate the interest that we've had in this proceeding and we believe that it will be a very interesting and enlightening procedure. Just a second.

MR. CORONER:

This inquiry will come to order. All those having evidence or interest in these proceedings please draw near.

Thank you for being here today. My name is Richard Tate; I'm the coroner of Lewis County. If you are a visitor in our town, we would like to take just a second and welcome you to Hohenwald and we hope that you will find this an enjoyable and pleasant visit. I would like to take a few minutes in the beginning of the proceeding to explain the procedures and the guidelines that we'll be following.

First of all, because of the high level of the press coverage this issue has received, it's been brought to my attention that there is some speculation as to whether these proceedings are in fact legal and in order and of a serious nature. As for the legality I will allow our able counsel to address that issue. As for the seriousness, I assure you this office takes this issue before us as important and serious, the death of Meriwether Lewis is a part of our history. History is a part of our past that we must pass on to our children and to our grandchildren. We feel very—every effort should be made to make sure that history is as complete and as correct as is humanly possible.

Having realized there are many new scientific means of forensic examination, it's my pleasure to convene these proceedings in answer to a request presented by affidavit to the District Attorney General's office by Professor James E. Starrs of George Washington University.

I would like to introduce to you two gentlemen who will be

conducting the questioning today. They are both Tennessee District Attorneys General, first is General Joe Baugh from Franklin and he is the District Attorney General for the district that includes Lewis County. Second is General Paul Phillips of Oneida, Tennessee, who serves as district attorney for five counties in east Tennessee. I would like General Baugh at this time to address the legality of these proceedings and also, if you would, please outline to the press, if you would, the guidelines that we'll be following and finally I will ask you to brief this jury as to their responsibilities.

GENERAL BAUGH:

Thank you, Mr. Tate. This coroner's inquest is convened pursuant to Tennessee Code Annotated Section 38-5-101 and following. Although a coroner's jury is somewhat of an unusual occurrence in the investigation of a death, it is a recognized procedure in the State of Tennessee for making an investigation. The coroner convenes a jury of seven people, which he has in this case, plus alternate, and those people are sworn to take an oath by the coroner to inquire who the person was and when, where and by what means such person came to such person's death and to render a true verdict thereon according to the evidence and arising from all of the circumstances. The verdict will be produced in—ultimately in writing, signed by all of the members of the coroner's jury.

This case is truly a mystery of 187 years duration. We have assembled here today some of the most preeminent historians and scientists to present evidence to the coroner's jury.

Members of the jury, as you know in the State of Tennessee, you are not required to believe or disbelieve any witness but you are the judges of the credibility of all witnesses. You are—you must weigh their testimony as you would weigh the testimony of any trial witness. However, science has changed and may be helpful to us in being able to focus the facts of history and make a determination. One of the witnesses pointed out to me before this hearing that on this day in 1805 the Lewis and Clark expedition had reached a fork in the road, actually it was a fork in the river, and members of the expedition wanted to take the north fork of the Missouri River. Lewis and Clark wanted to take the south fork of the river. Ultimately, of course, they explored both forks but we in the sense today are making that same kind of decision.

As we celebrate our 200th anniversary as a state, we have throughout history used the judicial system to resolve the problems and difficulties and disputes and sometimes yes mysteries that we have had from our history and yes, today is another step in that process.

MR. CORONER:
At this time, I would like to swear in the jury for this inquest. I'd ask all jurors to stand with me. Raise your right hand. Do you, each of you, swear or affirm that you will inquire into the question of who the person was who is the subject of this inquest and when, where, and by what means such person came to death and render a true verdict thereon according to the evidence offered so help you God. (All respond in the affirmative.)

MR. CORONER:
Are there any opening statements? Call your first witness.

GENERAL BAUGH:
Professor Starrs before you get suited up, I want you to raise your right hand, face Mr. Tate, and he will swear you in, sir.

JAMES E. STARRS

having been first duly affirmed was examined and testified as follows:

DIRECT EXAMINATION

BY GENERAL BAUGH:
Q. Would you state your name and spell your last name for purpose of the record, please, sir?
A. My name is James E. Starrs, S-T-A, double R, S.
Q. What is your occupation?
A. I am a professor of forensic science and a professor of law at the George Washington University.

GENERAL BAUGH: Can everybody hear him? Maybe just a little bit louder, if you could.

BY MR. BAUGH:
Q. Where do you live, Professor Starrs?
A. I live in northern Virginia.
Q. How long have you been with George Washington?
A. I have been with George Washington University as a professor for 33 years.
Q. What relation do you have to the affidavit that was filed in this case?
A. I am one of the persons who swore to and signed the affidavit filed for the convening of this coroner's inquest.
Q. What sort of area of expertise do you bring to this inquest?
A. I bring a combined interest and expertise in legal matters as well in scientific matters for the purposes of resolving disputes

concerning issues where forensic science can play a role.

Q. What are your qualifications as far as forensic science is concerned?

A. I have been a professor of forensic science at George Washington University for the past 25 years. Indeed, I am one of the—I am the sole surviving father of the Department of Forensic Sciences at George Washington University. I am a member of the American Academy of Forensic Sciences. Indeed, I recently was given the honor of being named a distinguished fellow for the American Academy of Forensic Sciences. In addition, I'm on the Editorial Board of the *Journal of Forensic Sciences* and have been for some years. I have been on the board of the Governing Board of the American Academy of Forensic Sciences. I have published one of the leading texts coauthored in the field of forensic sciences, *Scientific Evidence in Civil and Criminal Cases*. I have coauthored for some 20 years a quarterly review entitled *Scientific Sleuthing Review*.

Q. Have you ever testified as an expert witness before?

A. I have testified as an expert witness in both federal cases and in state civil cases.

Q. In your particular area of expertise?

A. I have testified specifically on a number of matters that we are concerned with here. For example, issue of identification by way of DNA analysis in the John Wilkes Booth matter in Baltimore recently on the question of legitimacy of an exhumation in order to resolve a historical dispute.

Q. Did you bring copies of your curriculum vitae with you?

A. I did.

Q. Would you make those available to the jury by way of submission after your testimony?

A. Yes, I will.

Q. Thank you very much. Does your experience include experience as a forensic scientist on the question of death as a result of suicide, homicide, or accident?

A. One of the particular specialties in which I've worked over the years is on precisely that question, the question of whether a death resulted from suicide, accident, or homicide or indeed by natural causes.

Q. Under that kind of subcategory—do you have particular experience with death by firearms?

A. I have particularly looked into a number of cases, both of a current nature as well as a historic nature on the question of firearms casualties.

Q. Are you familiar with the accounts of the death of Meriwether Lewis?

A. I am very familiar and have been for some years with the conflicting, confusing, and contradictory accounts of persons who were secondhand witnesses and not actual eye witnesses to the death of Meriwether Lewis.

Q. Why were you interested in that?

A. I felt that Dee Brown—a famous author, a western author who in 1990 was asked by *American Heritage Magazine* to stipulate what was the most important issue in American history that he felt needed to be resolved—and I agreed with him when he said the death of Meriwether Lewis. Among ten of the leading historians in the country, who were asked their particular focal interest, he pointed out the death of Meriwether Lewis.

Q. What about the opinions about homicide, suicide, etcetera presented in the past by historians?

A. I have prepared a brief summary for the coroner and the coroner's jury of the various conflicting accounts. Those being either homicide, suicide or uncertainty and I'll be glad to distribute that for the purposes of indicating the historical research that I have done as to what historians have had to say on the matter.

Q. Now there are people that have done biographies of Lewis in the past. Have you been in contact with any of them?

A. Yes, indeed, I contacted Richard Dillon who did I think

the first comprehensive biography of Meriwether Lewis, and asked if he would be kind enough to attend these proceedings. He indicated by reason of ill health he could not do so, but he sent me a letter in which he indicated in that letter that he maintained the same view that he had held when he did his biography some years ago and that was that the death of Meriwether Lewis was a result, as he put it, of murder in the book and as he did in his letter as well. I'm prepared to submit a copy of that letter today.

Q. Very well. We'll accept it after your testimony, if that's satisfactory or you can read portions of it if you would like, I don't know which you would rather do?

A. All right. It's a very short letter, if I could find it.

Q. Yeah, go ahead.

GENERAL BAUGH: Mr. Coroner, I think we're probably feeling the heat of this room but, I understand if we turn the air conditioning on, we won't hear anything. We may have to just suffer through that.

THE WITNESS: The short middle paragraph of his letter to me dated May 6th, 1996 is and I quote,

> (Reading:) It is my personal belief after much research that he—I take it meaning Meriwether Lewis--was a victim of murder and was not a suicide as is sometimes believed.
> (End of reading.)

That is a statement from Richard Dillon, biographer of Meriwether Lewis.

Q. The accounts of Lewis' death are conflicting, there's no question about that. What—do you have an opinion about the death?

A. My opinion as a scientist starts with a hypothesis. I would hypothesize that there is a strong case that can be made in behalf of this being a homicide.

Q. How did you arrive that opinion?

A. I viewed the individual letters and statements rendered, the historic accounts of which I have copies of the three major ones. First, the letter of Major Neely to Thomas Jefferson; second, the letter of Alexander Wilson, to a fellow ornithologist; and third, statements some years later of Major Gilbert Russell, a statement which was not forwarded to anyone that we know of, simply given in the form of an affidavit. Those three particular items seem to be the preeminent items in the historic account.

Q. But what sort of impact do you think that forensic science would have on these historical questions, or how could it contribute to resolving the death of Lewis?

A. I can give a graphic description of how forensic science in fact has in a very recent case put to rest a historical mystery of 120 years duration, and I refer to the case of Jesse James and the exhumation that I conducted on the remains of Jesse James just in July 1995.

The question that was raised in that case among others was whether when shot from the rear the bullet did exit. There were pictures of Jesse James in death showing distinct laceration over the left eye. The question and indeed there has been a hole in the wall in the house still preserved in which he lived and was killed, so it was said, in St. Joseph, Missouri. The question then was did the bullet exit or not and we found—if I may show?

Q. Please. I understand you brought a representative of an artifact of James —

A. Yes, I did. I bought a cast of a reconstructed skull of Jesse James and we have the top of the skull and all after having been painstaking reconstructed. We have the frontal portion with see the facial portion having been decayed away. According to the historians, many historians' accounts, the bullet had exited over the left eye. As anyone can see there is no exit wound over the left eye. The left eye being in this area, upper orbit and there is no exit wound of any kind.

Q. Would you make that available to members of the coroner's jury so they can get an idea, although, I understand we're not going to go into depth about Mr. James' murder today.

A. This signifies my view the telling an important contribution that forensic science can make in resolving a historical dispute in the case where a person was in the ground badly decayed for 120 or more years and nevertheless we came up with this among other findings.

Q. There's some tales of an inquest at the time or there are some historical accounts, there are many differing historical accounts, what could science do to make—to resolve that suspicion and mystery and make things less trouble?

A. A number of the individual scientists who are here today can speak to individual items relevant to their particular specialty, so the firearms experts can speak to the question of the nature of a bullet that might be found, the nature of a wadding that might be found, and the important ingredients in resolving disputes from those items; and physical anthropologists can speak to what the bones will tell us overall; a variety of other aspects that each one of the individual scientists can explain. We have document examiners also to explain as to whether or not the handwriting of Meriwether Lewis indicated any significant items of mental decline, defect, or derangement. These are items that are dealt with by forensic scientists on a regular basis.

Q. Well what kind of handguns do you think that Lewis had when he arrived here in Lewis County?

A. In the research that I've conducted on that question of what handguns Meriwether Lewis might have had, there are numerous gaps, but I started with the expedition and the acquisition of handguns for that particular expedition across the country. I think it's safe to say, start with the basic premise that if Meriwether Lewis killed himself he did not do it with a rifle. I start with that basic premise that it had to be a handgun.

Q. He had a rifle with him, didn't he?

A. He had a rifle with him, described as a rifle gun. I suppose that means a rifle long gun.

Q. Yes.

A. He also had pistols with him as described by Major Russell in his letter to President Jefferson. The pistols however are not further defined. However, we do know that he had two horseman's pistols of a very large caliber variety; of course, all handguns in those days were of large caliber.

Q. How large a caliber?

A. We're talking—if I may show the coroner's jury.

Q. Yes, please?

A. A particular item.

Q. You've checked and made sure it's not loaded I presume?

A. Indeed, I'll go further than that; I will point it at the floor or myself.

Q. Oh, no, don't do that. Unfortunately, I've had experience with people shooting unloaded guns.

A. This is a replica, a working model.

Q. If you don't mind, could you come down in front of them and sort of show it to them?

A. Yes. This is a replica working model, actually operated, of a 1799 North and Cheney. The 1799 North and Cheney, otherwise known as a horseman's pistol was a pistol that the government bought in 1803 for the purposes of—or 1802— for the purposes of providing whatever needed weapons there would be to persons who are using government issued weapons and ammunition. There were 500 of these made. This weapon, if it were an actual weapon, would be the single most valuable handgun in the United States today, the entire history of the United States, it is so rare to be found today.

Q. Do you propose to have one of the firearms examiners and experts fire that weapon here?

A. We propose to have this flintlock in the adjoining room, the firing range, today to demonstrate if this was the gun used, and it is the single most likely gun in my view that might have been used, what would happen if simulated human flesh had been struck by this bullet.

Q. And we're going to have a simulated human?

A. We're going to have a demonstration of that later today.

Q. Great. Apparently from history there is a site here in Lewis County that is said to contain the skeletal remains of Meriwether Lewis; is it not?

A. I'm sorry.

Q. Apparently from history there's a site here in Lewis County that is said to contain the skeletal remains of Meriwether Lewis?

A. Yes, indeed, if I may show that site on some slides that I have here.

Q. Great.

A. For the purposes of demonstrating the chronology of the site on 1848 to the present.

Q. You have been to the site?

A. I've been to the site a number of times. First let me start with the overhead here.

(Slide presentation).

This is the front piece of the report to the governor, message to the governor for the—covering the period 1845 to 1857. It specifically refers to the report of the Lewis monumental committee in—which was initiated in 1848 and it refers to the monument and its design and its height and I would particularly draw your attention to the fact that there was an effort made in 1848 to examine the skeletal remains so that the grave for identification purposes was reopened and the upper portion of the skeleton examined and witnesses were called, certificates taken to be assured that we have death and the site of the death of Meriwether Lewis.

We know therefore from this report that in 1848 that Meriwether Lewis was not dust; that we had skeletal remains that were available for the purposes of identification. You also see all of the descriptive features concerning the monument

itself at that time. Then pictorially show the monument itself.
(Off the record.)

BY GENERAL BAUGH:

Q. You are ready.

A. This is a photograph of the Lewis grave as it was the earliest
photograph I was able to discover at the monument and the
grave back in the—at the courtesy of the National Public
Library back in 1920, early 1920s. This is the monument at or
about the time of your Governor Peay.

Q. Peay?

A. Back in 1924 just at the time when the National Park Service
took jurisdiction over that monument. I point out to you there's
a line that I've drawn across the monument horizontally. That
line is drawn there for purposes of showing that all below that
line at the present time is underground, so that the monument
that you see today is this upper portion, all of the rest of it that
you see here is under the ground. In 1933 the monument was
visited by Dr. Anderson standing here and in 1933 you see the
cannonballs around the periphery of the monument.

Dr. Anderson on the birthday of Meriwether Lewis August
18, 1933 had that photograph taken.

Q. Dr. Anderson is a relative of —

A. Relative of Meriwether Lewis.

Q. And I believe he is here today; is that correct?

A. Dr. Anderson's—one of Dr. Anderson's descendants is here
today. Nephew. (See photo on page 275.)

Q. Glad to have you.

A. This is the monument as you see it today and we have around
the monument four feet of backfill. Those four feet of backfill
was put, in according to my best understanding of the records,
by the Civilian Conservation Corps in—between 1933 and
1935.

There were adjoining the monument at that time many
monuments, grave headstones of many of the pioneers of

the area. We have up in the corner here Meriwether Lewis' monument and all these other notations or 107 other grave sites at that location. This is a description by the National Park Service itself.

What happened to those other graves and those other headstones? Those other graves and headstones according to the reports I received from living persons who were alive at the time informed me that those headstones were removed by a bulldozer and you see them here today, many of them here today as they have been for the past 60 years or so against the side of the maintenance shed on the premises of the Meriwether Lewis monument.

Q. What effect would the condition of the monument have on the remains of Lewis?

A. The monument in fact acts as an umbrella so that the monument would be an umbrella protecting anything below it from intrusions of water, intrusions of organic material that would leak from above into the monument area. In addition, as in the case of Indian mounds we have four feet of mounded backfill around it providing further protection at least since 1933.

Q. What is this taphonomic effect business?

A. Well archeologists and anthropologists use fancy terms to define the effects of various environmental and other factors on human remains when buried. The term used is taphonomic effects. What we're talking about here is the soil mineralogy, soil acidity, the incline, the location, how high, in this case we're talking about 900 or more feet, the highest possible location in the area where there would be plenty of run off. It is perfectly poised taphonomically to provide for reasonable protection for human remains.

Q. And do you have someone that is going to or is there going to be someone who testifies about these effects?

A. Dr. Stephens and I did a mound penetrating radar at the site again on the birthday in 1992 of Meriwether Lewis—

on August 18, 1992—and he will report on that and other geological factors we took into account at that time.

Professor Starrs taking a reading at the monument

Q. Have you had any experience before this in revisiting historical controversies, other than Jesse James you told us about?

A. It's been something of forte of my mine for the past 15 years to try to put forensic science to the use of resolving historical mysteries where the question is whether a person died by one manner or another. So that the death of the five prospective victims of Alfred Packer some 120 years prior to my exhumation of their remains in the high hills of San Juan Mountains in Colorado was conducted.

Q. Is that the one they had the purported cannibalism?

A. In that case we had reported supported significant cannibalism to the remains. In that case we found remains that after 120 years were perfectly in condition for scientific analysis. We could actually see the cut marks on the bones even before we removed them from the grave.

In addition I exhumed the remains of alleged assassin of Huey Long; Dr. Weiss in Louisiana and we found significant evidence of items that had been missed, over looked, or in dispute historically.

Thirdly, I did an exhumation of Dr. Olsen who died as a

result of a failed CIA LSD experiment going 13 stories to his death at a hotel in New York. Once again, found evidence that had been overlooked, missed or misconstrued over the years.

And then finally, last year in the case of Jesse James not only did we identify the remains as those of Jesse James to the exclusion as far as science can go of anyone else, but we proved that he had one bullet, we proved that the bullet did not exit and we proved for the purposes of historical recollections that he was buried face down in a most unusual finding I don't think that we find on usual occurrence.

Q. Do you believe that in your experience that the various forensic sciences or science—areas of science you have been talking about, can shed light on a controversy such as the Lewis case?

A. I have no doubt of that. These scientists and the scientific tools they can put to bear on this could shed considerable light. Give you an example of one such item. From the recent, most recent biography of Meriwether Lewis, we have Stephen Ambrose, the author on page 177 of his book describing the marksmanship of Meriwether Lewis. And then defining it he says,

> (Reading:) If the target, I quote, was within
> a hundred yards and bigger than a mouse he
> usually got it. (End of Reading.)

Now here's a man who according to his latest biographer couldn't miss anything larger than a mouse in a hundred yards, he nevertheless couldn't kill himself by shooting himself at close range with a high powered and high caliber weapon twice, once in the head and once in the chest. There is something wrong with these two possibilities.

Q. Excuse me, but haven't there been times in historical cases where you have actually testified against exhuming bodies?

A. Yes, indeed. I am to some extent on the question of exhumations a purist, or to put it differently I respect the rights of the dead and the relatives of the dead and I do not think exhumation should be conducted frivolously or unnecessarily or without regard to the rights of other persons who may be buried in the area and therefore, I testified against the exhumation of John Wilkes Booth so called in Baltimore. And in part on that basis I'm sure—of my testimony and that of others, historians and so on—that exhumation was denied just a year or so ago.

I'm a great believer in the fact that one must have all of his cards in line' scientifically speaking and historically speaking before one goes forward to disturb the dead of anyone, historical figure or otherwise.

Q. Why wouldn't you—why did you have that opinion in the Booth case?

A. In the case of John Wilkes Booth, the issue was whether or not he had survived the shooting at Garrett's Farm in Virginia after the killing of Abraham Lincoln; and whether he had then surfaced in Granbury, Texas, along with Jesse James, so called in Granbury, Texas.

Q. And Elvis Presley?

A. It's kind of a tourist industry in Granbury, Texas and the question therefore was whether or not John Wilkes Booth, in fact, was buried and had been shot at Garrett's farm. The major problem that I had was that we didn't have the scientific tools available. There was no opportunity to do DNA analysis. There was no opportunity to do anything but facial superimposition and that is still in its infancy scientifically speaking and therefore, I felt that was not suitable.

In addition, there were six other unidentified graves in the area that we would have to look for John Wilkes Booth. There would be five other people who would have to be disturbed, I'm sorry, six other people that would have to be disturbed if you have my Irish luck and didn't hit the right grave until you had gone through six others. Therefore, I felt that it was not justified particularly since there was the considerable percolation of water in the site from —

Q. That would affect the remains?

A. And the remains would altogether likely to be in poor condition.

Q. Mr. Starrs what would you—if you were allowed to take the remains out of its location, what would you do with them, where would they go?

A. The remains would in first instance be x-rayed, radiographically x-rayed at the site before moving them away. We would not want anything to be lost by reason of moving the remains. The second step we would move them to a suitable laboratory for analysis and of course, we'd want to take them to a Tennessee laboratory and I would propose Dr. Bass could speak to the question of the availability of his laboratory at the University of Tennessee in Knoxville for that purpose and of course, for Dr. Bass could conduct the microscopic and other analyses on the bones.

Q. Have you solicited the opinion of people with experience and knowledge about this case about what they think about it think about—

A. I have solicited a number of opinions from persons of prominence and note both in scientific fields and historical fields on the question, one on the death of Meriwether Lewis; two, the value of an exhumation. I am prepared to submit along with the Richard Dillon letter an endorsement of this proposal for exhumation from the Lewis and Clark Trail Heritage Foundation; from the Lewis County itself, an endorsement from the Lewis County Historical Society, a more detailed and exact scientific appraisal and endorsement of Dr. S.Sone, then of the Navy University of Armed Services at AFIP, Dr. Besant-Matthews, private pathologist from Texas; the coroner Joshua Perper from Pittsburgh, Pennsylvania also specifying their particular detailed endorsement and approvals of a proposal to go forward.

Q. Professor Starrs, what I would like you to do is, this lady here, Mrs. Polk, transcribing this, I would like you to submit those to her to have those marked as collective exhibits to your testimony and then she'll submit them to Mr. Tate if that is all right with you Mr. Tate.

MR. CORONER: That will be fine. (*Exhibit #1-Letters were marked.*)

BY GENERAL BAUGH:

Q. I think we're getting close to the question and answer period so if anybody has any —

EXAMINATION

BY CORONER TATE:

Q. I have just a couple if things I would like to ask you, Professor Starrs. This first question may be kind of rhetorical, may be something you've already answered, maybe I just missed. What proof do you offer in the testimony that you've just given concerning what gun, or why you think this particular gun was used in the death of Meriwether Lewis?

A. I have not gone into the particular details with respect to this gun. There were only very few high caliber weapons but they were all high caliber at that time. So for example, I have a picture on a slide of a 58 caliber Harper's Ferry, a 69 caliber carrying a 68 caliber ball North and Cheney. They were all high caliber. They would all have the same results if fired into a human body, tissue, bone or otherwise because of the nature of their high caliber and they're all flintlocks and they're all black powder at that time.

I can not precisely say this is the weapon or one of the two weapons that he would have had at the time, but we do know this that when Mrs. Grinder reported according to Major Neelly that she heard two pistols there is no way she could know, absent from seeing, that Meriwether Lewis or anyone else was firing two pistols, it could just as well have been one pistol reloaded and fired the second time. My research into the federal archives also reveals that there is no record of Lewis having returned the horseman's pistols requisitioned to him for the Corps of Discovery.

That's the kind of thing that a knowledgeable firearm's expert can bring to bear on a case of this kind: these inconsistencies in the historical record.

Q. Also concerning the exhumation of the remains in 1848, do you have any kind of indication as to what was the extent of the examination of those remains at that time?

A. Unfortunately a very close and detailed review of all of the records both the archives of Tennessee as well as the public library historical society comes up with no further information than this report that I showed you on the overhead transparency.

Q. What was available at that time as far as scientific ways of examining the remains, was there very much?

A. Forensic anthropology, which of course is the key stone of the examination of skeletal remains, as a well formulated discipline, didn't come into existence until Dr. Bass and a few, a very few of his fellows, came on the scene in the early 1970s and made their mark on the science of forensic anthropology by establishing a subsection within the American Academy of Forensic Sciences. Consequently, 160 or more years before that, there literally was not an organized profession of forensic anthropologists; and, in addition, there is no indication from the local or Maury County records that anyone with anthropological training was called to give was called to give any scientific evidence at that time.

Q. What was the purpose for that exhumation?

A. The purpose at that time one can only presume was to identify the location of the remains so that the monument would be properly placed at that site where the remains were located. If there was no interest in locating the monument on the remains, there would have been no need to expose the grave and to identify the remains, they could simply have put it any place in that pioneer cemetery.

Q. Okay. In your testimony you've given us a lot of information concerning an exhumation of the remains of Meriwether Lewis. My understanding is that is not under the authority of this coroner's inquest—why would you give us this information, what would you hope to obtain from giving that information to this jury?

A. My purpose is to give the coroner's jury, and Lewis County through the coroner's jury an opportunity to have its say on the manner of the death of Meriwether Lewis and if it so feels, what should be done to clarify the matter of the death of Meriwether Lewis. Any finding in that regard would be advisory, or persuasive and certainly not compelling because Meriwether Lewis is buried in federal land, a national park, and therefore, it would be an advisory opinion as to what the best wishes of Lewis County through its coroner's jury might be.

MR. CORONER: Any questions from any of the other jury members?

EXAMINATION

BY MR. TURNBOW:

Q. A few. After viewing the record of 1848, are you satisfied that they found the remains of Meriwether Lewis?

A. I am satisfied to a limited extent that in 1848 the remains were those of Meriwether Lewis, but obviously, I'm not going to—as a scientist—live or die on that; so if an exhumation were conducted, one of the first items of business would be to identify the remains by way of a signpost that Dr. Bass will testify about later on, as to what we can find from the skeletal remains. My particular forte, I am canvassing the question of whether we, have living relatives today who have the same mitochondrial DNA that could be found in those bones so we can do for Meriwether Lewis what I did for that scoundrel Jesse James and identify the remains within the narrowest range of scientific probability as being those of Meriwether Lewis.

Since the Coroner's Inquest, Professor Starrs reports he has located direct, mitochondrially linked descendants of Meriwether Lewis's sister, Jane, who have the same mitochondrial DNA (mtDNA) as Meriwether Lewis. Two qualified molecular biologists have independently tested this descendant's mtDNA making it ready for immediate comparison to the mtDNA from the remains found at the Lewis Monument to insure their identification as those of Meriwether Lewis.

Q. If you were able to locate the remains of Meriwether Lewis what would those remains tell you that might relate to whether he committed suicide or murdered?

A. Well it doesn't take anyone with very great scientific knowledge to know that if we find an indication of an entrance wound someplace in the back of Meriwether Lewis, that it is highly unlikely to have been a suicide. If we find that there is a 58 caliber ball and a 69 caliber ball, two different weapons having been used, there's something wrong.

So that if we find, for example, there is no evidence at all of black powder, the residues of black powder on well preserved remains where they should be for a close in shooting, then there is a question as to whether or not it was suicide or not. But these are items that will be testified more specifically and with more scientific acumen by other scientists speaking after me.

MR. CORONER: Any others?

EXAMINATION

BY DR. BOULDIN:
Q. Dr. Starrs, going back to before Meriwether arrived on the Trace, do you have any indication or any record of what took place at Fort Pickering?

GENERAL BAUGH: His question was, was there any indication about what happened at Fort Pickering.

THE WITNESS: The only indication that I have are the recitals made by Major Russell and other military persons who were on or about Fort Pickering but I would propose that Dr. Guice and other historians could better speak to that question if I may defer to them, if that would be okay.

GENERAL BAUGH: Anything else? Anyone?
(No response.)

GENERAL BAUGH: Our next witness is Arlen Large. Thank you. Professor Starrs.

(WITNESS EXCUSED.)

GENERAL BAUGH: Mr. Large, if you would raise your right hand, Mr. Tate is going to swear you in please.

ARLEN J. LARGE

having been first duly sworn was examined and testified as follows:

DIRECT EXAMINATION

BY GENERAL BAUGH:

Q. Would you state your name for purpose of the records and spell your first and last name, please?

A. Arlen J. Large, A-R-L-E-N, L-A-R-G-E.

GENERAL BAUGH: Can everyone hear him? You might need to speak up just a little bit louder if you would.

BY GENERAL BAUGH:

Q. Where do you live, sir?

A. In Washington, D.C.

Q. What is your occupation?

A. I am a retired newspaper reporter

Q. Who did you report for?

A. *Wall Street Journal* for 30 years

Q. You were with the *Wall Street Journal* for 30 years; is that correct?

A. Yes.

Q. What interest do you have in Meriwether Lewis?

A. A broader interest actually in western exploration. The Lewis and Clark Expedition probably was the most important of those explorations. The Lewis and Clark Trail Heritage Foundation has about 1,500 members, people who are similarly interested in western exploration in the Lewis and Clark Expedition.

Q. Did you ever hold any position with the Lewis and Clark Trail Heritage Foundation?

A. I'm past president. I was president in 1984.

Q. Have you written any articles about western exploration, and specifically the Lewis and Clark Expedition?

A. The Foundation publishes a quarterly magazine and I have written something like 30 articles for them.

Q. How has—how have historians treated the Lewis and Clark Expedition and specifically—well Meriwether Lewis specifically his death?

A. In a great variety of ways. There are historians who are absolutely sure that Lewis went crazy, was constantly drinking at the end of his life, and killed himself. There are other historians who take great offense at the idea that a national hero could do such a thing and believed that he instead was murdered.

Q. Well, isn't the controversy over Meriwether Lewis really just ancient history?

A. It should be I think. But as Dr. Starrs mentioned, the very first full length biography of Meriwether Lewis was written 30 years ago. There's only been one other, it was published this year. The first one the author said murder. The most recent one the author said suicide.

Q. Why hasn't the argument gone away?

A. Because I think many of these authors want to have the last word. For example, Olin Wheeler writing in 1904, in 1904 said that the time has come to clear Lewis of this great stain on his reputation and —and absolve him from the sin of suicide.

Q. Do you have a personal opinion about whether it was suicide or homicide or accidental?

A. Yes, I think it was suicide.

Q. Why do you think that?

A. That is based on conjecture, on—on supposition partly on the actions of William Clark who was a close friend of governor of the upper Louisiana territory. Clark believed immediately that Lewis had killed himself and that was based on recent personal contact. Both of them had jobs in Saint Louis. They'd been talking back and forth to each other prior to the time that they both left for Washington, and partly on the immediate supposition of Thomas Jefferson that Lewis had killed himself, but remember Jefferson and Lewis had not been together for two years prior to the Governor's death.

Q. What makes you think Jefferson thought he killed himself?

A. Jefferson wrote in 1813 a short biography of Lewis in which he pointed out that the Lewis family had been subject to fits of depression in various of its branches and he claimed that he saw this in Lewis a little bit while Lewis was working for him as his private secretary in the White House prior to the expedition, and that Jefferson said this depression symptom returned after that. Also Jefferson had heard from Lewis' servant, Pernier, Pernier's account of the death of Lewis. Pernier was at the site although he may not have actually seen the shooting.

Q. Was there anybody that actually saw the shooting that you are aware of from history?

A. If it was murder then the murderer was the only surviving eyewitness. If it was suicide there were no eyewitnesses surviving.

Q. Have you read the various versions and public journals about Lewis and Clark and accounts of the assertions of the people that were around Lewis at the time of his death?

A. Yes, I think Major Russell has the most volume—he wrote the most about what he observed of Lewis when Lewis was at Fort Pickering on the Mississippi River.

Q. What period of time before Lewis came here to Lewis County had Russell seen him and how?

A. I think a couple of weeks prior to that time.

Q. Where did Russell first see him?

A. In Memphis at Fort Pickering.

Q. How long a period of time did Russell have to see him, do you know that?

A. It was about ten days I think.

Q. What about Major Neelly?

A. Major Neelly if he had not meet Lewis before, there's no indication that he did, came to Fort Pickering on some Indian agent business apparently.

Q. Was Nee

ly an Indian agent?

A. Yes, he was for the Chickasaw tribe.

Q. Where is Fort Pickering located by the way?

A. At the present site of Memphis.

Q. It's in Memphis?

A. Yes, that's the general location.

Q. Did any of these men accompany Lewis here to Lewis County?

A. Major Neelly did.

Q. Was he with him at the time he was shot?

A. He was not. He had stayed behind on the trail to try to find a couple of horses that had strayed away. Lewis came on by himself followed rather quickly by two servants, Lewis' own servant and apparently Neelly's slave.

Q. So is there anything in these journals that indicates to you that Lewis had a tendency to be suicidal.

A. Major Russell wrote a report, a statement it was called, saying that when Lewis came down from St. Louis on a boat on the Mississippi River that the crew of that boat when they arrived at Fort Pickering had told him, Major Russell that Lewis twice had tried to kill himself. This is one statement. As far as I know it is not corroborated by anybody. I mean, it was the only report on the scene.

Q. Have you—in reading these journals have you seen indications that Lewis may have been suffering from some physical disease, such as malaria, neurosyphilis, something otherwise that could have affected his disposition other than perhaps depression?

A. The answer to that, you wouldn't believe, it's very controversial and there are some malaria people who say Lewis was debilitated physically and showed all these symptoms because he had malaria. There's another theory —

Q. He had stopped at New Madrid, hadn't he?

A. Yes, he did.

Q. On the way down the river to recuperate?

A. He wrote a letter to William Clark, which has not been found, nobody has ever seen it which Clark characterized that letter, you could almost—I think Clark interpreted it almost as a suicide letter because he said to his brother Jonathan, this is William Clark writing to his older brother right after learning of Lewis' death and Clark said I think he killed himself and my reason for thinking it possible is found in the letter I received from him at your house and then later he wrote to Jonathan, saying, please send that letter along, I have need for it. Nobody has ever seen that letter; nobody knows what was it in. But Clark apparently interpreted it as something —

Q. You're talking about—does the letter between William Clark and his brother Jonathan Clark, does that letter exist?

A. Yes, it does.

Q. Who has that letter?

A. The Filson Club in Louisville, Kentucky.

Q. Did Jonathan live in Louisville?

A. Yes, sir.

Q. Now the letter that you don't know or no one knows about is a letter supposedly written by Lewis in New Madrid to Clark in Louisville?

A. William Clark. Lewis knew that Clark was en route to the east, that letter intercepted William Clark in Louisville while he was staying with his brother Jonathan.

Q. Why was Clark going east?

A. Clark also had some business to conduct with the government. He did not feel himself, I don't think, in any kind of financial difficulty with the War Department over government bills that perhaps were improperly done. Lewis thought he had to defend himself against that, but I think Clark wanted to do other kinds of government business, and he had relatives in Virginia and probably had to stop off and see them.

Q. Well, so what, if this is suicide why exhume him?

A. As I tried to indicate at the beginning, the Foundation takes an interest in the whole expedition from beginning to end, from the planning phases in 1803. It's one of the most documented events in American history. There are volumes and volumes of handwritten manuscripts describing all of the planning leading up to the expedition, events during the expedition itself, and historians really are in luxury in being able to read through all this documented stuff. Documentation for the death of the leader of that expedition three years later is much skimpier and it has been chewed over, it has been woven in and out by anybody with a theory. The documents have led to a dead end.

As far as the death of Meriwether Lewis is concerned if there is physical evidence that could add to the knowledge that the documents don't say, then I think it is worth while exhuming the body. Let me give an example of the kind of evidence that is needed. Now here is Dawson Phelps writing—

Q. Who?

A. Dawson Phelps.

Q. Dr. Phelps?

A. A historian for the Natchez Trace Parkway writing 40 years ago,

> (Reading:) In the absence of direct and pertinent contemporary evidence to the contrary—which not a scintilla exists—the verdict of suicide must stand. (End of Reading.)

Phelps was a big suicide man. People focused on the last little part about the verdict will stand, but overlooked I think because it's hard for just exactly what is being discussed here. Direct and pertinent contemporary evidence if that can be found in Lewis' grave, I'm for it.

Q. This is going to be my last question so you might prepare for any questions you have for Mr. Large. Was there something indicative about William Clark's reaction when he found out, he was in Kentucky, was he not, was Clark in Kentucky when he found out about Lewis' death?

A. Yes.

Q. Was there something about Clark's reaction that would buttress your opinion about suicide?

A. It is what he didn't do later on. If he had had the slightest inkling that Lewis had been murdered by some kind of assassin or robber, and remember that Clark was the head of the militia, he was general of the militia of the Upper Louisiana Territory, Clark was governor of the Upper Louisiana Territory (sic).

Q. You mean Lewis was?

A. Yes, Lewis was governor of the Upper Louisiana Territory. Clark could have claimed all kind of jurisdiction to lead his militia into Tennessee to catch the murderer. Clark never throughout the rest of his life gave the slightest indication that there was a murderer to be caught.

GENERAL BAUGH: Mr. Tate, that's all of the questions I have.

EXAMINATION

BY MR. CORONER:

Q. Mr. Large, if your opinion is that Meriwether Lewis committed suicide and realizing that is your opinion based on history, can you give me a brief line up of the events that you would think contribute to you having that opinion from history records?

A. Well, I think Lewis was in or thought he was in difficulty with the government over the contested bills. There are people I think other than Russell, I think Jefferson believed it very quickly that Lewis had developed a drinking problem. He showed no signs of it really on the expedition. The documents for the expedition show no signs of Lewis having problems with drinking. But after the expedition and after Lewis began to run into difficulties, political difficulties in St. Louis, and governor of the territory then he got busier. A significant reason I think is for Lewis being extremely depressed and riddled with guilt was his failure to produce the narrative book, the description of the expedition that he had promised Jefferson from the outset. He was three years late. Jefferson kept writing where's the book, where is the story of your expedition, and Lewis had not written a line, and I think that weighed very heavily on his mind.

Q. Thank you.

MR. CORONER: Questions from the jury?

EXAMINATION

BY DR. BOULDIN:

Q. My question again, is do we have any indication that he was so called treated at Fort Pickering and if so, in 1809 how would they have treated him at the outpost for a mental disorder?

A. Well, according to Major Russell he simply dried him out. He wouldn't let Lewis have access to anything except light wine. See from the standpoint of alcoholism, you are not even supposed to do that, but that's what Russell claimed that he dried the governor out.

Q. Was he taken off a boat, was not his intention to go to New Orleans and catch a ship there and sail around to Chesapeake, between St. Louis and Fort Pickering he was actually taken off the boat and put as you said drying out at Fort Pickering?

A. Yes, sir.

Q. Then decided to walk to Washington instead of sail to Washington?

A. That's correct, except (inaudible) his plan decided to go over land.

GENERAL BAUGH: Could you restate that, I think the court reporter missed part of that.

THE WITNESS: Lewis had planned to go to Washington by

steam, to go down the Mississippi to New Orleans, catch a ship go around to Washington through the Chesapeake Bay. At Fort Pickering he changed his plans and decided to go over land on the Natchez Trace.

MR. TURNBOW: You stated —

GENERAL BAUGH: If you don't mind let me follow-up.

EXAMINATION

BY GENERAL BAUGH:
Q. Why did he do that, do you think?
A. Well there are conflicting explanations about that. He told President Madison in a letter that, well there had been political diplomatic difficulties with the British; I don't want them to catch me and my valuable papers that was one of his reasons.
Q. He had his journals with him?
A. Yes, he did, also he cited to Madison reasons of health, you know, I've not been feeling too good.

GENERAL BAUGH: That's all.

EXAMINATION

BY MR. TURNBOW:
Q. You said that Jefferson concluded that Lewis had committed suicide based on the account of Lewis' servant, Pernier. Do you know what happened to Pernier following Lewis' death?
A. I have read and I've not really checked this out.

GENERAL BAUGH: He asked what happened to the servant Pernier after Lewis' death.
THE WITNESS: I have read that Pernier himself committed suicide.

BY MR. TURNBOW:

Q. Was there any reason given; does anyone know why Pernier committed suicide?

A. Not that I know of. There are members of the Lewis family who continue to think that Pernier was the killer. So there are many, many theories. There are many, many murder suspects other than— than the suicide.

Q. Do you know what the relationship was between Lewis and Clark at the time of Lewis' death; were they still on friendly terms?

A. They were on extremely friendly terms. I think the best proof of that, early in 1809 while they were both in St. Louis, Clark's first born son arrived and he named his first son Meriwether Lewis Clark, a guy doesn't do that to somebody on the out seat.

Q. Was there an account by a son or nephew of Clark's that indicated that perhaps Lewis was murdered?

A. I have read that a niece of Clark later thought that her uncle had changed his mind about that, but I've never seen any kind of documentation and for the rest of his life if Clark had changed his mind he never acted on that. The statute of limitations was running all of the time in a case of murder and Clark at any point had he thought that his friend had been murdered could have started making a lot of trouble.

Q. You said that there was some indication that Lewis may have had trouble with alcohol while governor in St. Louis. Is there any historical record that documents any alcoholism prior to the time he left St. Louis on his way to Washington?

A. No, I—none that I know of, I don't think there was.

MR. TURNBOW: That's all.

MR. CORONER: Any other questions?

EXAMINATION

BY DR. BOULDIN:
Q. Was Lewis' servant York with him also or what happened to York?

GENERAL BAUGH: He asked what happened to servant York that was Lewis' servant.

THE WITNESS: No. York was a slave of Clark, William Clark. Pernier was a hired free servant of Lewis. As far as I know York was still in St. Louis at Clark's home.

MR. CORONER: Other questions?

EXAMINATION

BY MR. FLYNN:
Q. Do the documents show how many rounds were used in Lewis' death?

GENERAL BAUGH: I couldn't hear that question.
BY MR. FLYNN:
Q. How many rounds of ammunition were used—fired in Lewis' death?
A. According to Mrs. Grinder which is only the account that has reached the record, there were two shots, both apparently from a pistol, either one pistol or two pistols, two shots.

EXAMINATION

BY MR. TURNBOW:
Q. If Lewis had been traveling the area on his journey from St. Louis to Washington, would—was it the common practice that someone could give him alcohol as a treatment for malaria?

A. For a guy who's thirsty, you could say, hey, I need my medicine for Malaria, but no, I wouldn't think you would treat a patient with Malaria by loading him up with booze, doesn't sound right. That's a question you might ask a couple of the doctors when they testify later.

GENERAL BAUGH: Anything else? Thank you, Mr. Large.

(WITNESS EXCUSED.)

GENERAL BAUGH: Just one moment.

GENERAL PHILLIPS: our next witness is Dr. Guice. Dr. Guice, if you will raise your right hand, the coroner will place you under oath.

THE WITNESS: Just one second, get kind of situated here. Someone else—

JOHN D. W. GUICE

having been first duly sworn was examined and testified as follows:

EXAMINATION

BY GENERAL PHILLIPS:

Q. Sir, would you please tell the coroner and the coroner's jury your name?

A. Yes, my name is John David Wynn Guice, that's spelled G-U-I-C-E.

Q. Thank you, Dr. Guice. Where do you live?

A. I presently reside in Laurel, Mississippi and I teach at the University of Southern Mississippi in Hattiesburg, Mississippi.

Q. All right, sir. Welcome to Tennessee.

A. Thank you. Thank you.

Q. What position do you hold with the University of Southern Mississippi?

A. I've been a professor of history or to use a redundancy, a full professor of history since 1976 and I've been there since 1969.

Q. All right, sir. Professor, have you also served at the University of Southern Mississippi in the position of director of their American Studies Program?

A. Yes, I have and I've been president of the faculty and held many positions of leadership on the campus.

Q. Professor Guice, we appreciate you being here today and as understand it you are not being compensated for being here?

A. That's correct.

Q. Nor are any of these witnesses. Is that your understanding?

A. As far as I know.

Q. This is not being done at public expense. You all are volunteers here with your services?

A. Yes. Not only did I volunteer, I convinced my department chairman to take my classes today so I could be here.

Q. Very well, that's great. Professor Guice, could you tell us what academic preparation you have had to prepare yourself for your job as a history professor?

A. Well my baccalaureate is from Yale University. I have a masters in history from Texas, El Paso and a Doctor of Philosophy and History from the University of Colorado at Boulder.

Q. And Professor, have you had occasion to specialize to some extent in matters involving the Natchez Trace?

A. Yes, sir. For the last 15 years I have been researching on what some people call the southern frontier, some of them call it old southwest because it was the south west during the early days of our republic.

Q. All right.

A. And I have—I have written a book, *Frontiers In Conflict*, which gives the history of that portion of the country, that is from Tennessee to the Gulf, and from central Georgia over to the Mississippi River. And more recently, I'm writing a comprehensive history of the Natchez Trace and in terms of this particular topic, in October of '94, I read a paper at Albuquerque for the Western History Association for a crowd about like this with about eight other sessions going on I might add and that paper was published recently in the *Journal of Mississippi History*. Prior to that, I had a publication in another journal dealing specifically with violence on the Natchez Trace.

Q. All right. Professor, in addition to the books and articles which you have published, have you also written entries for various encyclopedias dealing with historical matters?

A. Yes. Not particularly having to do with this topic.

Q. I understand.

A. But I have a number of entries in encyclopedias. I don't want to read my resume.

Q. Yes, sir, your curriculum vitae would you object to our filing it as an exhibit?

A. No, I'm not ashamed of it.

Q. Well, it is some 12 pages so we won't belabor it, but suffice it to say among your many writings, are you the author of the study, "A Fatal Rendezvous: Mysterious Death of Meriwether Lewis," published recently in the *Journal of Mississippi History*?

A. Yes, I just referred to that

Q. You're also the author of the forword—are you the author of the forword to the well-known treatise, *The Outlaw Years* which dealt with—

A. Yes, sir, that is true.

Q. — some violence on the Natchez Trace?

A. And I might add that my attitude towards violence on the Natchez Trace has changed somewhat since I wrote that and my attitude on the piece, "A Trace of Violence," which I mentioned a moment ago published in the *Southern Quarterly*, my ideas have evolved, but yes, I felt those things.

Q. All right, sir. And professor now, more specifically to the point at issue here today, could you address when and why did you become interested in the death of Meriwether Lewis and how long have you studied this question?

A. Well I first became interested in the death of Meriwether Lewis in the mid 1980s when I was writing this book *Frontiers in Conflict* which has a chapter on Natchez Trace. I must confess that, you know, my previous scholarship it all dealt with the Rocky Mountain area and as I was moving into the old southwest, I felt kind of stupid. I had forgotten that Meriwether Lewis had died on Natchez Trace. So I entered into this project sort of with a lot of innocence, I mean, I had no preconceived notions about —

Q. You were open-minded?

A. Very open-minded, yes, sir.

Q. Almost vacant minded?

A. I don't like to say that. At times it's pretty vacant, just ask my wife.

Q. I understand. She is very lovely. You obviously are a man of great taste. Doctor—professor, could you give us your views, now after your extensive research that you have published in the Southern Quarterly and in these books, would you give us your view of the historical controversy surrounding this issue?

A. Yes, sir. Thank you. First I want to back up a minute, my early scholarship was on the territorial history of the Rocky Mountains published by Yale University Press and that has given me a certain background to look at some of the problems that Meriwether Lewis encountered as a territorial governor. So it's given me a little perspective about the kinds of activities he engaged in and his successes and purported failures in upper Louisiana. So I come at this, not as a scholar of Meriwether Lewis, I make no pretensions of being an expert on the expedition, I want to make that abundantly clear but I feel there's very few people, if any, to my knowledge have studied as much the question of how historians have dealt with the death of Meriwether Lewis.

Q. Very few have dealt with it as much—as extensively as you have?

A. I don't think so, if so, I'm not aware of it.

Q. Well, Professor, give us your view then of this historical controversy?

A. When I first started writing a chapter which will appear in the *History of the Natchez Trace*, I was sort of astounded that historians were so willing with such scanty evidence to come to such firm conclusions about suicide. The evidence that they had was highly suspect, blatantly circumstantial and of the faintest kind of hearsay. Most of their decisions were made on the basis of—pardon me, of letters, which purported to report the words of Mrs. Grinder, I understand it was Griner, but everybody calls it Grinder and the jury has these documents, several of these documents before you, the Neelly letter, the Wilson letter, Russell letter and there are such obvious discrepancies in those letters. And I particularly was troubled with the conduct of which Mrs. Grinder attributed to herself in the letter which she dictated to Mr. Wilson. And please forgive me if I tend to lecture to you but I need to explain.

Q. Professor, we can expect no less than a lecture from you.

A. I hope it's a good one. Let me say that to my knowledge there have been few frontiers in the history of the United States that had greater violence on them than Tennessee. In terms of problems between the native Americans and European Americans and it was just a rather violent frontier. And the Natchez Trace was quite violent, particularly in its early years. And anyway Mrs. Grinder was a frontier lady. She was used to staying here some by herself. Her husband would go to another farm. Her behavior as described in the account to Mr. Wilson just didn't stack up with the behavior of a good old frontier gal. I mean she wouldn't render any service to him. At one point she said she's frightened. Well if Natchez Trace was so dog gone safe, you know, why was she so afraid. So there were a lot of inconsistencies that attracted my attention, that just didn't seem to stack up.

And I can recall when I was writing the first version of this chapter back before I ever heard—I apologize that I didn't know more than about him, but Jim Starrs, before I heard of his activities I had written in that draft wouldn't it be wonderful if we could have a forensic examination of the remains to determine, you know, whether or not the shots were fired according to Mrs. Grinder's several versions.

Q. So you reached that conclusion yourself as a historian before you ever heard of Professor Starrs of George Washington University?

A. Long before I ever heard of him.

Q. What is your opinion of the existence of evidence sufficient to reach a conclusion on the question of suicide or homicide?

A. I'm sort of repeating myself, we simply—historians simply will be unable to resolve this question unless we can find some physical evidence which would result from a forensic examination of the scene of the remains.

Q. What are some of the biases that you have observed in the writing of historians or why do you feel that their conclusions regarding the suicide are flawed?

Why do you think there's a need for further investigation as far as the conclusions of other historians?

A. Well there are several reasons. One is the impact that's already been mentioned by one of the witnesses of the statements of Thomas Jefferson. His word was sort of taken as impeccable, unimpeachable, unchallengeable, authoritative, and, of course, I venerate this man. I can't think of another American who I admire more greatly than Thomas Jefferson. I've spent many, many hours in his home. I talk about him a lot in my lectures. But he was not a saint that he was, you know, certainly a human being and just because he very readily accepts this, does not mean that he could not have erred and it's also the question of—of—if Jefferson knew all this stuff about Lewis, why did Jefferson put him in charge of the project that meant more to Thomas Jefferson than any other thing in his presidency?

The Louisiana Purchase occurred almost kind of as an accident but he had been interested in this project long before he became president. He had begun to—a plan for it before the Louisiana Purchase and of course, the Louisiana Purchase legitimized his project and made it possible for him to do it openly, and above board. This was his greatest thing. I can't imagine he would appoint as the leader of the co-leaders a man if he knew that man was an alcoholic and if he knew that man was unstable. It just does not make sense.

So then you ask yourself a question why would Jefferson have responded to the death of Meriwether Lewis as he did. And I think that's an easily answered question. It was a clean way to deal with it. And I don't take the matter of suicide lightly. One of my nephews who was a, you know, one of these Vietnam veterans who came back with great emotional problems killed himself. But in the 19th Century suicide was certainly considered, you know, in a bad light. I might even use the word disgraceful.

We have more tolerance toward it, better understanding of it now, but the easiest thing to do for Jefferson was to accept it as a suicide and I think with all due respect to any local officials who may be listening to me now, we even see evidence of this today, that officials if they're able to declare a homicide a suicide it's a much cleaner operation. You don't got to have an investigation, you don't have to have trials, you don't, you know—so it's not hard for me to understand why Jefferson might have accepted that. But it certainly would be inconsistent with Jefferson's early, early relationship with Meriwether Lewis.

Now, some historians, you know, approach a project from a particular philosophical disposition or background. Let me talk for a moment about the historian who's mentioned so frequently, Dawson Phelps. I've read everything he's written. I've copied 11,000 of his notes cards and taken to my university. I have the utmost respect for Dawson Phelps as an—as a researcher.

But Dawson Phelps was trying to prove a point. He and one of his colleagues, named William D. Hamilton who trained at Duke University, they were out to prove that the Frederick Jackson Turner's frontier hypothesis was wrong. Every time Hamilton could knock the frontier, he knocked it. He didn't believe Mississippi was a frontier, but he had a great influence on his long time friend Dawson Phelps, and both of them were trying to debunk a book called *The Outlaw Years*. This book had the greatest impact on writing of history of the Natchez Trace of any book ever written and it is a book fraught with errors.

It is true that the Natchez Trace was terribly violent in its earlier years with the Hawk Brothers, Mason and Hair and these people from 1800 to 1805 Natchez Trace was a dreaded place to be. It was not quite that violent after 1805.

But Dawson Phelps to suggest that the Natchez Trace was safe in 1809 just does not stack up with what I find in my research over 15 years.

So Phelps had a little axe to grind, if I might say—He had two axes to grind. He wanted to go along with his buddy, William B. Hamilton and disapprove the theories of Frederick Jackson Turner and he wanted to put down the work of Coates and these outlaw years. So he did have a predisposition to try to—to act like Natchez Trace was safe in 1809 when it certainly was not.

Q. Based upon your own research and your survey of all historians on this issue, do you recommend further investigation concerning the death of Meriwether Lewis?

A. I surely do because most of the historians have written on this start over here with this premise, it was suicide. And then they go look for the salient quote that backs them up, you see. And I can take a lot of the same things that they say are so salient and turn them around and say, guys this shows Lewis was a very sensible man. A man who's coming down the Mississippi River who thinks he maybe going around through the Gulf and the Atlantic or the Natchez Trace, who doesn't write a Will if he wants to leave his property to his mother was certainly indiscreet. So the fact that he writes a Will on the way down the river enhances him in my view. It doesn't show he's getting ready to blow his brains out.

In Memphis, he writes a letter to his old army buddy, Amos Stoddard. It says, send me my money, send it to Washington and I'm going to get everything straightened out in Washington, I'm going back to St. Louis. That's not a man who is thinking seriously about killing himself.

Q. Incidentally, did he have good reason to change his plans and not travel to New Orleans?

A. Surely he did. As we all recall our high school history and college history, you know, our relationship with Great Britain at this time was leading up towards the War of 1812 and the

British were interfering with our shipping on the high seas and he did indeed I think have—if he wanted to kill himself he might have gone on and let the British do it for him. I mean, the fact that he changes his route shows he is a pretty sensible person. It doesn't show us that he's out of his mind. It doesn't show, you know that —

Q. He had all these journals with him, did he not, that he had painstakingly compiled?

A. Yes. We have almost no evidence. Russell writes a letter that some guys on the boat said that Lewis tried to take his life. All right. Lewis was the biggest hero in America on that date, let's get this in perspective. This wasn't John Guice floating down, or one of my ancestors who were on the Mississippi at that time. This wasn't just any ole Joe on the boat. This was Governor Meriwether Lewis, the biggest hero since George Washington. Surely if those gentlemen on the boat had watched him try to kill himself two or three times as they floated down the river as they stopped in Natchez and were drinking at Natchez under the hill they would have talked about this, as they got down to New Orleans hanging around the wharf, they would talk about this. We would hear some more, you would know a little bit more about his attempt to kill himself on the boat in my opinion if, in fact, he did do that. It would be talk of the wharf. It would get in the New Orleans newspaper. You can't keep things about big shots a secret like that.

Q. And you say he was the greatest hero of the day?

A. He surely was.

Q. He was of the Neal Armstrong of the day?

A. You can say that. I think he might have even in the eyes of Americans, we have so many heroes today, I think in the eyes of Americans he might have even been on a higher pedestal because they had so few.

Q. He was described by President Jefferson as being that hero of undaunted courage?

A. And when he came back you can't believe how he was wined

and dined and feted, they had celebrations. The national—the Poet Laureate of America wrote this big poem about him. You can't believe how they celebrated this man's return.

So, all I'm saying is that I have a lot of problems with Russell telling us that the men on the boat said he tried to kill himself with no details, did he try to jump overboard, did he try to hang himself, did he try to stab himself, did he try to shoot himself, I'm not going to place a great deal of stock on the fact that some of these boatmen many of whom were wonderful people but many of whom were not necessarily the greatest witnesses in the world. Do I have time to address some of the things that an earlier witness said?

Q. Yes, sir please say —

MR. CORONER: May we take a break before we do that, if that is all right with you Professor, if we could take about a 15 minute break and come back.

THE WITNESS: Wonderful.

MR. CORONER: The jury will retire to the jury room.
(Recess.)

MR. CORONER: The Inquest is called back to order please.

BY GENERAL PHILLIPS:
Q. Thanks. Thank you, Mr. Coroner. Professor Guice, prior to the break you were about to address some comments you would like to make concerning matters indicated by other witnesses. Would you do that, please?
A. Thank you, sir. Early this morning we were—we listened to discussion of some of the problems he was having in upper Louisiana, and I would like to address that very briefly and also would like to address the question of William Clark's letters also very briefly.

Let me first deal with the letters. Of course, you know, when we write we—it's only human nature for us to want to quote those things that tend to best support our case. I'm not quite convinced that Lewis Clark (sic) was—William Clark was so totally supporting of the idea of suicide, because here's a letter that he wrote, if I can find it here, let's see, William Clark wrote,

(Reading:) I think that it will all be right that he...

Meaning Meriwether Lewis,

...will return to fine colors to the country.

Because much had been made of Clark's response in reading the news of Lewis' death in the newspaper and in part he said,

(Reading:)I fear this report hasn't much truth, though it may have no foundation, my reason for thinking possibly founded on the letter I received from him.

Which we don't really have that. But what I want to address very briefly and I don't want to break that out and take up too much time but we are here on a very serious matter. Many of the people who argue for suicide try to dig- up reasons why he, you know, may have committed suicide and they've made much over so many things. How much time did he spend in Philadelphia before he reported to his position as governor? You know, most people say that the reason he committed suicide was because he didn't find a girlfriend or a wife, which he did not. But I think that we could surmise that Meriwether Lewis may have been having a big time in Philadelphia, just a little R and R. He'd been out in the wilderness for all these years. We know from letters to his buddies, we know he'd been drinking a little bit and the point I'm making is we're wrong to assume that his time in Philadelphia was a sad time. Just because he said I'm still a bachelor many of us in this room probably have said that on one occasion.

So but specifically I want to talk briefly about what was going on during his governorship and this is often used by people who argue suicide as a reason for his purported despair.

First of all, compared to most territorial governors and this is something I do know something about, he performed very well. He was particularly successful in dealing with Indian relations after he got there. He did get into some financial trouble with some land speculation but basically, this was par for the course. Okay. This is not just something that Meriwether Lewis did. Virtually all of the territorial official ships, why do you think that people wanted to be appointed to a territorial position, they got paid very, very little and you had to go live out in the territory under the worse possible conditions. I mean, one of the reasons many people wanted a territorial appointment was to get out there and make bucks on speculation, good old American activity. I'm not criticizing it. But he did have a cash flow problem toward the end but he was not facing bankruptcy.

He did—he did have a problem dealing with the bureaucracy in Washington. Every territorial official did. Russell wrote that letter from Fort Pickering. He wanted to go to Washington with Meriwether Lewis to resolve a very similar question about the challenging of some of his expenses but his bosses would not let him leave Fort Pickering.

I think there's strong evidence that Lewis was performing well in the territory was Frederick Bates who was the territorial secretary who had preceded Lewis to the job by a year or so. Frederick Bates was about as much of a pain-in-the-neck as anyone could have been for Meriwether Lewis. I hate to use the words, he despised Meriwether Lewis. He was jealous of him. He was envious of him. He did everything he could to hurt Meriwether Lewis, but yet no where can we find any evidence that Frederick Bates accused Meriwether Lewis of incompetence nor can we find that Meriwether Lewis was accused of being an alcoholic by Frederick Bates. And if your worse political enemy, if your worse political enemy is not going to bring to the attention your mental incapacity, who in the world is.

So I just thought that I would bring that out to show that people who argue in favor of suicide start generally with the assumption and work back to find everything conveniently falls into its place.

Thank you.

Q. Dr. Guice, I want to ask you to address now briefly two other scholars who I think may share your view or have shared your view that further investigation is warranted and would be historically significant. First Vardis Fisher, would you address him?

A. Yes, I will. Vardis Fisher, I'm sure many people in this room are aware of who he is and may have read his book but in 1961, I believe it was, he wrote the book called *Suicide or Murder? The Strange Death of Governor Meriwether Lewis*. And Vardis Fisher was much maligned after publication of this book by the great scholar Donald Jackson and Julian Boyd, who had together written the Jefferson Davis papers and when I first got interested in this subject I read his book and then read where people put him down. Then I read it again and then I went up to Yale University and researched in the letters that Vardis Fisher donated to Yale University, you know, after as he finished each project he would donate all his letters and work to Yale University. And after reading the correspondence at Yale University between Vardis Fisher and Don Jackson and between Vardis Fisher and Julian Boyd, I'm convinced, absolutely positively convinced that this man, Vardis Fisher, had an open mind. I'm convinced that he researched with incredible intensity and integrity and I'm ashamed that some of my fellow scholars who are my seniors maligned him so. I suspect that one reason they did was that he was a Ph.D. in history from Chicago, a wonderful graduate school at the time, the college there, but he did spend most of career writing novels and because he had written novels some of the historians have tried to look down their nose at his work.

If you haven't read *Suicide or Murder?*, I want you to know this book raises hundreds of questions about the death and I will say in all honesty he admits that he can't prove murder and he admits that, you know, he can't pick a particular assassin, but he certainly blows a million holes in the research of suicide people.

Q. Could you address the work of Dr. E.G. Chuinard?

A. Yes. I would like to point to you Dr. Chuinard was an orthopedic surgeon. He was a professor of orthopedic surgery in the Pacific Northwest and in 1991 he wrote a lengthy article in a journal called, *We Proceeded On*, which is journal of the Lewis and Clark Trail Foundation and I think if I had to pick a single work to read, I mean, if I read only one thing, I guess I'd read that, it's a little shorter than this, I think I would read these two things, but you know being a medical professor, professor of orthopedic surgery I think does a wonderful job of destroying some of the arguments for suicide in terms of the fact that he claims that Meriwether Lewis could not possibly have behaved in the manner that Mrs. Grinder said he behaved having been wounded as she said he was wounded.

Now he just said it's a medical impossibility for him to have behaved in the manner that she described in one of the letters that you have to look at. And he also brings out he was raised had on the frontier. He also brings out the behavior of a frontier lady. He says her behavior is just not consistent with a person that's been raised on the frontier since they were a child.

Q. Thank you, Dr. Guice. Now let me ask you this, this question is probably in the minds of many good citizens of Lewis County, and that question is: Why bother after all these years, why bother about this death that occurred in the early 19th century?

A. I'm smiling because one of my closest friends when I told him I was doing a paper on the death of Meriwether Lewis, he's retired a Navy man and so he used a mild cuss word and said, what in the blank difference does it make, so I've done a lot of thinking about it.

Q. What in the blank difference does it make?

A. And I've done a lot of thinking about that. And let me back up and very quickly remind you of the fact that we are dealing here with a person who was America's greatest hero since the American Revolution. We must keep this, in perspective and even if he were an unknown, I think we would owe it to that person to have rectified an injustice and I think it's an injustice for us to have assumed without very strong evidence, on very weak evidence, that he killed himself. So I think we owe it to his image as a great American hero. I think we owe it to his descendants. I think we owe it to our nation. I think this is a national—this is a national issue. I think we owe it to our nation to try to have as truthful history as we can write. And I think since we're standing in the great State of Tennessee during very special moments I think we owe it to the State of Tennessee since this occurred in this state and since the world is sort of watching us at this moment, I think the least that we can do is move towards an opportunity to resolve the question and basically as I understand, this is all Dr. Starrs is hoping for is not asking you to do anything more than provide the opportunity to gather some physical evidence. You are not coming—I think that's really, you know, an appropriate thing for him to ask and I'd like to close by thanking you for being good listeners. You have listened to me and I know that if you are on the spot right here in town, I know you walk around town probably passing one and I do want to thank you as an American and historian. Thank you very much.

Q. Thank you very much, Dr. Guice. If you'll wait just a moment Mr. Coroner may have questions or members of the jury?

MR. CORONER: Questions of the jury?

EXAMINATION

BY MR. TURNBOW:

Q. Dr. Guice, I think we need to base our opinion on the evidence that exists. Could you very briefly go over the reasons that have been given for suicide and tell us what evidence exists for those, for example, Lewis was distraught over not finding a girlfriend or wife, what evidence —

A. Well the evidence that is given for that are the letters that he wrote in which he does say, you know, I forget his exact words, I was never good at memorizing things like that but he does in a letter express disappointment that he had not yet found a wife. You know, but, I mean, I don't see that as I said a minute ago many of us in this same room have said similar things at some time in our life.

Q. Was there any indication in the letter that he was so upset over that that he thought of taking his life?

A. Not to my way of thinking about it, depends on how—what you think his predisposition is when we read the letter. If you start with the conclusion, you know, as does the author named Allen Goodson wrote a treatise on this, you know, and he starts with suicide and finds all sorts of little things in his life and later today or tomorrow you are going to hear, from a psychologist who I suspect will tell you that we could find in the life of anyone who had committed suicide that could point to it in the background.

Q. When was that letter written in relation to his death?

A. Somebody help me. It was written before he reported to St. Louis. I would guess it was written a year or two before his death, am I right? It was about—it was year and a half, or two years before his death. It was written from Virginia before he headed back—before he reported to—to St. Louis.

Q. Were there any letters written near the time of his death that indicated he was distraught over that?

A. The question was were there any letters written close to his death in which he belabored the fact that he hadn't found a wife I don't think so.

Q. The other —

A. As a matter of fact, I—I can't recall it.

Q. The other thing you mentioned was that he was having financial problems. Tell us what problems he was having, I assume he wasn't bankrupt?

A. You are going to have opportunity I believe to talk to Ms. Frick who knows more about that than I do. He had overextended himself in land purchases. Okay. But over a long—if you take that problem to an accountant he'll say, if we can just work this out, a little cash flow, you know, down the road you are going to be in real great shape when you start making money off this land. So when the government dishonored some of his warrants that he had to pay for personally, you see, that gives him a momentary what we call today cash flow problem, but I'm sure if you ask an accountant to look at what all his financial plans were, they would probably say he was—he was a pretty wise guy. This land speculation again in the United States of America land speculation was the number one activity for getting rich quick, ever since they landed in Jamestown at Plymouth we were a people of speculation.

Q. Someone else can address this question more directly?

A. About the amount of money he had and owed. I would hope so I'm not prepared to that.

Q. Let me ask one final question.

A. Because I would resolve that it was not a problem in my experience from observing other territories.

Q. Who should have conducted the investigation into Lewis' death and why did Clark not do it and why didn't Jefferson not do it?

A. I stick by my previous statement and I may have been speaking so fast I wasn't clear, I think that Jefferson as many, many officials do and he was immediate past president but had he encouraged this challenging wilderness—now let's keep in mind this is happening in middle of the wilderness and if anyone should have investigated it, it should have been a local coroner's jury and again, in this book there's a whole chapter about whether or not a coroner's jury did exist and you find people who think it did and the evidence has been destroyed.

So the answer to your question, I'm not trying to be a smart aleck, the death if it were to be investigated by anyone should have been investigated by a coroner of the jurisdiction in which he died.

Q. Would it not have been customary or appropriate for the government in St. Louis, the federal government to get involved?

A. Hardly. It's just like the other night and I started to say this in jest but I didn't want to offend anybody, the Natchez Trace is still not safe. Last night the car in front of me ran into an entire herd of cattle. We couldn't get anybody. The Rangers were out doing whatever they do on Sunday night. We called the emergency number. What I'm getting at, I don't see how a territorial official in St. Louis, Missouri, he would have nothing but some oral persuasion to write a letter to somebody and say, I'm—why don't you have a coroner's inquest. Certainly Clark was in no position as I see it to initiate any kind of inquest. Jefferson would have been in a position to write to his friend James Madison and say why don't you use the authority of your office to encourage a local official to make an inquest.

But again, my answer to this is, if—accepting a suicide, I might use the word quotation mark, a clean, easy way of disposing of a problem, and even today we read in the newspapers I think, we can find, you know, a tendency on the part of officials to avoid when, you know, a conflict and problem, hearings and pictures of this and pictures of that, and I just think that you should not base the entire question of a man's suicide on whether or not Thomas Jefferson said, particularly Thomas Jefferson earlier had placed greatest trust in the world on this person. I can't—I don't have a word to tell you, to express to you the significance that Thomas Jefferson placed on this expedition specifically. It's something he had dreamed of from the colonial days long before he became president and this expedition was, you know, the single most important thing in his mind and I suggest to you it is not likely he would put that expedition in charge of a person if he knew that that person had a history of alcoholism and mental problems and instability.

EXAMINATION

BY DR. BOULDIN:

Q. Doctor, does anyone besides Mr. Ambrose bring up the problem of syphilis?

A. Yes, sir. I believe —I believe that you will before wouldn't we hear —

GENERAL BAUGH: You will hear from Dr. Ravenholt about that particular area.

EXAMINATION

BY MR. CORONER:

Q. I have a question as far as this jurisdiction comes about, where in conjunction to the place where Meriwether Lewis died, where—who did have jurisdiction, what territory was that, who would have had jurisdiction there?

A. Well, that was inside the boundary of Tennessee, wasn't it? It was just across the line from the Indian boundary.

GENERAL BAUGH: I think it was in Indian land at the time. It was not? Maybe we'll ask some —

UNIDENTIFIED SPEAKER: Since 1796 we were a state.

THE WITNESS: It was Tennessee land, but you see, I'm

embarrassed because I thought you asked me what specific county and I can't remember, so I was trying to wiggle —

GENERAL BAUGH: I think pretty certain it was Maury County, the actual county but I think that there were—although, Tennessee was a state and I can—I don't know maybe Ms. Frick knows the answer to this, there were Indian territories within this state that were under the jurisdiction of men like Mr. Neelly who was an Indian agent, Mississippi Territory—

THE WITNESS: Wasn't this first stand outside of the Indian— believe this is—I believe, I stand to be corrected, I believe that Grinder's Stand was the first stand as you're going north outside of the Chickasaw.

GENERAL BAUGH: Do you know that, Ms. Frick?

MS. FRICK: I'm sorry, I don't.

MR. CORONER: Other questions from the jury? Thank you, Professor.

(WITNESS EXCUSED.)

MR. CORONER: Next witness.

RUTH FRICK

GENERAL PHILLIPS: Mr. Coroner, we call Ruth Frick. Mr. Coroner, in the interest of time I'm going to read a statement that Ms. Frick has provided us concerning her qualifications. Ruth Frick, who is before now and will be sworn in just a moment, is a descendent of John Colter of Lewis and Clark Corps of Discovery. She has researched John Colter and the men of the expedition since 1954. She is the author of a book soon to be finished concerning her ancestor, John Colter. The jury may recall that this is the John Colter who is credited with discovering the area of Yellowstone National Park I believe. Of course, we all know that the Native Americans discovered Yellowstone so I guess it would be the European Americans who discovered Yellowstone.

The past few years she has been processing the Grace Lewis Miller collection at the Jefferson National Expansion Memorial Archives in St. Louis. She does this at the national park there.

Now regarding this other lady whose papers this lady is an expert on, Grace Lewis Miller, spent 40 years, virtually her entire life studying and collecting information about Meriwether Lewis. Unfortunately, she was a perfectionist and although she wrote extensive drafts concerning the collection she had amassed, she never submitted them for publication, never having been sufficiently satisfied with it.

So upon her death, the Grace Lewis Miller papers which are voluminous—most of which concern her study of Meriwether Lewis—have been donated to the Park Service. This lady, Ruth Frick, has had the opportunity to study this collection of documents, letters and manuscripts and to organize and write the finding aid for this collection.

So Ms. Frick is here today for two reasons, first because she has researched Meriwether Lewis herself because of her interest in her ancestor John Colter, another explorer who is associated with Meriwether Lewis; and secondly, because Ms. Frick is conversant, perhaps the most conversant, with the voluminous papers of this perfectionist lady Grace Lewis Miller who dedicated her life to collecting and organizing information concerning Meriwether Lewis and his death.

With that Ms. Frick I'll ask you raise your right-hand to be sworn.

RUTH FRICK

having been first duly affirmed was examined and testified as follows:

DIRECT EXAMINATION

BY GENERAL PHILLIPS:

Q. Ms. Frick, where do you live?

A. I live in Washington, Missouri.

Q. Okay. Is that near some larger city?

A. It's near St. Louis.

Q. Okay. Welcome to Tennessee

A. Thank you, I'm happy to be here.

Q. Could you tell us, first of all, whether or not you have an opinion based upon your research and your knowledge of the Grace Lewis Miller materials concerning the death of Meriwether Lewis?

A. Yes, I have.

Q. Are you of the opinion that that death merits further investigation?

A. Yes, I do.

Q. Is that an opinion that Grace Lewis Miller also had?

A. Yes, it is.

Q. Did she commit that to writing at various times?

A. She wrote a response to Dawson Phelps' article that was in *William and Mary Quarterly* but it was never published.

Q. It is the same Dawson Phelps historian that we've referred to earlier in this hearing?

A. That's right.

Q. Now Ms. Frick, why are you of the opinion that this death merits further investigation and may very well not have been suicide?

A. I would like to show by the records that Meriwether Lewis was planning on living in the Louisiana Territory and was planning on returning from Washington.

Q. Okay. Go ahead.

A. The first letter that I would quote from was written December the 1st, 1808 when Meriwether Lewis wrote to his mother. He told his mother that he had bought 5,700 acres of land. He described the land and the buildings that he had planned for her residence and the only thing he asked of her was that she relinquishes her dowry in the plantation that she owed at Ivy creek. You must realize also that Meriwether Lewis being the oldest son owned this plantation in Virginia.

I'm not sure that you could call his buying of the land particularly speculation because he bought his land very carefully in the Louisiana Territory. The piece of land that he bought with the thought of having his mother come to live on was a thousand acres. He paid $3,000 for this land. He had put money down and $1,500 was going to be due in May. Now you have to remember that he was writing this December 1st, 1808. So this $1,500 would have been due in May of 1809 and then an additional $1200 would be due in May 1810.

He also described some land that he was renting out to someone, I think his name was Mr. Eastman, but don't quote me on that. But in this letter he specified how high the fences were supposed to be, also that the man would be allowed to tap the trees but he specified in what method he could use to tap the trees. He was tapping maple trees for sugar and he could only bore two holes in each tree. So that doesn't sound like a man that is going to go off and not come back.

On August the 21st, 1809, this is going to be just week before his fatal journey, Lewis and Clark settled their accounts agreeably. There's a record of this, that Clark will buy one half of the interest in the book that is going to be published but Lewis still retained one half of that book. When Lewis was in Philadelphia in the east—he wasn't just—I'm sure he partied, but he wasn't just partying. He was making arrangements for his book to be published. He was paying people to have portraits done, to study the mathematics so they could do the maps; he was busy doing these things.

Lewis had some bills that were, protested, but Clark also had bills that were protested, and also as you heard Mr. Russell had bills that were protested, so this was not unusual. I quote from Clark's memorandum book, that he wrote in October 1809, and I have copies of all of the documents that I'll be quoting if you want to look at that. Clark wrote that he had debts listed as $5900. He also lists the money that's due him as being $1445.

Now, Clark with a wife and child was in debt $4,455 in October 1809 by William Clark's calculations. In Clark's memorandum book he has Governor Lewis' debts listed as $2,750.72, and he lists the protested bills as being $1,818.50. Plus there's a bill, protested bill for Chouteau which amounted to $940 but according to Clark's calculations Lewis had already paid $500 of that. So what we have here is leaving Lewis' protested bills as $1,957.50, or a total debt of $4,709.22. I have not checked Mr. Clark's figure. I'm only telling you what he wrote.

Q. But according to Mr. Clark's figures, he, Mr. Clark, was in worse financial shape than Meriwether Lewis. Is that the point?

A. That's the point.

Q. That's the point. Thank you, Ms. Frick.

A. And the assets of Mr. Lewis he estimated that his land was worth $2,065.50 in the Louisiana territory. He also said that

Reuben, Lewis' brother, owed him $300. So the assets that William Clark calculated for Mr. Lewis being in the Louisiana Territory was $2,365.60 or the total debt including the protested bills was only $2,343.72.

Now Lewis had paid more than that, according to the records that I could find in his memorandum, he would have paid $2,065 for the land in the Louisiana Territory. He also owned approximately a thousand, acres of land in Kentucky. He also had his plantation in Virginia and he still had his $1600—1,600 acre warrant that was probably worth at least $2.00 an acre.

On August 24th, Meriwether Lewis acknowledged a debt of $30.75 to Dr. Antoine Saugrain, moneys which may be remitted to them by me or to be paid from a sale of his land but it sounds to me that if they were not paid he was still going to be responsible for them. On August the 25th, just days before his leaving on his trip, he gives William Clark a receipt for the land warrant number two which William Clark had for 1,600 acres with the promise that he will try to sell the land in New Orleans or deliver it to Daniel Clark, who I think was in New Orleans.

On September the 16, 1809, Meriwether Lewis's letter to President Madison, quote,

> (Reading:) I arrived in Chickasaw Bluffs much exhausted from the heat of the climate. Apprehension of the climate in the lower country and the fear of his original papers falling into the hands of the British endured me to change my route and proceed by land through the state of Tennessee, to the city of Washington.

Notes from Lewis' memorandum book August the 22nd, 1809, quote,

> (Reading:) Settlement Chouteau by returning

land and if note is paid by May next, the land
is returned.

August the 24th, 1809, he agrees to pay Mr. L. Bacon $100
next spring. And in his memorandum book, quote,

> (Reading:) Gave Judge Steward a deed for 408
> or 7 08... I couldn't make out the figure, . . . acres
> of land recorded to the Sioux conditioned that
> if I return him $750 with interest there will be
> by the 10th October in 1810 then the deed is
> to be void, end of quote.

Also quote, in the memorandum book,

> (Reading:) Directed my letters to be returned
> to City of Washington.

September the 17th, 1809, he says he

> enclosed my land warrant for 1,600 acres to
> Bowling Robinson of New Orleans for $2.00
> an acre or more if it can be obtained and the
> money is to be deposited in the branch bank of
> New Orleans or the city of Washington subject
> to my order or that of William D. Meriwether
> for the benefit of my creditors.

September the 27th, he in his memorandum book says,

> (Reading:)Borrowed of Captain Russell a check on
> the branch bank of New Orleans $99.50 and gave him
> a note for the $99.50, also gave him a note for $280 for
> two horses.

I don't want to skip anything. In the memorandum book he
also writes that he is confident—who is this letter too, excuse
me, looking for my notes and his letter to Amos Stoddard.

Q. In any event Ms. Frick, you feel these are not the actions of
either a man who is bankrupt or a man who's bent on suicide.
Is that your opinion?

A. That's my feeling.

Q. Let's give the coroner and jury a chance to address any questions?

MR. CORONER: Questions from the jury?

EXAMINATION

BY MR. TURNBOW:

Q. Is there any evidence of him being hounded by creditors?

A. The question was is there any evidence that he was hounded by creditors? I have not found any evidence. I have not found any evidence that there was a long overdue debt.

GENERAL PHILLIPS: any other questions? All right. Thank you very much, Ms. Frick.

THE WITNESS: Thank you for your attention.

(WITNESS EXCUSED.)

GENERAL PHILLIPS: Mr. Coroner, we call George Stephens. Mr. Coroner, prior to Mr. Stephens being sworn, in the interest of time, I would like to present to you Dr. George C. Stephens. He has a Ph.D. Degree from Lehigh University, a Masters from George Washington University, as well as a Bachelor's Degree from George Washington University. He is as we said here earlier today, a full professor at George Washington University as well as being chairman of the Department of Geology at George Washington University. He has a curriculum vitae, Mr. Coroner and members of the jury, that is about 20 pages that we'll submit to you as an exhibit but suffice it to say that he has been head of the Department of Geology at this esteemed university in Washington, D.C. since 1989, that prior to that time has had numerous appointments at other prestigious teaching institutions. He has received numerous grants from societies such as the National Geographic Society. He has received numerous grants from George Washington University, he's conducted research. He has publications that stretch for some seven pages, so we submit to you that he's well qualified in the field of geology and ask he be sworn at this time.

GEORGE STEPHENS

having been first duly sworn was examined and testified as follows:

DIRECT EXAMINATION

BY GENERAL PHILLIPS:
Q. Thank you, Mr. Coroner. Dr. Stephens, and we want to be as brief as possible, and you've indicated that you want to do that as well. Can you tell us briefly what is the role of geology in connection with exhumation in historical controversies such as this one, what's the role of geology?

A. Again, I realize, I might say, parenthetically, I realize I'm probably the only single person standing between all of us and lunch, so I will try to be brief. The role of geology is —
Q. You have had lunch?
A. No.
Q. Go ahead.
A. The role of geology in historical exhumation is really four fold as I see it. The first is to do a careful site mapping of a proposed exhumation site locating all other adjacent burials, monument stones, significant vegetation large trees, roadways, paths, and so on, so that when the exhumation is carried out we don't intrude on any other nearby features.

The second role is to do a physical description of the topography in the area because the topography or the landscape to some extent controls the soil moisture content in the subsurface and that in turn has a lot of bearing on preservation of human remains. The third major role of geology in exhumation would be to do a detailed soil analysis, including soil mineralogy, soil textures, soil acidities, and so forth, because the soil chemistry and the soil structure again has a great bearing on preservation of human remains.

And then the last step for a geologist in an exhumation is to aid in guiding the exhumation, proper guiding, to help guide the excavation of the remains and we do this in several different ways. One geological tool that we can bring to bear on this problem is geophysics, like magnetic surveys, metal detector surveys or ground penetrating radar surveys; we try in some way to remotely sense the location of the remains before we do any excavation at all. And then during the actual digging we can also, use geology, we can use the soil structure that we see exposed to guide us as we're digging, to keep us sort of on the right track and guide us towards the grave site in particular.
Q. Dr. Stephens, have you looked at the site of the grave of Meriwether Lewis here in Lewis County?
A. I have.

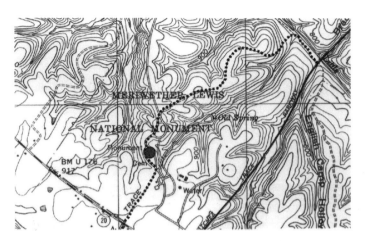

Marked on this topological map are the paths of the original Natchez Trace on the left, and the modern Natchez Trace Parkway on the right. The Meriwether Lewis National Monument & Gravesite is indicated by the black dot.

George Stephens and James E. Starrs at the site

Q. Have you conducted—have you given some professional attention to that site?

A. I have.

Q. All right. Now can you tell us from your standpoint as a geologist are the prospects good for the skeletal remains of Meriwether Lewis being in good enough shape to be examined if there were to be an exhumation?

A. Yes, sir.

Q. Why is that? Why is it a good prospective site for looking at skeletal remains?

A. Let me—let me try to illustrate that with one slide if I can.

Q. As a matter of fact, just show all of the slides, if you like, there aren't very many, are there?

(Slide Presentation).

A. Here is a piece of a topographic map from this area from Lewis County. This is the portion that shows the Meriwether Lewis National Monument and I don't see a pointer here, but perhaps you can hear me if I step back here. Here is the location of the Lewis Monument, marked by a small circle and that's also the burial site of Meriwether Lewis. This series of roads is a series of Park Service Roads. Here is the location of Grinder's Stand where Lewis was killed, where he died, and they are about 650 feet apart but notice, if you will, that the monument, that the burial site is surrounded on three sides, it's surrounded on the east, west, and the north by a series of ravines, by a series of valleys and that means that the monument site is the highest point of land in this vicinity and what that means geologically is that the ground water table is going to be very much depressed, very much lower than the monument site and so we imagine that the grave itself is in the so called zone of aeration within the soil column in a relatively dry portion of the soil.

The soil pH is slightly acidic but not overly so. We don't have any direct pH measurements from the burial site itself because that is Park Service land so we have some from nearby locations and they indicate the PH is a four and a half to five and a half which are slightly acidic, moderately acidic, or a normal pH.

The other two very favorable conditions have already been mentioned by Professor Starrs, one is the presence of the monument itself. It's got a large concrete base so we imagine that can act as an umbrella to protect the remains from direct infiltration of rainfall or snowmelt and the second has to do with this burial thickness of backfill that was placed over the monument site back in 1934 and 1935. At the monument itself we know that fill is about four feet thick. At other places on the site we have some estimates from our ground penetrating radar survey, says the thickest areas were two feet to eight feet and we think that the place where it's filled will probably also serve as an impermeable barrier to the infiltration of surface water.

Q. Dr. Stephens, on one of the occasions that you were at the site of the monument were you present when ground penetrating radar was done?

A. Yes, I was.

Q. Was there an indication on the ground penetrating radar that there may well be something under the monument, something other than soil under the monument?

A. There was. I might say that ground penetrating radar is a pretty straight forward technique but it works best when you can run your radar apparatus directly over the object you're trying to locate and in this case we have a large monument directly over the object. And so we use the radar to try to look obliquely beneath the monument, not an ideal situation geophysically but the person in charge, Dr. James Mellet from Subsurface Consulting Limited was fairly confident that he had detected some sort of anomalous condition beneath the monument which we imagine would be the burial itself.

Q. Dr. Stephens, on occasion when you were at the site was Dr. William Bass there with you the Tennessee Forensic Anthropologist, this gentlemen seated behind —

A. Yes, he was.

Q. Do you know who that is, know Dr. Bass he's a nationally renowned forensic anthropologist?

A. Yes, sir.

Q. We're proud of him here in Tennessee?

A. He's the governor of Tennessee [Obviously intended as a joke].

Q. He has a big orange heart. He's a professor emeritus at the University of Tennessee; do you know who he is?

A. I do.

Q. Do you say as a geologist say that him as a forensic anthropologist that the condition, that the geological conditions at that site are favorable for him finding a skeleton that would be good enough for examination purposes, is that your opinion?

A. Yes, sir, that's my opinion.

GENERAL PHILLIPS: Mr. Coroner, I submit him to you and the jury for further questions.

EXAMINATION

BY MR. CORONER:

Q. Dr. Stephens, in the tests that were done there at the park, is there anyway of having any kind of indication as to the type container or anyway that Meriwether Lewis might have been buried and placed there?

A. From the radar?

Q. From any of the tests that you've done was there any way to indicate if he might have been placed, for example, inside of a concrete container or a wooden container or whatever?

A. No, sir. I would have to say from our results there's no way of telling. The radar at best gives you kind of a shadowy ambiguous photograph of what might be present in some occurrences. In this particular case being blocked by the monument it was very difficult to get a good radar image, and so the best we can say is that there is some non-natural feature beneath the monument but beyond that I don't think I would characterize it.

Q. Probably need to break that down to where I could understand it, what is your opinion of what that object is, what would that be?

A. Let me digress a little bit and tell that you Dr. Mellet, who was radar operator on site thought that this situation was analogous to some sort of a void or a vault based on his experience. He's examined some underground vaults in New York City and he thought he had some pretty analogies of what he was seeing beneath the monument. My experience is limited enough that I would be hesitant to say.

MR. CORONER: Any other questions?

GENERAL PHILLIPS: Thank you, Dr. Stephens.

(WITNESS EXCUSED.)

GENERAL BAUGH: What time do you want to come back from lunch?

MR. CORONER: Take about an hour and a half.

GENERAL BAUGH: You think we can get back—well, however you want to do it. We've got several witnesses this afternoon.

MR. CORONER: Let's come back at 1:00 o' clock.

(Recess.)

GENERAL BAUGH: My next witness is Tom Streed. If you will face Mr. Tate and raise your right-hand he will swear you in.

THOMAS STREED

having been first duly sworn was examined and testified as follows:

DIRECT EXAMINATION

BY GENERAL BAUGH:

Q. Would you state your name, please?

A. My name is Thomas Streed.

Q. Where do you live, Mr. Streed

A. San Diego, California.

Q. What is your occupation?

A. I am a criminal psychologist, behavioral scientist.

Q. What caused you to be able to be a criminal psychologist and a behavioral scientist, what sort of education do you have?

A. Yes, I am educated in the field of human behavior. I have a Masters degree in that area and Ph.D.

Q. Can y'all hear him? Just a little bit louder, please?

A. I have a Masters degree and a Ph.D. in the field of human behavior. I spent a considerable amount of my professional career in the analysis, evaluation and study of criminal behavior.

Q. What sort of vocation did you have before you were a psychologist in that particular subspecialty?

A. I worked in the San Diego County Sheriff's Department for 24 years, the last 21 years of which I was assigned as a homicide detective. I worked in the field of death investigation from approximately 1970 until 1991 when I retired.

Q. Have you been asked to evaluate death from firearms in

order to determine whether the death was a result of suicide or homicide?

A. Yes, sir, on numerous occasions.

Q. And whoever is using the flash please don't, please stop. And have you examined the literature on the question of firearms as it applies to suicide or homicide?

A. Yes, sir.

Q. Tell us about that.

A. During the time that I was employed by the San Diego County Sheriff's Department and even subsequent to that point in time, I have both attended and taught at numerous different educational facilities throughout the United States. I have both attended and presented at national and international forum in reference to the various aspects of suicidal ideation and in terms of analysis and interpretation of various aspects of trauma.

Q. What is a psychological autopsy?

A. A psychological autopsy is a procedure for evaluating after death what was going on in an individual's mind, a victim's mind prior to the time of their death. It's essentially a biological profile of life-style, personality, stress factors, possible mental disorders and preoccupation of death.

Q. How common is a psychological autopsy—how commonly is it used by forensic psychologists and admitted in courts across the country?

A. Since 1958 a psychological profile has been an integral part of the evaluation of equivocal death. Under those circumstances where pathological evaluation, and possibly preliminary investigation, have not been able to reach a solid conclusion as to the matter or mode of death, a psychological autopsy may be conducted by various individuals involved in the death investigation. Since 1958 the psychological autopsy has been an integral part of death investigation.

In 1984 the C.D.C., the Center for Disease Control essentially endorsed the appropriateness of the psychological autopsy and it is well respected today as a vital tool.

Q. Are you familiar with the circumstances surrounding as much as history can tell us the death of Meriwether Lewis?

A. Yes sir,

Q. Does this historical record and the reports that you have been provided allow you to construct a psychological autopsy of Lewis?

A. To an extent. There is a limitation in terms of hard physical evidence, in terms of efficient death investigation that was conducted at the time, in terms of proper questioning and evaluation of the witness, the sole witness that was available at the time. As a consequence a psychological autopsy is as good as the information that you can access in order to glean a profile. Under the circumstances of the death of Governor Lewis, however, there are various aspects of his biological—biographical profile that provide an index that might be used to assess whether or not he was suicidal.

Q. Have you carried out such an assessment?

A. Yes, sir, I have.

Q. Did you reach an opinion about the death of Lewis whether it was homicide or suicide?

A. Yes, I did.

Q. What is that opinion?

A. My opinion is that there's a little degree, very little information that strongly and psychologically points to the fact that Governor Lewis was in fact, suicidal. I'll couch my opinion in these terms. I spent an abundance of years as a homicide detective; if today I saw this degree of information in a contemporary case I would be investigating it as a homicide.

Q. I believe you told me that you were able to reconstruct how many death investigations you actually participated in?

A. Over 2,000, sir.

Q. Now, what—and I think you have compiled something to assist us?

A. That's correct, sir.

Q. What is your—what is the basis for your opinion about the death of Lewis?

A. The basis is the historical record. The actual procedure that I used for purposes of the psychological autopsy is actually mnemonic, I used a tactic basically of understanding what sorts of factors and pressures might have related to an individual's potential for suicide. The word that I use is suicidal and each of the letters of that word actually equate to various aspects of suicidal ideation. Each of those letters, as a matter of fact, corresponds to the criteria that is accepted by the C.D.C., the Center for Disease Control. I just happened to rearrange the information to I think make it a little bit easier to follow and understand, if you like I'd be like happy to —

Q. If you would please?

A. — show you some slides of that. Might need the lights off. We'll take a moment to dim a light or two. (Presentation of Slides:)

A. This is a newspaper article— in 1986 I inadvertently got involved in the project, the investigation of the death of Meriwether Lewis. This is an article that came from a newspaper here in the State of Tennessee. This is the word that I alluded to suicide, and as you can see each of the letters corresponds to a certain series of the events.

S U I C I D A L

S The S, for instance—what sex was the individual that we are evaluating? Men commit suicide more frequently than women. The S also stands for the existence of either a support system or no support system. Subintention death has to do with risk taking behavior; suicidal thinking, I think it speaks for itself. And separating from life, I'm going to go into each of these criteria a little more thoroughly in just a moment.

Suicidal ideation in reference to pulling away from life. It's giving items of personal property away, communicating your thoughts of death with other individuals, illustrating that you have essentially ended life.

U The U stands for unsuccessful previous suicide attempts, prior attempts to taking your own life. We find that a large number of individuals that have attempted suicide or successfully carried out suicide have prior suicide attempts. The estimates run as high as 80 percent.

I The I stands for identification with others who have committed suicide, inquiring about death, isolation for the attempt and the intention of the individual to die.

C I CI stands for communicated intent. In other words, leaving information behind, notes, that sort of thing that illustrates that the person is in fact suicidal. No control, loss of impulse control is another factor, chronic illness, chronic injury, chronic illness' that is referred to contemporarily has to do with factors that cause or generate considerable amount, of despair or hopelessness on the part of the individual, such as heart disease, cancer, arthritis, and various things that we so frequently hear about. Chronic injury-has to do with injuries that the individual believes somehow or another destroyed or no longer enhanced the quality of life, possibly paralysis, that sort of thing.

D The D stands for depression, drugs, dichotomous thinking. Dichotomous thinking has do with saying, things are either this way or that way, there's no in between. There's either right or wrong, good or bad, and that's rigid dogmatic thinking. Delusion has to do with the implication of psychopathic condition, excuse me, a psychotic condition whereupon the person may be hallucinating.

A The A stands for alcohol abuse, inability to form an alliance, no future anticipation and

L the L stands for loss or lethality of method.

As I go through these slides very quickly, you'll see I believe that each of these criteria are fairly well explained in terms of a cautious analysis as to whether or not Governor Lewis happened to correspond to any of these particular criteria. At the end you'll see a highlighted series of data that give us an index as whether or not he might have been suicidal.

First of all, the sex issue. Males commit suicide three times more frequently than women, today at the rate of 22 per 100,000 versus women 6.6 per 100,000. Those statistics have not changed appreciably since the time of Governor Lewis' death.

No significant others or no support system. There was a newspaper article in reference to a support system that was written by Governor Lewis on November 16th, 1808, this is one year prior to Governor Lewis' death. He wrote the article for the *Missouri Gazette*, "The True Ambitions of an Honest Mind." "Were I to describe the blessings I desire in life"— I'm going to paraphrase this for the purposes of accelerating my presentation—"I would be happy in a few but faithful friends."

So to say that Governor Lewis didn't have a lot of friends or that he was not as benevolent, or as cordial or as gregarious as a non-suicidal person, I think it really flies in the face of his own profile of himself.

> "I would be in happy in a few but faithful friends. Business enough to secure me from indolence and leisure enough to always have an hour to spare. I would hate only those whose manners rendered them odious and love only where I knew I ought."

And the most telling statement of all in reference to this little profile, "and wait for that which will last for forever"— he's referring to death. "Wait for that," not go seeking it, not confront it, "wait for that which will last forever."

Another aspect of the support system consideration has to do with Governor Lewis' association with the Masons. He was very active in the Masonic organization. He joined the Virtue Lodge number 44 of the Masonic Order January 28, 1797. The Masons were founded in 1717. He was elected to various ranks in a very, very short period of time between January of 1797 and October 1799, he became a Royal Arch Mason. He named western rivers, the Philanthropy, the Philosophy and the Wisdom after Masonic ritual. He helped establish and became Master of the Masonic Lodge in St. Louis in 1808.

The Masonic belief has to do not with a particular affiliation to a certain church or a certain religious group, it has to do with the requirement that the members have a belief in God, and a belief in the rewards of a hereafter; and these factors, I think fly in the face, again, of an individual that has no regard for what the hereafter may bring to them. And I'll expand on that in a moment.

Other significant others, Lucy Meriwether Lewis Marks, his mother. He maintained a very strong and close relationship with her throughout his life. At the time of his death he had been anticipating moving her from Albemarle County, Virginia to his residence in St. Louis; she was 57 years of age at the time of his death.

A very long relationship with Thomas Jefferson. He was a life-long neighbor of Meriwether Lewis. He lived with President Jefferson as President Jefferson's personal secretary during the time—for a period of time in Washington. A letter from Jefferson to his daughter, Martha, May 28, 1801, about Mrs. Madison, who essentially served as the first lady,

> "Dolly Madison left us two days ago to com-
> mence housekeeping so that Captain Lewis
> and myself are like two mice in a church."

This is not an individual that had an obscure relationship with an individual.

His relationship with William Clark. He met Clark in

the army in 1794 at age 20. He was second in command of the Corps of Discovery. Now the interesting thing is that Meriwether Lewis considered William Clark the co-commander but as far as President Jefferson was concerned Meriwether Lewis was in charge and as a matter of fact, he outranked William Clark on the expedition. William Clark named his son Meriwether Lewis Clark, born in 1809.

Mahlon Dickerson was a very close friend, a Philadelphia lawyer, politician, became very active. I think he was ultimately governor of New Jersey and involved in federal politics as well. There are frequent references in Dickerson's diary regarding outings with Lewis and some of them had to do with their activity in Philadelphia, various—how can I say this gracefully, a little bar-hopping now and then. Let's not get too bound up in the fact that Governor Lewis was quote an alcoholic.

Amos Stoddard. Amos Stoddard was an Army Captain who Lewis met in 1804 at a port that's approximately 60 miles from St. Louis. He assisted Lewis in procuring equipment for the expedition. They maintained a close relationship.

> "September 22nd, 1809, I must acknowledge myself remiss in not writing you in answer to several friendly epistles which I have received from you since my return from the Pacific Ocean. Continued occupation in the immediate discharge of duties of the public station, will I trust—will I trust in some measure, plead my apology."

That's the nature of the relationship with Amos Stoddard. I could go on and go about this, but the bottom line is that he had considerable volume of very close friends as he attested to in this article of the *Missouri Gazette*.

Subintention death. Now, subintention death has to do with the unnecessary-involvement of risk taking behavior. An individual for instance that's a skydiver, may be said to engage in risk taking behavior but among other skydivers that isn't risk taking behavior. It's a very calculated, very precise sort of thing that's done. But if the individual that's a skydiver is told don't go up today, upper air turbulence is so bad that if you do this there's a strong possibility that you won't survive. If the individuals presses it and pursues that kind of risk taking then that may in fact correspond to subintention death or so the called death wish .

There are allegations of cautious behavior on the part of Governor Lewis. Cautious behavior.

> "My apprehension from the heat of the lower country and my fear of my original papers relative to my voyage to the Pacific falling into the hands of the British induced me to change my route and proceed by land in going to Washington..."

The point is this: This is an individual that's engaging in cautious behavior, not subintention death. He's concerned about the British. He's concerned about his papers falling into the hands of the British. An individual, who is in fact suicidal, doesn't much care about the worldly possessions that they are entrusted to control.

October 18, 1809 letter from Neelly to Thomas Jefferson. It appears that his first intention was to go around by water to the city but his thinking of the war with England probable and that his valuable papers might be in danger of falling into the hands of the British he was thereby induced to change his route. This is another confirmation of cautious behavior.

Suicidal thinking. There is no evidence in any of the data that I've researched for the past ten years that gives any indication of suicidal ideation. Suicidal ideation has to do with role playing, seeing how far you can lean out on the edge of the cliff before you fall over, placing weapons against the side of your head and dry firing them. Slumping into nooses. No preoccupation with suicide. Separating from life. There are no farewell expressions, saying good-bye, giving away property. The common statements that you might hear are things like you won't have me to kick around anymore, things of that nature. I know we heard President Nixon say you won't have Nixon to kick around anymore and he wasn't suicidal, so you just can't say automatically that the uttering of one particular comment makes an individual suicidal.

At the top we've already looked at the S. Unsuccessful previous suicide attempts. Now there is the key reference, this business that occurred on this riverboat en route to New Orleans whereupon there are allegations of at least two prior suicide attempts. There is no direct evidence of any suicide attempt during Lewis' life. As a former homicide detective, I can tell you, that if an individual is alleged to have attempted to take their life the most curious question, the most important, and significant question that people around that individual ask is: "How did he try to do it?"—and there is not one scintilla of evidence of anyone ever asking how did he try to take his life.

As a matter of fact, in the letter from Captain James Howell, who's also known in some of the literature as James House, writing from Nashville to territorial secretary Frederick Bates and perhaps the counsel that's here with us today, maybe General Baugh can make a comment on this, is whether or not this might be regarded as a significant piece of information and I'm going to just characterize this, Major Stoddard informed me that he saw a person who told him —if I were to present a prosecutor with that kind of information I would probably be driven from their office. That's third or fourth hand hearsay. It has absolutely no value.

Down here in the letter November 26, 1811, two years after the death, Major Gilbert Russell from Frederick Town, Maryland writes to Thomas Jefferson, about learning from the crew that he had made two attempts to kill himself—in one of which he nearly succeeded. Wouldn't you be curious if you were Thomas Jefferson how did this man attempt to do this?

There may be an explanation as to what the crew happened to see. But then again, that's a matter of historic speculation.

So in terms of the S and the U, we already have those articulated at the top. If you will notice the only word that's highlighted is the word sex because we know that males kill themselves more frequently than women do.

The I, identification with others who have committed suicide. There are no historical records as to anyone known to Lewis who committed suicide. Inquiring about death. There is no evidence that Lewis ever became preoccupied with death.

Isolation for the attempt. Most suicides, 96 percent as a matter of fact, and I've researched a lot of the literature in reference to this, are carried out in solitude or isolation and there are multifaceted volumes of reason as to why suicide is carried out in solitude or isolation. One of the biggest reasons is because the individual committing suicide has a purpose to insure a low probability of rescue.

Another reason is because suicide over the years has been linked with despicable conduct. It's not Christian behavior. It's a sign of weakness, and all of the rest of the stigma that's attached to suicide. So the individual that is in fact suicidal is preoccupied with taking themselves out of the public eye in order to do this.

Lewis' alleged suicide attempt in route to Fort Pickering via the Mississippi River interrupted by the crew of the boat. This is not carrying out suicidal activities or attempts in isolation of the crew that can rescue you. It's inconsistent then with a suicide attempt.

There are numerous isolated locations along the Trace. I think every one in the room has had the opportunity to look off to the sides of the road along the Trace and to just consider the absolute overwhelming volume of isolated locations whereupon an individual could walk off the Trace and very, very easily be in isolation and in solitude for carrying this out. At Grinder's Stand, there was Mrs. Grinder or Griner in attendance, possibly Grinder's children, Bethany age ten, possibly a son age unknown. Governor Lewis' servant Pernier and Neelly's servant as well. Again, this is not isolation.

Intentions to die. There is a notation in the journal after he was accidentally shot during the expedition by Peter Cruzatte. Lewis changes his opinion. First he thought he had been accidentally shot by Cruzatte. Then he suspected that the Indians had shot him. Here's his comment as recorded in the journal.

> (Reading:) "I now got back to the pirogue as well as I could and prepared myself a pistol, my rifle and air gun being determined as retreat was impracticable to sell my life as dearly as possible."

May the 28, 1811. The statement of Lewis as reported by Mrs. Grinder—and again this is hearsay information—to Alexander Wilson in his letter to Alexander Lawson.

> "0, madam, give me some water and heal my wounds."

Again, she changed her statement in a third account but nevertheless, this is a statement that is inconsistent with virtually every suicide investigation that I've ever conducted, which incidentally I figured out the other day I think the conservative account was 432 suicide investigations.

The CI communicated intent. There are no communications from Lewis that express morbid thought content; I can't go on, life isn't worth living, I have no worth. These statements do not exist. Suicide notes are left in an estimated only 20 percent and some researchers will say 30 percent of cases. Notes are usually left at the scene. One-third of those who leave notes leave more than one note, and notes often reflect the range of emotions of the suicidal individual. Suicide notes may give a variety of categories and depending upon the researcher they are categorized in different fashion.

There's a transitory note whereupon the suicidal individual says I'm going to a better place. There's an explanatory note wherein the suicidal individual says this is the reason that I'm doing this, I can no longer live with the shame or the humiliation or whatever the reason happens to be. And then there is an accusatory note which is, you rotten jerk, you deserve this, I hope you suffer guilt because of what you drove me to, those are the kinds of generalized categories and that's a bit of a reckless assessment I understand, but we're kind of in a press for time here.

This holographic will—and I think there are experts here that will testify as to whether or not the holographic will purported to have been written by Lewis was in fact in his hand. I bequeath all of my estate, real and person, to my mother Lucy Marks and it goes on to describe the necessity of paying the debts, a statement of which will be found in a small minute book deposited with my servant. Again, it's, not unusual for an individual embarking on a relatively hazardous journey and particularly one who now has property, as opposed to an individual that earlier had less property and was in the company of a large cavalry of fairly well trained men to write a holographic will.

The other aspect of communicated intent, control of impulses, CI, Control of Impulses. An impulse is a sudden inclination to act without conscious thought. Governor Lewis is attested to have been a bit of a hot head. Now that does not imply that he was acting without conscious thought. An impulse is an inclination to act that's not driven by a conscious thought. There is no evidence of Lewis' failure to resist an impulse drive or temptation to perform harmful acts.

CI, chronic illness. Now there may be another aspect of this that relates to potential for depression and it's labile if, in fact, it exists in a serious mode at all. Malaria in reference to Governor Lewis' experience with the disease was labile, meaning that it wasn't an ongoing and draining malady. It had spikes whereupon he would feel high fever, chills and other aspects of the actual disease.

Letter from president Lewis—from Lewis to President Madison September 16th, having taking medicine he's feeling much better and providing my health permits no time shall be lost in reaching Washington. He is also demonstrating future anticipation in the sense that he has a goal for the future. But again the important thing I think to remember in terms of chronic illness is the lability of the affliction itself.

Chronic injury, there are no debilitating injuries reported by Lewis. He had a complete recovery from the accidental gun shot wound to his hip which he suffered August 11th, 1806.

Again, we see the chart at the top illustrating—you can see the S, which again sex is the only thing we strongly recognize.

D, depression. No evidence of severe prolonged depression. Every one in the room at some point in their life is going to suffer mild to moderate depression. It's not mild or moderate depression that leads to suicidal ideation. It is severe depression, and there is no evidence of a severe prolonged depression. And particularly there's no evidence of any documents written during Governor Lewis' life.

One of the other gentlemen that spoke earlier, made reference to the fact that President Jefferson entrusted this individual with an expedition that was dear and close to his heart. Had this individual had any reservations in terms of depression that he observed in this individual or alcoholism or any other aspect of behavioral disorder, he would not have entrusted this extremely important venture to this person.

Depression is noted by disturbances of judgment, has to do with perceptiveness, insight acumen, orientation, these are the aspects that we look at to assess the degree of depression. Orientation, time frames become unimportant.

Now individuals have said Governor Lewis was not active and precise in terms of meeting deadlines and answering the responsibilities in publishing the journals. I'm the biggest procrastinator on the planet myself and I'm not suicidal. And I think that may have been a bit of the problem with the journals. Governor Lewis was extremely busy fulfilling the obligations of his governorship.

Intellectual function, impaired attention and concentration. There's no evidence of that. No evidence in terms of the memory deficit or difficulty in prioritizing his recollection, no evidence of blurred, flat or labile affect. Affect has to do with visual confirmations of emotional feelings that you can see on the part of an individual, crying, sadness, self-mutilation, these sorts of things. Thought content. No evidence of pervasive guilt. Hopelessness or helpless.

Drugs. Lewis did in fact use opium or morphine as needed for Malaria. There is no evidence of abuse; I know I've read some accounts that his dosage by one researcher's assessment was as much as a gram of opium per day. That is a horrific amount of opium. The question that rises that this gives rise to be exactly how pure was this opium, what in fact was the actual reaction that Governor Lewis felt to this. There's no evidence of abuse as evidenced by increasing dose levels. Individuals that abuse dangerous drugs, narcotics, report necessity for more and more of the drug in order to compensate for the dose level requirement. There's no evidence of overdosing or withdrawal syndrome. We don't see that. During the expedition Lewis frequently prescribed laudanum as a remedy, which is a mixture of opium and alcohol. There is no evidence of abuse, again, as evidenced by increasing dose levels, overdosing or withdrawal or the business of depression.

Here it is again [slide image of cartoon]

> (Reading:) "William [front page] Lewis and Clark Expedition declared a success. See what I mean. His name is always first. I'll tell you son, if you don't do something about this now, you're going to be playing second fiddle in the history books."

This is Clark's mother talking to him. Kind of—I think it's a ridiculous play on whether or not Governor Lewis might or anyone else near to him might have been distressed.

D also stands for dichotomous thinking. There is no evidence of rigid thinking. For example, right or wrong, good or evil, truth or lie. We often talk to children who engage in dichotomous thinking. You question a five or six or seven year old about something and they have two distinctions, either you told the truth or you told a lie. As adults we have the miraculous ability to kind of shade the truth a little bit, or we didn't exactly tell you everything or we weren't exactly honest. There is no evidence of Governor Lewis engaging in that kind of rigid thinking, again, that involves right or wrong, good or evil. People that plot a suicidal see only two operative—two applications, either I'm going to live or I'm going to die, there is no center ground.

Delusions. There is no evidence of hallucinations or psychotic behavior.

Inability to form an alliance. An alliance is an association formed for mutual benefit. Lewis formed several alliances shortly before his death. I think other researchers have alluded to some of this. He had a relationship with a publisher, a marketing individual, a historian, a person that is going to assist in terms of scientific description of plants, his painter Charles Wilson Peale, the engraver, artist, naturalist, the list goes on and on. He had numerous alliances with individuals. These are relationships formed again for mutual benefit.

July 22nd, 1808, he helped establish the *Missouri Gazette* with Joseph Charles. December 1808, he helped establish the St. Louis, Missouri River Fur Company and again, these are either one year or less than a year before his death.

His final alliance was with James Neelly. This is an individual who if he was anticipating suicide would probably choose to go off into the wilderness by himself and not make a relationship —establish a relationship with another person.

Future anticipation, another aspect of the A letter. Lewis's correspondence indicating future planning, "September 14th, 1809, providing my health permits no time shall be lost in reaching Washington"— that's a future anticipation.

September 26th, a letter from Lewis to Amos Stoddard, "you will direct to me at the city of Washington"—he's anticipating getting to Washington DC—"until the last of December after which I expect I shall be on my return to St. Louis." These are future anticipations again.

The A, alcohol. Twenty-five percent of all suicide victims are alcohol dependent and that's the operative word. It doesn't mean that they drink a lot, they are dependent upon alcohol. Lewis drank frequently but there's no evidence of dependency in the sense that he had to have a drink and then once he started it was impossible or difficult for him to stop. Are there indications of—let's call it raising a ruckus. Yes, there are, but is this alcohol dependence, there is no evidence of that.

Lewis is endorsed by President Jefferson as commander for Discovery. This again flies in the face of an individual entrusting a very important mission upon someone they might have had a lack of confidence in because of alcohol abuse. There is no evidence of alcohol abuse during the expedition. Lewis' harsh enemy, the biggest enemy that he probably had, Frederick Bates, never criticized Lewis in reference to his drinking habits.

Captain Gilbert Russell's observations, January of 1810, again this is after death has occurred, the fact is what you may— the fact is what you may yet be ignorant is that his untimely death may be attributed solely to the free use he made of liquor, he acknowledged very candidly, but an astounding aspect of this after writing or making these observations Captain Russell also remarks that he deprived him several days of alcohol except for a claret and some white wine. Again if an individual has a drinking problem, these aren't the sorts of things that one would not normally prescribe even in medicinal quantities.

L has to do with loss. As you can see we're almost to the

end of the mnemonic right here. Loss may be of two varieties, it can be a tangible loss or intangible. A tangible loss has to do with financial loss, employment loss, possessions loss, love ones loss, these sorts of things. Intangible losses have to do with loss of things you can't put your hands on, power, prestige, self identity, authority, those sort of things.

Lewis had financial difficulties which may be argued by some researchers and discounted by others, but appeared confident in resolving them. September the 16th letter from Lewis to President Madison, "I flatter myself they will receive both sanction and approbation" and he critiques the word sanction. What he's referring to here is payment of the warrants that he drawn on the government.

September 22nd, 1809, a letter to his friend Amos Stoddard, "an explanation is all that is necessary, I'm sensible to put all matters right." These are not the words of an individual that has a sense of loss that is so devastating that they see absolutely no sense of resolution.

L, lethality. There is a desire in the heart of suicidal individuals, those who intend truly in taking their life for efficiency in terms of the fatal blow. Males generally select a more lethal—I think a better word is more violent means of self destruction in the sense of the more -- they use more gunshot wounds (sic), more knife wounds, more falling from a height type of injuries than women do. Weapon, or method selected, may be symbolic depending on the type of a gesture that the suicidal individual is making.

If the individual is altruistic, for instance, they may chose to go out in a blaze of glory, i.e., the type of individual that blows themselves up at the Marine barracks in Beirut. Multiple weapon usage is very, very unusual. I think I have seen possibly in reference to over 400 suicide investigations that I have conducted, possibly a half a dozen applications of multiple weapon usage and usually both weapons are used at precisely the same point in time. And it usually involves something like the ingestion of an over dose of pills with slumping into a noose for purposes a asphyxia or possibly shooting one's self and falling from a height at the same time.

To administer one wound and then recover sufficiently to administer another wound is extraordinarily unusual. Has it ever happened, yes, it has, but it is nevertheless very, very unusual. Lewis's trauma was suicidally inefficient, but ultimately fatal. He was proficient as a frontiersman as a hunter, as a soldier, one would think that an individual skilled at survival in the wilderness who has these survival abilities about him would be able to administer a fatal wound, but apparently he was unsuccessful in doing that in the sense that the fatal wound struck him down with a sense of urgency and immediacy.

Finally, we look at all of these factors and I have to apologize for not being able to spend more time in elucidating what all these things mean. But look at the highlighted areas here. Yes, he's a male.

Unsuccessful previous suicide attempts. It's highlighted because of the letters that have been written regarding the crew on the boat that saved him. But there is no reliable information. There was a statement of one or more crew persons and we don't know anything about who these people were, exactly what they said or what they said Governor Lewis did. That is it not reliable information.

The D, drugs, yes he used opium for malaria, but there is again, no evidence of any kind of an abusive relationship or a dependency. So it's highlighted in the sense that there are researchers over the years that would say yes, the individual was using alcohol. There may be a bifurcated problem in the use of alcohol and drugs in the since that the combination of these things may result in some kind of synergistic relation, in other words, heightened reaction. But again, there is no evidence of this having occurred before.

There is evidence, however, of this state of derangement which was described by Captain Russell, "he appeared in a deranged fashion." In fact, that may have been a description of a delirium. A delirium is manifest by a couple of things, a clouded state of consciousness, misinterpretation of the environment, confused thinking, in other words. If Governor Lewis was suffering a bout of malaria, if Governor Lewis was suffering a delirium as a result of that, if Governor Lewis had ingested opium pills for controlling—I'm going to defer to Dr. Francisco later on, but I believe that it controlled diarrhea and if he were drinking a bit at the same time, this may have been interpreted to be derangement of mind, when in fact it's the effect is quite predictable.

Alcohol he drank frequently but no evidence of dependency and in terms of lethality of method again, the wounds were fatal but suicidally inefficient.

Again, this is the conclusion of the data that I wanted to present to you regarding the psychological autopsy, if we could have the lights back again, regarding the object of our concern Meriwether Lewis.

Q. You probably need a breather. There has been an article written in *William and Mary Historical Reporter*, I believe the Kushner article?

A. Yes.

Q. It took the opposite side. Do you have any comment on that?

A. It—Howard Kushner has an article that appeared in 1981. In addition, he has a book entitled *American Suicide* and Mr. Kushner is entrenched in terms of three specific aspects that he believes contributed to the suicide of Meriwether Lewis.

First of all, his financial condition; secondly, the fact that he abused alcohol; and third, the fact that he was unsuccessful in terms of acquiring a wife, but again, I've already addressed the business of the financial concerns as well as some other researchers. I've addressed the business of alcohol abuse I think and in terms I think of his desire to seek out and obtain a wife, I don't know how to say this humbly, but my experience has been that often the relationship that one has with a spouse leads to suicidal ideation more frequently than the lack of it.

Q. Thank you, Dr. Streed. Any questions from the members of the—?

MR. CORONER: Anybody have any questions?

GENERAL BAUGH: — jury.

MR. CORONER: No.

(WITNESS EXCUSED.)

GENERAL BAUGH: Thank you very much. My next witness will be Dr. Jerry Francisco. Dr. Francisco, if you will raise your hand and Mr. Tate will swear you in.

JERRY THOMAS FRANCISCO, M.D.

having been first duly sworn was examined and testified as follows:

DIRECT EXAMINATION

BY GENERAL BAUGH:

Q. Would you state your name, please, sir, when you get your papers in order and spell your last name for—first and last name, please—for purposes of the record?

A. Jerry Thomas Francisco, J-E-R-R-Y, Francisco, F-R-A-N-C-I-S-C-O.

Q. What is your occupation?

A. Pathologist, physician.

Q. Where is the seat of your practice?

A. University of Tennessee in Memphis.

Q. How long have you been so employed?

A. Since 1959.

Q. What does a forensic pathologist do?

A. A forensic pathologist provides information support to a death investigation, such as a coroner or a medical examiner as a part of this death investigation in order to render objective data that makes the determination of cause of death and manner of death based upon more solid ground.

Q. Did you have a position with the state, or do you currently have a position with the State of Tennessee as a forensic pathologist?

A. I had a position with the State of Tennessee as chief medical examiner for the state from 1971 until about 1988.

Q. I believe that you did the autopsy on Elvis Presley; is that correct?

A. That's correct.

Q. How does—how do the facts of the death and the pathologist's investigation meet together?

A. Well, let me use this cartoon to illustrate the elements that are available in death investigation, and there basically are only three areas. One is an examination of the scene. In this particular case, that is not possible. It cannot be done. The other is the interrogation of witnesses, and in this particular case there is only one witness, albeit that witness having been interpreted, reinterpreted, reinterpreted and reinterpreted over and over again until you come away thinking you're hearing several stories when, in fact, you're only hearing one story from one person repeated multiple times, a single witness. And the third is the examination of the body, and in this particular case, there was no known recorded documented examination of this body. None.

There are observations of witnesses that say I saw this or I saw that, but these are not same as examination of the body. The body examination is something that is to be undertaken by someone experienced in body examination, not a witness who happened to see this or happens to see that. For instance, there is one statement attributed to this lady that says the brain was exposed. Well, I'm not sure she knows the difference between brain and blood. She might have seen blood, and since it was the head knowing that the brain is inside the head, therefore, brain was exposed, but I submit to you that is not a reliable observation. It is an observation that is, by it's very definition, suspect.

The phenomenon of a gunshot wound to the head and then a gunshot wound to the chest is, by definition, an unusual type of suicide, if indeed suicide it was. You can have multiple shots. I personally have a case in which a person fired a gunshot wound to his head four times, bang, bang, bang, bang, and it wasn't until the last shot, had been fired that he was incapacitated and died.

There's another case in which a person fired a shot across the right side, sat in his car waiting to die, didn't, changed hands and fired a shot to the left side. This time it struck the brain appropriately and he died so that there were four holes in the head, an entrance/exit on one side, an entrance/exit on the other side. Fortunately, the gun was still in his lap. Therefore, it was possible for the investigators to say hmmmm, possibly this is not a homicide, but without the presence of the gun, it would have been considered a homicide.

So there are unusual suicide phenomena, but be that as it may, it is clearly unusual. It's the kind of unusualness in which once it occurs the investigator has the tendency to report it, to tell the world this is what I saw because of its unusual nature.

Q. What is the importance of the examination of the body? What can it tell you?

A. It is vital because there are many things that it can show. And let me—you're looking for trauma, injury, abnormalities to the body. There are things you may find that will tell you how it did occur. For instance, was it to the left side; did it come out the right; or did it, indeed, graze across the forehead not entering the skull at all; when did it occur, an interval, how long did he survive. If indeed it was a crease to the scalp only, there was essentially no brain damage and, therefore, there was ample opportunity to fire the gun to the chest maybe trying to find the heart, but I would suspect that you cannot prove he probably knew where the heart was. I think all of you know where the heart is. You can feel it beating. Because you feel it beating, you know where it is. If you are going to make a shot, you are going to fire where the heart is beating. In this particular case, the description of the path of this wound—again, by this one unreliable witness -- is into the chest, out low in the back, which means it's coming downward, not toward the heart itself but away from the heart.

Now, the point is: The credibility of where these wounds, were, you cannot get from a witness, you must get from an examination of the body itself, and that is the one thing that we are lacking. And as a scientist, it really kind of puts me in an unusual position, but I usually don't testify to anything unless I have something to see. In this particular case, there is absolutely nothing that I can see. All I have are statements, observations, interpretations, secondhand interpretations, third hand interpretations, fourth hand interpretations all without the one prime phenomenon that can give objective data, and that's the body itself. It's not seen, it cannot be seen at this date, at this point, and yet it is probably available to be seen.

Significance in death causation. Again, let's go back to the head. Did it go across and come out here? That being the case, the brain, the significant parts of the brain are in between. Therefore, it must have gone through a significant part of the brain. If it went through a significant part of the brain, there is no way for a second shot to the chest. It cannot be done. And if there is no second shot, to the chest that can be done, how does he make the observation— give me water—look?

What was produced? What kind of wound was produced? Bullets, by and large, travel in straight lines inside the body. Therefore, if you know your anatomy of the body and you know a start point and you know an end part, you know what it went through, because they don't travel zigzag lines inside the body. The only exception to that are gunshot wounds to the head that come in here, they will strike the inner part of the skull, they will circle around and come to rest on the opposite side, but with that exception, they travel in straight lines.

What was the direction? And this, again, becomes very, very important in this particular case. Was it left to right? Was it right to left? Was it front to back? Was it back to front? Was it contact? Is there powder present on the skull; because if it was contact, that powder is going to be present on that skull, even today. It will stay. Does it exist? Was it left to right? Was it right to left? Again, the skull is there for examination.

Bones are preserved for hundreds and hundreds and hundreds of years.Egyptian mummies being the prime example, of course. The bones are still there. The bones are still examinable. The bones can still be x-rayed, the bones can still be photographed, the bones can still give you information that is vital and important in coming to a decision of what is the manner of death.

What was the quantity of force? Now, this really gets outside of my field, because I know nothing about guns. All I know is you point them, shoot them, they go bang, and something happens, but that's about all know. There are other people to talk about quantity of force, but a gun with a 50 caliber is a pretty significant bullet and if, in fact, it has sufficient force to penetrate the skin, penetrate the skull, it is going to produce a lot of damage. And if it goes into the brain, enough damage will be there that the capacity of the person to produce other conscious, intentional actions are gone, and, therefore, the shot to the head, if it was first, if it indeed blew out the front of the skull, if it indeed did that, it probably produced significant brain damage, and if there was significant brain damage, there was not time or consciousness to inflict the second shot.

That's basically what I have to say, except for one thing.

Q. Well, let me ask you about—what about the skin? Does it—does it remain over a long period of time?

A. The skin is less likely than the bones, but because skin that's dry, is by definition, leather—and leather has a good survivability—if, in fact, the location is dry enough, as was mentioned that appears to be above the water table and, therefore, if it stays dry, skin is also going to be preserved. If the skin is preserved, that's a second organ to allow an examination and an observation to give objective data that would be very significant in rendering an interpretation regarding both cause and manner of death.

Q. What about time of death? Is there —

A. Time of death? Well, I'm sure you've seen Kojak on TV saying 7:32. I'm lucky if I can say sometime between April and May. It is an art form, it is not a science, and you have to take everything you have into consideration in order to deal with a time of death. There are certain injuries that by their very nature appear to be instantly lethal, but there are documented events in which they are not instantly lethal. There is a documented story of a fellow in Kansas who wanted to commit suicide and laid down in front of a train, the train came along and cut him in two. People arrived, he was still alive, alive long enough to tell them that's what he did, and put an "X" on a piece of paper after dictating that he did intend to do it.

Now, this seems incredible, but it can occur. However, it is unusual. There are certain wounds that by their very nature you say that's got to be fatal, and that's got to be fatal within a relatively short period of time. One to the body would not necessarily be fatal rapidly, because it's a function of what organs were damaged and how rapidly was the bleeding, because the bleeding is going to be the cause of death, and it has to be a large vessel and the bleeding to be rapid for death to be rapid.

Q. What about diseases such as malaria, syphilis, things like that?

A. Well, disease is constantly with us. Everybody has got one disease or another. A mole is a disease. It's a deviation from normal, so all of us have moles. At this time in history for a person to be without disease was kind of unusual, but there are all sorts of diseases out there. Diarrhea was even more common. Infectious diseases of various sorts were common. Malaria, typhoid, all of these diseases were common. He may very well have had some of those diseases, but that by itself is not necessarily a significant event if, if examination of the body says this was not a contact gunshot wound. It has significance if, in fact, you have evidence that there was suicide. And from what I know about the events, from what I know about the circumstances and from what I have learned today, and I've heard a lot of interesting information today, in my judgment, there is insufficient information to claim that this was suicide or this was a homicide. I don't think I could do it. I would have to say I don't know.

Q. Could DNA be recovered from a body that had been—from

skeletal remains 197 years old?

A. Yes, probably.

Q. What could that tell us?

A. Well, the DNA that's recovered from skeletal remains has been most useful in the examination of what is called mitochondrial DNA. The mitochondrial structure, which is the structure inside the cell, has a separate genetic machinery than the DNA of the cell nucleus, and there are a lot more of those structures inside a cell than—there's only one nucleus, but multiple mitochondrial structures. And, therefore,, if you can determine the sequence of the DNA in the mitochondria and if you have the maternal line available of this person, then you can establish an identify with this particular maternal line.

This was the way in which they finally concluded that the bodies recovered in Russia were indeed Romanovs was by the matching of material DNA of the bodies with the maternal line, because the mother passes it on to each offspring unique from the mother to the offspring.

GENERAL BAUGH: That's all the questions I have, Mr. Tate.

EXAMINATION

BY MR. CORONER:

Q. Dr. Francisco, is there any connection between a person's dominant hand, the hand that you would use most often, and the wounds that one might receive —

A. None that I'm aware that is very useful, because commonly a right-handed person is going to use both hands to pull the trigger. And very commonly in our environment using our modern guns, it may be upside down with the thumb pulling the trigger with both hands on the gun. With this particular type weapon, upside down is not necessarily the favored way of doing it, because it just doesn't work very well upside down, but the dominant hand is what I would call a secondary characteristic, whether it's right to left or left to right, and you discover which is right-handed and which is left-handed. Number one, it is hard to get that information, because relatives don't necessarily know what is the truth. You ask them were they right-handed, yes, they were right-handed. Well, they weren't necessarily right-handed, they may have seen them use the right hand, and it's very-hard to get good data about which hand did the deceased favor. That's a very hard thing to get. Even if you get it, there's no guarantee that a person is going to have used the dominant hand.

But you have to remember one thing: Suicide is not a rational act, at least not in our society. When you start thinking rationally, you're creating problems for yourself because you can't come to a rational conclusion about an irrational act.

Q. Would you address the issue of the frequency of two shots being used in suicide?

A. In my experience, probably less than one percent of the time that multiple shots have been used.

Q. And what has been your experience with examination of cadavers that have died over a long period of time ago that have already been buried and —

A. The bones and the skin are the two most preserved parts of the body. The soft tissues, in the absence of embalming, probably beyond a couple of years would not be useful, but even a hundred years, 200 years, the bone and the skin are commonly preserved. Egyptian mummies, there are a little bit different circumstances in that there was embalming present and it was a dry, cool—dry, hot climate, however the pyramids were a little cool, but the preservation of the bones and the preservation of the skin, they are very sturdy structures and would last—my personal experience was with Egyptian mummy about 2,000 B.C.

Q. Would the mode of burial have something to do with the outcome?

A. Mode of burial will have some outcome in the sense that if it is dry, the body will last longer because dryness—or should I say the other way, moisture is the facilitator of decomposition, and, therefore, in the absence of moisture, preservation is for an extended period of time. In the presence of moisture, it leads to degradation at much faster pace.

MR. CORONER: Any other questions from the jury?

EXAMINATION

BY MR. TURNBOW:

Q. Dr. Francisco, you said that if a bullet penetrates the head, it's a good probability that there is damage to the brain?

A. That's correct.

Q. And there's also a good probability that that would render any judgment or ability to function impossible?

A. That's correct.

Q. Now, in Major Neely's letter to Thomas Jefferson he said that there was hole in the head, and he must have seen that because he helped bury the body and directed that it to be done. We know that that was the case. That was Ms. Grinder's statement. If there was a hole in the head, it means that there was likely to be brain damage. In certain things, if she had a conversation with Lewis after he was shot, is this suspect?

A. Yes, it's inconsistent.

GENERAL BAUGH: His question was about the observations of the hole in Lewis' head, how would that affect the ability of Lewis to hold a conversation with Ms. Grinder or anyone else after the time that he had been shot?

THE WITNESS: That's part of the problem when all you have is the statement of witnesses. Number one, you run into all sorts of inconsistencies. You may be able to explain these inconsistencies if you had a good examination of where was the hole, was it forward, was it mid part, was it back, but without knowing that, you can't choose—I can't choose between the —

GENERAL BAUGH: Anyone else have any? Dr. Ravenholt?

DR. RAVENHOLT: I would just like to modify one thing that Dr. Francisco said. He indicated there was only one witness. There were actually three, Mrs. Grinder and Pernier and the other servant, and they were present when he died at daybreak.

GENERAL BAUGH: Good. We've got controversy already.

THE WITNESS: True, there was another witness, but to my knowledge, there is no documentation from the other two. There is no statement, there's nothing that we know that they said. We only have one witness that talked.

GENERAL BAUGH: Any other questions? Thank you, Dr. Francisco. (WITNESS EXCUSED.)

GENERAL BAUGH: Our next witness is Lucien Haag.
Mr. Haag, if you will turn around and face Mr. Tate and raise your right hand, he will place you under oath.

LUCIEN C. HAAG

having been first duly sworn was examined and testified as follows:

DIRECT EXAMINATION

BY GENERAL BAUGH:

Q. Would you state name and your occupation, please, sir?

A. Lucien C. Haag. I'm a criminalist and firearms examiner for my own consulting firm.

Q. Where do you work?

A. Carefree, Arizona.

Q. Must be a nice place.

A. It's a nice place.

Q. What is a criminalist?

A. A criminalist is a forensic scientist that deals with the evaluation and examination of physical evidence as it relates to some law or science question. Basically, the work you see depicted in a functioning crime laboratory.

Q. Can everybody hear him? Maybe just a little bit louder. And by whom are you presently employed?

A. I have my own consulting firm at this time called Forensic Science Services.

Q. How long have you worked as a criminalist?

A. Be 31 years this month.

Q. Have you ever received any type of certification as a criminalist?

A. Yes. There is certification available through a number of organizations now. I've been certified through the California Association of Criminalists.

Q. Who did you work for before you had your consulting firm?

A. I worked for the City of Phoenix Police Crime Laboratory for about 17 years both as a criminalist and later as technical director of the Crime Laboratory.

Q. What did you do for the City of Phoenix Crime Lab?

A. Well, I did all the basic things you see done in a crime laboratory. I worked in all the sections, I later supervised them. My area of special interest was the firearms unit.

Q. What are the types of firearms examination that you've done in the last 17 years or so?

A. Well, they range from the basic things, again, you see depicted in films, so examining a bullet or cartridge case with the submitted firearm. There are other aspects of the criminalist. You deal with such things as powder residue, that you heard a little bit about from Dr. Francisco, distance determination, determining the type of gun that fired the bullet if we don't have a firearm already submitted, whether it was an accidental discharge. Oftentimes, suicide can be discriminated from a homicide by physical evidence generated by firearms, both antiquity and modern.

Q. What sort of educational background do you have that will entitle you to be declared an expert witness in this field of firearms examination, criminalist?

A. Most criminalists have a degree in one of the physical sciences, usually chemistry because much of what we do is applied chemistry. My degree is from the University of California at Berkeley in chemistry, I have some specialized training beyond that in criminalistic firearms examination, microscopy, other courses over the years after I graduated.

Q. What sort of training have you had in firearms examination?

A. Well, I received some college level training after my chemistry degree, but then after that, on-the-job training at the Crime Laboratory in Phoenix through an organization in the United States called the Association of Firearms and Toolmark Examiners. I think to date I've attended 20 to 25 of their training seminars, other training courses through organizations such as the FBI, McCrone Institute and so on.

Q. Have you ever conducted any research in the area of criminalist?

A. Yes, I have. To date, I've presented and/or published

over a hundred scientific papers, most of which focused on reconstructive aspects of shooting.

Q. Have you written any articles or given any presentations on the subject of criminalistics?

A. Yes, I have. A number of times.

Q. Give us an estimate of the number of articles that you have done?

A. I think to date there's a little over a hundred to date.

Q. Have you done any specific research in the area of black powder firearms in the past?

A. Yes. Besides being familiar with black powder firearms and owning a number of them and shooting them over the years, there are on occasion, even in this age after the century, crimes involving black powder firearms. I have worked on at least three such cases, and as a consequence did some basic research in that area, published several papers having to deal with black powder and modern black powder substitutes.

Q. Do you have any special offices or positions with the organizations that study criminalistics?

A. Yes. I served in a number of committees, groups appropriately for this presentation here today. The most important organization in this country is the Association of Firearms and Toolmark Examiners. Actually, it's an international organization. I served on a number of committees, I am a past president of that organization, I served on the board of directors, the scientific advancement committee, a number of other functions of that group.

Q. Have you ever been declared an expert witness in any state or federal courts in the United States?

A. Many times.

Q. Give us an estimate.

A. Several hundred occasions in the last 25, 30 years.

Q. Have you testified in criminal and civil cases?

A. That's right.

Q. Prosecution and defense?

A. That's correct.

Q. Prior to leaving your employment with the Phoenix Crime Laboratory, did you work on shooting cases for other agencies?

A. Yes, sir. I was basically loaned out on city payroll to work on cases for other agencies. Oftentimes, the military that had several training bases, in fact, still do in the central Arizona area.

Q. Have you worked with Mr. Fackler one of our other witnesses here in times past?

A. Yes. Dr. Fackler is a professional colleague and good friend. He and I have consulted on a number of cases over the years that I have known him.

Q. Have you continued to write on the subject of criminalistics?

A. Yes.

Q. Have you ever worked on reconstruction of crime scenes and reconstruction of the firearms usage in a crime scene?

A. Yes, many times, both while I was at the Crime Lab and since I've left.

Q. Give us some examples of how you would do that.

A. Well, you start with what we know about an incident, what has been reported, statements and observations of any witnesses, if there is a surviving suspect, if the suspect is alive and they have an account, and we look at the physical evidence as a sounding board for that information, neither believing it or disbelieving it simply saying here is this individual's account. How can the physical evidence test the credibility, the accuracy of that account? If we have another account, or even if it's just a hypothesis or a theory. It might be posed by the police investigators, it might be posed by the county attorney, it might be posed by the subject's defense attorney, but what if, how about this. Hopefully, all of those can be addressed by the available physical evidence, and more hopefully, it may be possible to exclude, to refute all but one particular account and, in fact, to lend support to that one particular account. That's not always the case, but that's the ideal approach, neither buying into or rejecting any particular version of the event, but using what we can see and touch and feel and get into the laboratory to evaluate.

Q. What are carbonaceous deposits, if that's the right word?

A. That is the right word, and it is simply a chemist's term for carbon, for soot. If we have charcoal briquette and rubbed it against a nice white shirt, you know that is very hard to get out. That's carbonaceous material that's not soluble in anything and very difficult to remove, and, of course, gunshot residue, whether it be modern day cartridges, or in this case, cartridges of black powder produces a lot of carbon that's very indelible.

Q. From your study of weapons, can you tell the members of the jury what types of weapons would be in use and any specific examples of weapons that would be in use during the period, of Meriwether Lewis' life?

A. All of the firearms of that era used the same propellant, black powder. It's a physical, mechanical mixture of potassium nitrate, carbon and sulfur. The differences were the granulation. Some of you may be present day shooters of black powder firearms. There is a very fine granulation that is uniquely used for the priming pan, the pan charge in the flintlock arms. That's the next point. All of the firearms of that period were flintlock firearms, whether they were pistols, shotguns or rifles.

Finally, in so far as handguns and pistols are concerned whether they're a Cheney and North, a Charleville pistol, a Harper's Ferry pistol or many other manufacturers of the period, they were all talking about so-called horse pistols, large pistols for personal protection, large caliber.

Substantially larger than what we see today. One of the outstanding features, as you will see, they would range from 54 caliber, that's one of the Harper's Ferry pistols, a 58 caliber on up to 69 caliber, the type Professor Starrs showed you earlier today. Those are all very large caliber, and they shot a spherical projectile. This was before the time of bullets, about the time of the Civil War, conical bullets, bullets with elongated shapes came into being. At this time, at the time of Meriwether Lewis' death, all the projectiles were round spheres, basically of pure lead.

Q. What does that 58, 69, what does that denominate? What kind of measurements are those?

A. That is the dimension. You have the micrometer, a good measuring tool, of the inside diameter of the bore of the gun. And I should have added that most, not all, most of these firearms in so far as the pistols are concerned, would have been smooth-bored, no rifling. Basically, the barrel looks like a piece of pipe and we would measure the inside diameter, and in the case of pistol that Professor Starrs showed you, that would nominally measure 0.69 inches, less than three-quarters of an inch across.

Q. Now, you had opportunity to examine that weapon?

A. Yes. The exemplar, the demonstration pistol?

Q. Yes.

A. Sure.

Q. Have you actually fired that weapon before?

A. Yes. Professor Starrs came to my laboratory several years ago and did a substantial amount of test firing, there are slides of which I will show you, measuring velocity penetration, generation of sooting residue and an item that I haven't yet told you about called a patch in regard to its ballistic performance.

Q. How would you compare the weapon that Mr. Starrs showed the members of the jury and the weapon that most probably Lewis had there at Grinder's stand?

A. In so far as caliber, it's the most likely choice. It can't be concluded at this juncture since the trail of the brace of pistols that he described as taking through the Trace have never been found, but a gun either that type of gun, Charleville or Cheney and North, are the most likely candidates, but in effect, it doesn't really matter. If it was a Harper's Ferry, we'd still be dealing with a large caliber gun, a large ball (for the projectile) and black powder (for the propellant).

Q. What is a brace of pistols?

A. Today an antiquated term meaning a pair. A pair of pistols and they would, of course, be of the same caliber because you need to carry the projectiles around and you wouldn't want to mix sizes any more than a modern day person would want to carry a nine millimeter in one hand and a .357 in the other. More importantly back then, the difficulty in loading these things or it's time-consuming, involved, it would be a set, same caliber, usually the same brand.

Q. I believe you brought some slides to illustrate the function of these weapons?

A. Just a few to orient us mostly with the ammunition characteristics compared to modern cartridges and these guns in particular.

Q. Mr. Haag, let me ask you a logistical question. Once you show us the slides and you show us about that, are you then—you want to do the demonstration, or do you want to wait until after Dr. Fackler's testimony?

A. That would be fine. When Dr. Fackler is talking, I can be making sure everything is set up to be real efficient realizing the time crunch.

GENERAL BAUGH: We're going to take a break—what time did you want to break, Mr. Coroner?

MR. CORONER: Any time.

GENERAL BAUGH: He wants to take a break about 2:30ish. If you want to after the slides—are you fairly close to the—is the slide— are the slides the end of your direct testimony?

THE WITNESS: It is, but it is more dependent upon you, because I think the slides will summarize the differences between what the folks here probably know about cartridges today and what we're dealing with.

GENERAL BAUGH: I'm going to guess, then, that we would want to see the slides and then probably take a 15-minute break and then ask you some questions and then put Dr. Fackler on.

THE WITNESS: That's fine. If we can turn down that light, we'll finish up with a brief presentation.

Depicted on this drawing is simply modern ammunition. It falls, basically, in two categories, shotgun shells—we're clearly not dealing with in this case by any indication—and fixed ammunition, some kind of a cartridge, modern smokeless powder and a singular projectile. These are some contemporary-examples. Most of the police officers you've seen in here today are going to have a cartridge something like one of these. A pistol cartridge. Again, you've got a cartridge case, a modern very efficient smokeless propellant, and a modern conical shaped bullet that will either have an expanding, what we call a hollow point., or a full metal jacket. These are some intermediate rifle cartridges, and that's a very large caliber rifle cartridge, and finally again the shotgun shell.

These are some of the projectiles that typically come from modern, present day ammunition. They range from lead bullets to copper jacketed bullets, even to bullets that have aluminum jackets. And as far as handguns or pistols and revolvers, those are two choices in modern day guns. Basically, about the close of the Civil War we had revolvers available to us that have multiple cartridges and revolving cylinders or semiautomatic pistols started coming into existence at the end of the last century, about 1897.

And what we typically expect in police work and as readers of news accounts, the things such as drive-by shootings, and all other types of misuse of firearms, is some kind of a cartridge case being ejected and left at the scene. In the case of Meriwether Lewis, there was not a bit, any kind of a cartridge case available.

Here are the types of firearms we are actually dealing with. This is the pistol that Professor Starrs produced this morning, this is a replica of a Harper's ferry pistol, also a Charleville as a possible contender, a possibility. At the time, these are both large caliber guns that shoot a spherical lead projectile, they have a flintlock ignition system where a fine granulation of black gunpowder is placed in a thing called a pan. That will show up with the demonstration after the break.

The main charge of black powder of a coarser granulation is placed down the muzzle, step one. A patched ball, meaning some sort of cloth or thin buckskin, and the ball of a smaller diameter than the bore is forced down on top of this powder charge. That's step two. Step three would be to prime the pan, that's to be done immediately or you can reserve that for a situation where you felt you were in danger or about to get upon your quarry, the deer, the elk, whatever it might be, but that would be the last step. Prime this pan to lower this piece, raised on this gun, lowered here—this piece is called frizzen—and then cock back what we today call the hammer. Then it was called the cock sometimes. In that hammer is held a piece of flint, and upon pulling the trigger, the flint strikes the frizzen, hurls it upward exposing the priming charge and a shower sparks—if this all works right back then and today—go down and ignite the powder charge in the pan. That will cause flash, flame and smoke. There is a small hole going from this pan into the chamber of the gun. It's a little bit bigger than a paper clip. That's called a vent hole or touch hole in the cannon. That flame, then, the idea is, will be communicated on into the main powder charge and the piece will fire.

If my demonstration doesn't go as well as I'd like to—I was watching the recent remake of James Fenimore Cooper's film—
Q. *Last of the Mohicans.*
A. There's lots of flintlock, rifles and pistols being fired in that and it's well done.

Black powder soot is very tenacious as well. Any recovered patch can give you some idea of the caliber of the gun that was fired—even though the ball may have gone completely through (a victim) and elsewhere.

And just so you might—if you are wondering what black powder looks like, the upper portion of this photograph, it looks like lumps of coal. It looks black because of all the carbon.

This is the pistol that Professor Starrs brought. The previous patches were nicely cut, professionally cut. This is a field expedient cut patch, where I would just place the ball on his pistol, seated it, and cut the patch with a patch knife or just skinning knife. So it is very irregular. We could match that back to the piece (of cloth) that goes next to it.

Here's a fired patch. Then this ball is of interest because it has imprints from this tool. It may have been a separate tool called a ball starter where you get the ball started down in the gun and then finish the business with this rammer (ramrod). This ball has both an imprint from the ball starter and an imprint from this ramrod. And here's actually a fabric imprint from hitting the clothing.

Again, we only have the Grinder account to interest us. I'm not saying rely upon, but the wounds are described as through and through. If an exhumation is ordered and carried out and we find a ball inside the body. We now know the account of the exit wound is incorrect. And we may see something like this on such a ball would be a stripe of clothing. If he was buried with clothing and there's no soot on it, it's not a close or a contact shot.

There are a couple of slides of all the mess (debris/gunshot residue) that these things (black powder pistols) create. This is Professor Starrs behind my laboratory about to fire the pistol he brought today. We've got a witness panel right here. We've got some chronographs here to measure velocity, and a box that has a couple of panels of soft body armor to capture the balls so we can look at them later.

That was before, this is during. As you can see, Jim is engulfed in sooty, smoky material. The box is blurred because it is in motion now having taken on the 68 caliber ball. And here's an example, of what I will hope to show you in just a moment. We had to actually extinguish the fire. This is where the term powder burns come from. Black powder will set things on fire. Modern powder will not. This is burned out, the soot from that shot of only about two feet away.

Here are some other examples 12 inches or so. So, again, we don't know how this man was buried. If he was buried in the clothes in which he died, there is the opportunity, depending on how time has taken its toll, you can see such material, either a black hole or a very sooty deposit either in the skin or in garments or in both.

I think this is last slide. This is also what I intend to show you. The tremendous scorching and sooting power of this material. This is a material called Ordinance gelatin developed by your next speaker, Dr. Fackler. It is a tissue simulant, and you are looking at about 28 inches of this material. The shot was fired about two or three inches away of a piece of cotton on this end so you can see now a black stellate (star like) tear from the blast and tremendous soot deposits. This is black from carbon, and it's even followed the wound track, two feet into gelatin. And there's the ball, and I've at this point recovered the patch, which is about right here, few inches into the wound track.

That's the end of the slides. So break and then questions after?

GENERAL BAUGH: Yes, if that's all right.
(Recess.)

(The following proceedings and the firing of a gun were conducted in the firing chamber of the National Guard Armory.)

THE WITNESS: Are we ready, Mr. Coroner?

MR. CORONER: Yes.

THE WITNESS: What I propose to do is just go through the loading process and explain what I'm doing, what would be involved in preparing one of these firearms for discharge.
At the present time, the pistol is empty. We have the hammer with the flint down, normal, we tip the frizzen out of the way,

that's this piece, now even if somehow we receive a blow here we can't create a spark.

The first step is going to be to dole out some powder charge. There are a number of tools for this. I have one from about the time of the Civil War. I'm simply going to load this gun with a charge of 50 grains of 2F black powder. The F has to do with the size of granulation. This is a coarse version, much like you saw in the slides. Simply pour it now and then until it's essentially filled, turn this piece, shave it off, this is going to be poured down the muzzle, since it's a muzzle loader, and if I were really diligent, I'd look and make sure the charge is now in the gun.

I'm going to use the field expedient method. Now, I'm going to take one of our projectiles, and this is 68 caliber ball for a 69 caliber gun. In the American system, during our revolution and afterwards, you could shoot an undersized ball with a patch around it to hold it in place, secure it on the powder charge so I could have some pillow ticking and just a little pouch, a little bag like this one, or I could use my own clothing if I were desperate.

Set this on the board. I'm fortunate enough at one point in time I had a ball starter here—this tool. Okay. Now, the ball is flush with the muzzle. My skinning knife or my patching knife, in this case my buck knife. Now, from a science standpoint, we have just created an irregular edge from this random process that has value because we can match it back to this. Like fitting a jigsaw puzzle back together.

I'm going to continue ramming the ball down. It is almost on the powder. I'm going to use the ramrod that comes with the pistol which is going to leave another mark; the tool I just used has already left a mark. The ball is seated against the powder. Now, we're two-thirds of way there.

The next step is to prime the pan. This is where we start getting into the potential misadventure area. That hole is the little touch hole back in here. I've got to fill this tray with powder. At this point, I'm going to put my ear guards on, not because the gun is going off, but because I don't want to have to set it down

Professor Starrs at the firing range.

Close up of ramrod and ball starter imprints on lead bullet

.69 caliber pistol, ball starter, ramrod, fired ball and patch

and look like any more maladroit than I might already. Now, we're down to needing to prime this gun with the fine powder. That is the 4F. I want it to be back in that vent hole, and fill the pan. Okay. The pan is filled.

I'm going to lower the frizzen, and now we still don't have quite a ready gun. We have to manually cock it back, and we're ready to go. The first shot of the two I'll attempt here today is going to be through 29 inches of Ordinance gelatin. This is the material Dr. Fackler, I assume, will talk more about. I'm going to have the muzzle nominally about 12 inches away just for demonstration purposes.

The last thing I'll tell you before I fire this shot: Don't count on it going off on the first try. These are very fussy items, particularly this system, but we'll give it a try and I'll give you a chance to get a view. I'll let you know when I'm ready to fire. Cock the hammer, the frizzen is down. All right. All right. First attempt. Second. For those that are counting that was three.
(Additional firing attempt.)
Okay. I'm going to do one procedure here and that is to freshen the frizzen. During the handling of these, if you get oil from your hands on them, it prevents the spark, although I could see some sparks.
Another try. I'm going to have to reprime this in a moment.
(Additional firing attempts.)
Well, this is one of the embarrassing moments when you should have been here yesterday. Okay. I'm going to reprime it. We can go on standby, if you'd like, for a moment.
I'm ready to give it another try. Well, my apologies to you all.
All right. Let's just go on standby and let me readjust this flint.
(Recess.)

THE WITNESS: Remember we have a loaded gun here, so no one gets out in front of the table. Now, I've just adjusted the flint a bit. Give it another try.
(Additional firing attempts).

Well, it's true we're getting sparks, but we're still not getting a fire. I'll tell you what, I'd say put your next witness on and let me work on this.

(Recess.)

(The following proceedings were held in the courtroom.)

GENERAL BAUGH: If everyone will take their seats, please.

GENERAL PHILLIPS: Mr. Coroner, as I understand it, you are going to revisit the firearms expert after you hear some more witnesses, and let him have a chance to work with the firearm.

MR. CORONER: Yes.

GERALD B. (JERRY) RICHARDS

GENERAL PHILLIPS: That being the case, we'd like to call Jerry Richards.

Mr. Coroner and members of the jury, once again in the interest of time, I would like to present to you Gerald B.(Jerry) Richards and tell you just a little bit about his qualifications. Most significantly, he is a retired FBI Special Agent. He has over 20 years of experience in the FBI laboratory and he was the head of the FBI's Document Operations and Research Unit at one time, and also he has been the head of the FBI's Special Photographic Unit. He has academic preparation, as you might expect, for his expertise. He's a graduate of Southern Illinois University with both a Bachelor and a Master of Science degree. He has had additional training at various universities. He is presently a private consultant since his retirement from the FBI. He is certified by the FBI as being a questioned document examiner. He's also certified by the FBI as being a forensic photographic examiner. And as I said, he has during his FBI tenure been head of each of those units.

He has been accepted as an expert witness in both state and federal courts on numerous occasions. Since retiring from the FBI, he has been a consultant. He is adjunct professorial lecturer at George Washington University. He has a number of articles that have been published in his area of expertise. He has presented a great number of papers. We will be submitting to you his curriculum vitae.

With that as an introduction, Mr. Coroner, I submit to you to take an oath to testify as an expert witness in this case Mr. Gerald B. (Jerry) Richards.

If you will raise your right hand, please.

GERALD B. (JERRY) RICHARDS

having been first duly sworn was examined and testified as follows:

DIRECT EXAMINATION

BY GENERAL PHILLIPS:

Q. All right, sir. Could you tell us as a consultant and also as an FBI agent and head of the two mentioned FBI lab units, tell us what a questioned document examiner does?

A. Well, basically, a questioned document examiner conducts analysis on a document, any type of analysis on a document. In this particular case, handwriting analysis. In order to conduct this type of examination, a side-by-side comparison is conducted, usually of known or questioned-known compared to questioned items.

In this case, I conducted handwriting examinations on a number of documents that were forwarded to me—and also a little unusual in my area—to determine if there was any distortion or perhaps areas of the handwriting that would suggest either a physical or mental malady of the writer.

Q. All right. Now, in the work that you performed in this case, did you receive some documents— of course, they would be copies of documents—that were identified to you as being documents that some historians had relied on as being Meriwether Lewis' authored documents?

A. Yes, sir. I received nine documents that were purported to be initially upon receipt as being known exemplars, known writings of Meriwether Lewis. In addition to that, I received five documents that were purported to be known handwriting of one Major Gilbert Russell, and in addition to that one, document purported to be the known handwriting of a Jonathan Williams.

Q. All right. Focusing now first of all, on the Meriwether Lewis documents, would you tell us what the nine were and whether or not you designated for comparison purposes some of those nine as being known writings of Meriwether Lewis?

A. Yes, sir, I will. Would you like me to enumerate them in order?

Q. Yes.

A. The first one that I examined—this list in chronological order—was an April 13th, 1801 document. This was a proclamation by Meriwether Lewis naming Reuben Lewis, his brother, as his attorney. The second one was an August 20th, 1804 document which was a list of promotions. The third document was a March 2nd, 1807 document which involved a resignation of a military appointment by Mr. Lewis. The fourth document was a February 6th, 1809 document which was a letter to James Madison beginning "three days after." The next document was also a February 6th, 1809 document to James Madison this one beginning, "my bill of," and then continuing on. The next document was an August 18th, 1809 letter by—or purportedly by Meriwether Lewis to the Secretary of War, William Eustis. The seventh document I received was a September 11th, 1809 document which was purported to be his last will and testament. The eighth document was a September 16th, 1809 document which was a letter to James Madison, and the last was a September 22nd, 1809 document which was a letter to Amos Stoddard.

Q. Tell us what examination you did with respect to these documents and what conclusions you were able to reach.

A. All right. Well, basically, again, they were all purported as known. And fortunately, the question that was asked is were they, in fact, known—was it all written by the same person. Upon examining these documents generally I could immediately see that they were not all written by the same person; so I had to make a determination at that point, and based on my best judgment, I took three of the documents which internally were totally consistent. In other words, the handwriting itself was totally consistent, there were no variations or major variations or differences in them and I determined those were the three I was going to use as a standard to compare the rest of the documents against.

Now, to do this very unusual in the document world, but

here we're dealing with documents that are 200 years old, and in this case, extremely poor, poor copies of those documents. It's a case where you have to work with what you have. You are not going to get any more documents from the individual you are trying to determine whose handwriting it is.

The documents I chose as known I felt were probably the least questioned as to whether he wrote them or not. The first one was March 2nd, 1807, the resignation of the military appointment. The second one I chose was the September 16th, 1809 letter to James Madison which there was another question about. This particular document questioned as to whether his physical or mental condition was in question on that one. His handwriting wasn't. And then the last one, the September 22nd, 1809, the letter to Amos Stoddard, I used as basic known to compare the other documents.

Q. All right. And these three documents, which if I understand correctly, two are from 1809 dated shortly before his death and one from 1807. These three are all internally consistent with each other?

A. Yes. When you compare them side-by-side. Again, this is a side-by-side examination. There is no real variation or differences. There's no differences whatsoever in the handwriting and the variations are quite consistent. The style of writing, the line quality, the rhythm of the writing, are all quite consistent between the three.

Q. Now, tell us about what observations you were able to make about the other six in comparing the other six to the three— I'm going to call them known at this point?

A. At this point. I'll just go down the list again. It's probably as easy to take the next six. The April 13th, 1801 document, basically the body of the letter was not written by Lewis. He had nothing to do with that. It appears only the signature was his. He didn't write the document as a whole. He just signed it, even though to my knowledge, most historians have taken that as his entire handwriting.

Q. What kind of letter was that?

A. This was a letter that Reuben Lewis would be his attorney, his brother, basically. The next one was a list of promotions —

Q. Excuse me, just a second. So it may be—I'm just suggesting a hypothesis here—it may be that he dictated that letter, someone else took it down in their handwriting and he signed it?

A. In all probability, that's exactly what happened.

Q. Now, that's the first of the six. Now, would you discuss the second?

A. The next one is a list of promotions that I mentioned on August 20th, 1804, and this list of promotions was not written by him, and he did not write—he did not write the signature portion of the document on it, either. The name Meriwether Lewis is on there, and in a few moments I do happen to have a slide of that, but it was definitely not written by him. Somebody else wrote his name under the promotion list.

Q. Is this one of the documents that says signed Meriwether Lewis?

A. No, it is not.

Q. So this may be—this may be a document—it could be a document that he dictated, or it could be a copy made by a clerk of some original that he wrote; is that correct?

A. Yes.

Q, But to the best of your knowledge, this is the best original that exists for historians?

A. For historic purposes. However, the crux of this is that many documents get into circulation as being known documents of these individuals or known signatures, many times they are not. They didn't have Xerox copy machines back in the 1800s, so the only way copies could be made was by hand, and most of the—important Majors or important Captains or important Generals didn't have to make their own copies. They had people to make for them.

Now, some of the problems that did occur with this from time to time—if changes were made, you would never know what those changes were, or rough drafts came into play. Many times we may be looking at rough drafts thinking this is the final document or vice-versa. There may be rough drafts that are around, so you never know what stage this document is in or what its basic revisions could, or would, have been.

Q. Okay.

A. Then I can continue on.

Q. What are the other documents?

A. Okay. Very briefly, again, two September 6th documents were both written and signed by Meriwether Lewis. No question about that. Excuse me. February 6th, 1809. The August 18th, 1809 letter to the Secretary of War is a perfect example. The entire body of the letter was not written by Meriwether Lewis. However, he signed it and then above the signature, the next two sentences, and materials to the left of the signature, he did write. He actually signed it after. It was probably a file copy, probably not the original one, that was sent because of the notations.

Q. So a reasonable hypothesis would be a clerk wrote the body of the document, but Meriwether Lewis himself signed it and he made some notations on it in his own handwriting?

A. Yes.

Q. Okay.

A. The last one here is the last will and testament, and in the last will and testament the notation in there and the second paragraph in it says basically three witnesses swore by oath that this was the true and accurate handwriting and signature of Meriwether Lewis when, in fact, he not only didn't sign it, he didn't write it, either. He didn't write it or sign it; however, that is in the court records as his last true will and testament. He had—his hand never touched it, in all probability.

Again, not a tremendously uncommon type situation in that it is probably a copy and somebody who filed it didn't know which was which and that's the one that got filed as his true will and testament.

Q. But to the best of your knowledge, this is the so-called holographic will, which is obviously not—at least the copy that historians have at their disposal is not—is obviously not his holographic will?

A. It is not written by him nor signed by him.

Q. All right, sir. Now, let me ask you this: You have referred to this 1809 letter to the President which you're taking to be written by Governor Lewis?

A. Yes, sir.

Q. And you're aware that this letter has been the subject of much historical controversy and some historians have based the manner of writing of this letter, they base that on thinking that he was disoriented or under the influence or out of his mind or something when he wrote this letter?

A. Yes.

Q. Now, do you find anything unusual about the writing in this 1809 letter compared to the 1807 resignation or the other 1809 letter to his friend Amos?

A. As far as the writing goes, the style of the writing, the relative size, the speed, the quality of what we call the rhythm of the writing, it's all totally consistent with the other two examples. The only difference and it's a the very noticeable difference, is there are numerous—and this is what the historians mostly dwelled on—there are numerous corrections, cross outs, additions, deletions throughout the entire document; however, the handwriting itself is stable, it is solid as he has ever written it before, there's no tremor, there's no signs of quiver at the end of the lines or at the end of the words, there's no indication of any physical distress in the writing itself.

Now, let me stipulate right now we cannot tell any type of mental disease, nor can we tell any type of physical disease as a rule from handwriting. All we can do is see what those things reflect in the handwriting as much as the handwriting will deteriorate with some types of mental and physical disease. I see none of that deterioration. It all looks perfectly similar except for the corrections, and as I said before, it is much more apparent to me that this is what it is, it is a rough draft. There's no indication on the letter this was the one that was ever intended to be sent to the—I believe that was to Madison, James Madison.

Again, it was a custom to always keep or to make rough drafts. As a matter of fact, Thomas Jefferson, every letter he wrote, he made a second copy of it as a rough draft for his file copy. This very well could be the file copy. It may have never been sent, but historians have grabbed this, for the most part, and made a tremendous amount of out these corrections, which really in my opinion don't appear to be anything, but what they are. Corrections.

Q. Okay. Now, did you—also, you referred to documents that you received concerning Russell. Tell us what documents you received concerning Russell.

A. I received five documents. As I mentioned before, a January 4th, 1810 letter to Jefferson; a January 31st, 1810 letter again to Jefferson; a statement by Russell, and this was supposedly—it was sent to me to determine the handwriting on it, so I would say it was a statement by Russell, and this is a statement where he describes Meriwether Lewis's death to—I believe it was probably to go Jefferson, but anyhow, it's supposedly it's got a signed at the bottom and it's signed Gilbert Russell and then below that is another statement and then there's a signature J. Williams below it as a statement that he received it from Gilbert Russell. The fourth document is an April 18th, 1813 receipt, it's just an unknown receipt from New Orleans supposedly in the handwriting again of Russell; and the third one is a letter to James Monroe on March 8th, 1850.

In this particular case, I used four exemplars to compare with the November 26th, 1811 letter since that was the one in question and was designated to me as the one in question.

Q. What conclusions were you able to reach concerning these writings of Major Gilbert Russell?

A. Well, I could probably best illustrate that with just a few slides very quickly that I brought along, if I might.

Q. Fine.

A. You'll have to excuse me if I'm not projecting quite well. I have a little hay fever I'm dealing with. Basically, this is the signature on the Russell statement of November 26th, 1811. One of the things I would like to quickly point out that I want to show you are a number of pieces of writing one right after another was, first of all, there's no middle initial in this particular document. In this -- in this particular document there's no middle initial. In addition to that, note the way the "R" is positioned here. Coming up -- as you can tell, these are very poor photocopies. We're missing actually half of the letter up here. And, also, right at the end this e-l-lcombination— actually this is an "l", but it looks more like an "e". That's how I described it. e-l-l with the last "l" which actually looks like an "e" and then circumvents way off to the left and back into the "r" formation again.

The next line, or the next paragraph in this document is the name Gilbert Russell written supposedly by Williams. And if you'll notice we have the same characteristics here again. "R" over here, the double "s" actually in those days they wrote, the first "s" looks like an "l", the second one looks like a normal "s", so this is actually an "s-s" combination. So, s-s-e-l-l, and again, the lower case "l" looks like a lower case "e" that actually represents the last "l".

When we look at the three other signatures, these are three other signatures on three of the other documents that I had. We can see that—is there another pointer here. If we'll notice on the end here, Russell himself actually uses two different "e" formations. A Greek "e" here. Notice how the "l" does not look like an "e" whatsoever, and in here where the "l"s are, the same identical size, for all practical purposes. These are just a few of the characteristics that led me to the conclusion that Russell did not sign the name; however, the same person wrote the name on that document twice, the signature and then the name in next lower paragraph.

Below that is the signature—below that second Russell signature was the signature of J. Williams -- was the signature J. Williams, and as you can see on here, particularly the "J" on here coming into a very, very simple "W" formation. The one exemplar I have of Jonathan Williams, he doesn't use "J". He uses the full Jon—actually, this is an abbreviation, for Jonathan was J-o-n, and then there was the "W" formation, it is totally different, has a flourish first on here. We're missing part of it because it was poor copy—it comes back and then it makes—a little flourish downward again. In examining the rest of the letters in there, I pretty much came to the conclusion that he probably did not write that signature Jonathan Williams. Someone else wrote it.

In addition to that, I looked at the body of the letter itself, the document itself. Now, this is a document—remember that Russell is trying to describe what happened two years previous to Meriwether Lewis. And just to show you how a document examination is conducted, what I did was just to isolate two of the letter formations. Now, we cannot compare apples to oranges. You have to compare the same letters to the same letters. So I cannot compare "A"s to "T"s. I have to compare "T"s with "T"s and "G"s with "G"s.

In this case just for illustrative purposes, I chose the "th" combinations. And the next line I marked them for you here. What I would like to do is just to show you the difference in the handwriting on here. The "t" formation as you can see in almost every case was just a straight vertical line. The crossbar comes across horizontally into the "t" and through the "h", and in most cases, the upper stroke of the "h" starts halfway up the "h" and continues around making a fairly fine loop of the "h".

In Russell's signature, we find the same "th"s. Again, I've marked them for you to make it a little easier. As you can see, these t-hs the "t"s come down and there's a very distinctive connecting stroke. In many cases, one or two strokes, an up stroke, a down stroke and it connects directly in to the "h" formation. Based on these characteristics and numerous other ones I found throughout the writing, it became very obvious that Russell did not write the Russell statement that's purported to describe what happened to Meriwether Lewis.

In addition, I took a look at Jonathan Williams' "th"s, he didn't have near as many in his letter, and again I marked them and here we can see a completely different formation of the "t"s. Almost all the "t"s are on one stroke down which forms into a very, very wide arch that forms the—actually, the top of the "h" in most cases. We do have one exception down here, but in almost all of the cases here, we actually don't even form a loop and the "t" itself is just a vertical stroke. Again, based on this characteristic and numerous other ones , it was the determined that Williams did not write the Russell signature.

So what it amounts to is we have a report written supposedly reported by Russell who was not an eyewitness to the situation. He had to hear it from someone else. He told the story to someone who wrote it down here who was another fourth party perhaps who wrote this document out. Neither one of the people whose purported signatures are on the document wrote them.

Just for illustration this is a slide showing Meriwether Lewis' handwriting. See the different "t" strokes that he makes? He makes the "t" like little bullets. These are very, very distinctive from the other writers. What I did want to show you, though, is the signature. This is the signature on the promotion list that I mentioned to you that was not written by Lewis nor was it signed by him. Look at the "L" formation in Lewis here and the "s" formation particularly on the end. This is a genuine signature of Meriwether Lewis. His "L" formations are totally different. As a matter of fact, his signature is totally different all the way across, and it is very, very distinctive. So, based on the four documents that I use for comparison purposes, Russell did not write the questioned document or his signature, and Williams, did not write his signature.

Q. All right. Do you have other slides?

A. No.

Q. So, Mr. Richards, is it, then, your opinion that many times the documents that historians take to be original writings of the author, such as Meriwether Lewis, are not that but are, in fact, copies made by someone else?

A. Yes. Many times they are copies made by someone else. And again, as to what generations, since they aren't originals, what generation those copies are very, very hard for us to tell.

Q. Or how reliable?

A. How reliable the information is due to there may be more than one generation or one copy.

Q. More importantly, though, you find no inconsistency in these recent letters that he wrote just before his death and his earlier writings. You find nothing significant there and no significant degrading of his writing?

A. No. I do not, and even if I did, I would give it very little significance because anybody who knows who has been seriously ill with malaria or anything else for a period of time, when they write and they aren't in the best of condition, that can deteriorate their handwriting to some degree. So trying to identify a malady from the handwriting, be it a mental malady or a physical malady is virtually, for all practical purposes, really not possible based on the handwriting. All you can say is it's degraded. For all you know, he might have written it on a log, and it then be attributed to mental illness.

Q. But these writings are not degraded?

A. But these do not show any indications —

Q. In fact, the letter to the President appears to you to be a rough draft?

A. If—when I first looked at it, that was my very first impression, and it still is.

Q. All right. In addition to that, the four Russell writings that you took to be known, they were all consistent with each other; is that correct?

A. Yes, sir. Internally consistent.

Q. Internally consistent, but if I may refer to them as that, they are not—they are not the important documents, are they?

A. No.

Q. Not the documents that bear upon the death of Meriwether Lewis?

A. No, that's correct.

Q. They are simply samples of his handwriting that have survived through history?

A. Yes. I believe—I don't recall the content of all of them, but, I know one of them is regarding money, but I don't recall the exact content.

Q.. You had four?

A. Yes.

Q. But they were all consistent with each other?

A. Yes, they were.

Q. But the statement of Major Gilbert Russell where he purports to say how Meriwether Lewis died, you found that to be inconsistent and that is why you say in your opinion he didn't write it?

A. It's totally inconsistent, and in my opinion, he did not write it.

Q. And it's also your opinion that Mr. Williams is not the author of it?

A. That's correct.

Q. Even though it purports at the end that he is?

A. It's his signature at the end indicating, or suggesting at least, that he received this information from Russell.

Q. But based on other examples of Williams, it doesn't appear that—

A. Yes. Based on the one example I have.

Q. All right.

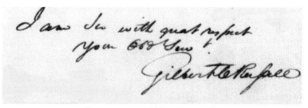

Gilbert C Russell (authentic)

Gilbert Russell (November 26, 1811 statement)

J. Williams (November 26, 1811 statement)

Jon. Williams (authentic)

For a discussion of these signatures see pages 133-37.

GENERAL BAUGH: Mr. Coroner, do you or members of the jury have questions?

MR. CORONER: Any questions from the jury?

BY GENERAL PHILLIPS:

Q. Now, one other question: Besides your examination, Mr. Richards, of these documents, did you learn that Professor Starrs asked another documents examiner to also make, independent of your work, an examination of the same material?

A. Yes. Because of the unusual problems we have in this case, one; we are dealing with old documents, ancient documents; number two, we are dealing with very, very poor copies, and a number of areas such as, like I say, the physical and the mental attributes of the writer. Professor Starrs wished that two of us take a look at this particular set of documents and that we provide independent opinions regarding the documents.

Q. Okay. And do you now know whether you and Dr. Dillon reached the same conclusion?

A. Well, Dr. Dillon will be speaking to you a little later, but basically, our conclusions when we finally discussed them yesterday, were virtually identical.

Q. But you worked independently?

A. To be honest, I didn't meet him until yesterday.

Q. But you independently reached the same conclusion?

A. Identical.

GENERAL PHILLIPS: Any other questions?

MR. CORONER: Any other questions?

GENERAL PHILLIPS: Thank you.

THE FIRING RANGE

GENERAL BAUGH: I think we're ready to shoot again.

(The following proceedings were conducted in the firing room.)

MR. HAAG: First of all, of course, as soon as you left, the first try it fired. Here's the projectile that hit the steel back stop. Remember, this is not tissue or bone, but there's what our piece of lead looks like. It started out like this, but more interestingly; this was just a shot that I fired down range after I changed the flint in the gun.

By eye you can follow me, here is the patch, and I didn't moisten it, so it actually has sat here and burned a little bit, physically burned, another little piece of it over here. I'll hold it here.

Let's see. Let me try this again. I've got the gun loaded, it's not primed, new flint, everything else the same. We should be able to get at least one into the block of gelatin and look at a close range discharge.

My nose is used to it, but you may be able to smell the sulfurous odor in this room from the discharge.
Okay. All right. Okay. Okay.
(Gun Fires.)

Let me get my sectioning knife here. First of all, we do have a safe firearm, but this is truly the smoking gun. There's still a little bit of smoke curling out of the muzzle, and any of you who wish to take a smell of it, in a few moments you get the idea, probably, in this room as it is.
Look at the physical evidence here. Again, the gun is safe if you any of you wish to move forward. It's a single shot gun; no way it can fire again. We have some scorch here, that's from the pan, even though it mostly went that way. You can obviously see all of the carbonaceous material. Now, this is a distance of about a

foot. Much of it, of course, missed this block. As Dr. Francisco mentioned, these bullets generally embedded in tissue follow essentially straight paths. Here's our path going right along here. Oh, you might notice some what appear to be BBs. Those are for calibration purposes.

We've got—well, I need to have a tape measure. We've got, roughly, 13 inches of penetration. We need the fire department. I'll explain that in a moment, but I wanted to show you this. Our projectile, you can probably see, very nice shape. Incidentally, it should have really penetrated further. That felt like a fairly light charge. There's basically an undeformed ball.

Again, I think both of the doctors who deal with wounds will tell you bodies are seldom much thicker than that, so there is an opportunity, if no hard structure to hit, it will go all the way through. And, again, if any of you wish to see that, you can see the marks from the ramrod where I struck it and those could be compared if we were so lucky to recover a ball with the types of ramrods that were available.

That patch, apparently even over that short distance, it went enough to one side to miss the gelatin. If I had been essentially contact, it clearly would have gone in the wound track. Most individuals, if they were going to load one of these guns and immediately fire it, would do what's called a spit patch. I didn't do that. That was just an oversight. They literally put this in their mouth and get saliva on it to soften the powder fouling and to soften it on the way out. If you don't do that, you literally can set them on fire as we could clothing. Now, if you wish to stay around, I'll quickly load this and we'll try a direct shot into cloth, like clothing, so you can see a powder pattern.

I will send this back if any of you wish to look at that. This is the one that struck the steel. I'll start setting the gun up for one more attempt.

Dr. Starrs asked to me to comment to you-all, what you've seen here is something where we demonstrated approximately what we would expect if there was just soft tissue struck, skin, intestines and so on. Bone, of course, is much harder and Dr. Fackler, I'm sure, will talk to you about what we could expect to see with this kind of missile and projectile, but hopefully, we should see someone's account or the physical, evidence, lots of this material, insoluble carbon driven right into a wound or into skin and/or bone, but he'll talk a little more about that.

I'll load and prime it—this pistol one more time and try to get you a shot. If you elect to go back, I can bring it down and show it to you unless you wish to stay and see it.

MR. CORONER: Let's go back.

GENERAL BAUGH: Martin Fackler please. Dr. Fackler, if you would step right up there and raise your right hand, turn toward Mr. Tate, and he'll place you under oath.

MARTIN FACKLER

MARTIN FACKLER
having been first duly sworn was examined and testified as follows:

GENERAL BAUGH: Have they wired you for sound?

THE WITNESS: No sir, they have not.

GENERAL BAUGH: Well —

THE WITNESS: I can speak loudly or you can wire me. It's up to you.
GENERAL BAUGH: I think we can probably —

THE WITNESS: I can speak loudly.

DIRECT EXAMINATION

BY GENERAL BAUGH:
Q. Would you state your name, please, sir, and spell your first name and your last name for purposes of the record?
A. Yes. My name is Martin Fackler, M-a-r-t-i-n, second name, F-a-c-k-l-e-r.
Q. Where do you live, Dr. Fackler?
A. I live in north central Florida.
Q. What is your occupation?
A. I'm a surgeon and a wound ballistic consultant.
Q. How long have you been employed in that kind of occupation?

A. Well, I was a career military officer as a surgeon and retired from the military after 31 years of active duty in 1991, and since I have been out of military, I have been self-employed as a consultant in wound ballistics.

Q. Now, which branch of the military were you in?

A. Actually, I was in two branches. I was 15 years and six months in the Navy and 15 years and seven months in the Army. The last was in the Army.

Q. Are you also a medical doctor?

A. I am, yes.

Q. Where did you go to medical school?

A. Yale University in New Haven, Connecticut.

Q. Do you have any kind of specialty in the practice of medicine?

A. Yes. I'm a board certified general surgeon.

Q. Now, what exactly is—I don't know which is correct—wound ballistics?

A. Wound ballistics is the study of projectiles striking and penetrating the body.

Q. How long has that been an area of expertise?

A. You mean a recognized specialty, or my area of—recognized specialty?

Q. Recognized specialty.

A. Actually, there have been books written on this subject as early as the last part of the 18th—actually, the 1800s. You might consider the fact that surgeons have been publishing their reports of the wounds they treated during war time for ever since firearms have been invented, and you might consider that the beginning of wound ballistics, but actually formalizing it and doing some experimental work and publishing this probably started about 1870.

Q. Well, how would you—how would you study wound—wound ballistics methodology if that's a wound profile methodology in Florida, for example?

A. Well, actually, I didn't start in Florida. I started the last ten years of my military career after I had quite a bit of experience operating on people in Vietnam in 1968 and being interested in trauma, penetrating projectiles. I was asked to go to San Francisco and set up a laboratory for the study of gunshot wounds at the Presidio Army base, and I did that and was there from 1981 until 1991, at which time I retired and that was the same time the Army base was closed.

Q. What did you do after you retired from the Army?

A. I went back to Florida, and one of the reasons I went to Florida was in order to continue my research by going into the Medical Examiner's Office in Miami, Dade County and actually taking measurements from gunshot wounds in—I'm going to be wired.

In taking measurements from wound paths in the human body. The reason I did this is because we had set up the methodology when I was at Letterman Army Institute of Research and tried to quantify the gelatin that you saw Luke Haag using just recently. Gelatin had been used before but in more of a qualitative sense with some high speed photography and it pops all around and is impressive, but there are no measurements that were realistic one could take from it.

So we calibrated the gelatin against living pig muscle tissue and then derived our wound profiles from that, and I'll show you a few wound profiles in a minute, but the criticism had been by some people saying well, is pig muscle—living pig muscle the same thing as living person muscle, and so it was necessary to take measurements from living people and calibrate them and then compare them with the actual wound profiles we had developed in the gelatin which had been developed from pig muscle, and it did show to be a very close correlate and that paper has been published and verified.

Q. How does that work? How would you do that? Would it be the same caliber, the same loads, the same—in the experimental—?

Q. Yes.

A. Actually, I could just explain with some slides, if I might.

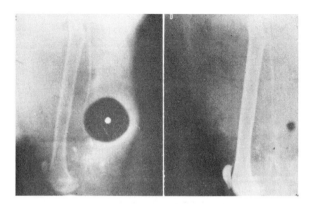

Two x-rays showing the same bullet wound in a cat thigh: temporary splash cavity on the left and bullet wound after cavity closes on the right.

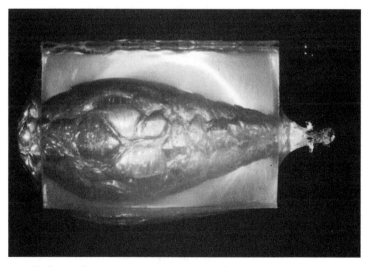

High speed stop action photo at time of maximum expansion of the temporary cavity, with bullet exiting on the right.

Cracks radiating out from bullet's path through gelatin.

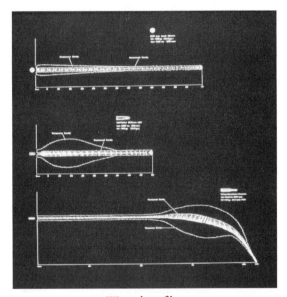

Wound profiles

(top)
69 caliber soft lead ball, shot from a horse pistol like Lewis's
(middle)
 cone shaped soft lead bullet spun by rifling (1850's–1870's)
(bottom)
hard metal jacketed bullet spun by rifling (1880's onward)

Q. Go ahead.

A. First, we need to explain that there are really only two things that happen when a projectile enters the body. One, it's a single bullet, that's obvious, and secondly, it makes a bit of a splash in the tissue. Here you can see on the 9:00 o'clock position view, which is the x-rays through the leg of a cat. This research was done during the second World War and published in 1962, in a book entitled 'Wound Ballistics.' You can see how this x-ray was taken right down the line of fire. So you can see how the tissue has been pushed out of the way temporarily, and then if you go over to the 3:00 o'clock position on the right, you can see there's a little hole but it's not nearly as big as the temporary cavity. The temporary cavity is called "temporary" for a reason: the tissue moves outward and then comes back. Given that muscle is pretty much an elastic tissue. So these are the two mechanisms, and these are the only two things that bullets do, and so all we had to do is, one, have calibrated gelatin so we could get the same kind penetration depth; and two, then all we had to do was measure the penetration and the temporary cavity.

Now, this is courtesy of Winchester. It's a high speed photograph to stop action at the point of maximum expansion of the temporary cavity with the bullet going through. This shows the way one can do it. If you look at the end of that gelatin after the temporary cavity of any size goes through, you see these cracks radiating outward from the bullet's path. I think probably you could see them in Mr. Haag's demonstration. These are a little larger cracks because this is a much higher speed projectile, but what we do with the crack, we cut the gelatin and we can measure the crack. It's very easy to see the difference between the center, which is a granular appearing area and that was what was actually hit by the bullet, and the cracks are very easy to discern and very easy to measure. So we measure these and we put them on what we call wound profiles.

Now, the wound profile—here are three—essentially, is almost a graph in a way. There is a centimeter scale down there at the bottom. We use centimeters because medical journals prefer that, so all the profiles are in centimeters. This is sort of a historical look at profiles. The top profile is very, very similar to the one that Mr. Haag shot, the 69 caliber ball going at about 540 feet per second. And as you can see, it penetrates very deeply; however, splash (temporary cavity) is very small.

Now, as I say, that's sort of a look at history, because that was the earlier ones, back in the 1700s and early 1800s. Then people developed a conical shaped bullet, which was spun by rifling, the next one down is a typical soft lead bullet from the 1850s to the 1870s. This happens to be a Vetterli -- a military rifle used by the Italians and the Swiss. This soft lead bullet hitting about the speed, of a 22 long rifle bullet (about 1300 feet per second), flattens, shortens, and doubles in diameter. So by doubling its diameter, it makes much damage. You can see the larger permanent cavity, and it also doesn't penetrate as deeply. All of the hollow point bullets used today are given basically that same kind of wound profile. The only difference is how deeply they penetrate, how much the bullet expands and how big the cavity is.

And the bottom wound profile is an example of the first generation of jacketed rifle bullets. The lead is soft and you can only get so high in velocity with lead before it starts stripping off in the barrel, and that velocity is maybe 16 to 1700 feet per second. So about 1880, the full metal jacketed bullet was developed, which is a bullet with a lead inside but outside was covered with a harder material so it can be shot much faster and spin. And it happens that the invention of smokeless powder came along about the same time.

So what happened between the last two profiles here, the velocities just about doubled. We went up over 2,000 feet per second and because of the fact that if at these over 2,000 feet per second velocities, if we shot the same large weight projectile as we had before, no one would have been able to tolerate the recoil, so the projectile size had to be reduced. So, basically, it was a progression of sizes coming down as velocity increased.

Actually, it might be of interest that this lowest projectile you see here is a projectile called the 6.5 Mannlicher-Carcano. You may recall this is what was used to assassinate President Kennedy., the same projectile.

But you see the deep penetration at that velocity. At the time, most doubted that projectile could have gone through two people. Actually, as measured from the wound profile, it could have gone through three. Very deep penetration was characteristic of the first generation of full metal jacketed bullets. This is an example of how we use the wound profile: we superimpose them on the body. We can often accurately predict penetration depth. I'm working on a case right now. A police officer got shot with a projectile, that first went through his arm, then went through his entire body, came out his skin and in fact, just stopped under his bullet proof—his body armor, went in under his body armor on the other side. A very long penetration and there were two possibilities: One is the person that shot him was using a non expanding bullet that goes very deeply and the police officer— the defense is saying well, the police officer's buddy, his other officer shot him. Well, the officer is using an expanding bullet that went about half that penetration, so we can just show by the penetration depth that it wasn't the police officer's bullet, that's just one example of how we use the wound profile.

Q. That seems to curve down?

A. That one—that particular one does. The ball tends to go very straight. The expanded bullet goes very straight. Expansion is sort of called mushrooming, because the bullet ends up looking a bit like a mushroom. Now, a mushroom has its center gravity forward. The undeforming jacketed bullet being either pointed or rounded on the front, the center of gravity will be more towards the rear, so sooner or later in tissue they will—it not only curves in its path as it yaws, yaw meaning the changing in the long axis relative to its line of flight. Every pointed bullet if it is not deformed in tissue, if you have enough tissue to catch the entire bullet, it will turn over 180 degrees and then end its path with its base going forward and pointing backwards. As you can see, it's not easy to see, but this one did that.

Generally, when they are turning over, they tend to change direction a little bit, but this would be—this direction would not be clinically significant, because it would have already passed through any projection of the body. That would go two feet straight ahead before this yaw takes place with this particular bullet.

Q. What about the considerations of tissue disruption patterns in the 68 caliber that may have been used?

A. Tissue disruption pattern is, as you can see on the top profile, the great majority of the damage is caused by direct crush of the—by the projectile. Now, you must remember this is in gelatin. It simulates soft tissue, hasn't gone through any bone. So certainly if this projectile passed through something hard like a skull, it could well flatten and this could cause more damage and this could cause the—because the bullet would deform and it might not penetrate as deeply. So you would have to do some experimentation to see at this speed whether or not this projectile deformed when it hit the bone. It would deform somewhat. I don't know exactly how much.

Q. What kind of experimentation are you talking about? How would you perform that experimentation?

A. Find—you go down to the butcher shop and find a piece of probably cow pelvis or and something like that and shoot some—put some gelatin behind it and then shoot through it and see how deeply it penetrates in gelatin and how much expansion or how much deformation you get.

Q. When you worked for Mr. Davis who is the Medical Examiner in Miami, how many wounds would you see in a week, approximately?

A. Miami —

Q. Gunshot wounds I'm talking about.

A. They did an average of 12 gunshot wound autopsies a week. Now, some of them would not be especially interesting and they'd be calibers that—but, you know, I spent enough time down there, eight or nine weeks, and I would find a person shot with a projectile that I already had a wound profile made for and so then I would take the measurements and I would put these on graph paper and match them with the projectile.

Q. What about the—how would the human skeleton affect wound profile projections?

A. Generally, any penetration through most anything that's skeleton, certainly any of the large bones, will deform the bullet, or even if it doesn't deform the bullet, it certainly slows the bullet down because a bullet uses a certain amount of its potential to poke through the bone. Ribs don't do much because ribs are pretty—you know, they're not really very substantial compared to the big bones of the leg, for instance, but the usefulness of this methodology in, for instance, in a case that—like the one in question is an exhumation, if you found holes in bones you might be able to reconstruct a path through the body and then with the path through the body, we could go to a great number of good cross-sectional anatomy books today and then we could establish a very good guess at which organs were perforated, and from that, we could give, I think, a pretty accurate estimation of how rapid would have been the incapacitation or death from that.

Q. Because you could project organ damage from these niches —

A. Yeah, this is some wishful thinking. If we certainly—there might be an exhumation which we don't find much and can't really identify, but, you know, given the best of situations if we find, you know, entrance through the second rib on the right and out through the ninth rib on the left, we could establish a very nice path.

Q. Do you have some interest in history besides being interested in wound profile methodology?

A. Well, I'm interested in especially the history of warfare and how wounds were treated and the results of wounds throughout history. I collect books on that subject.

Q. Now, what sort of limitations would there be on the action of a bullet or bullet that might figure out from organ disruption?

A. There are certain differences in the way these various temporary cavities, for instance, affect organs. The temporary cavity of most handgun bullets would be—modern day handgun bullets would be the size of a grapefruit, for instance—no, a little larger than that—and a shot through the abdomen with one of these, the forces would just tend to push the bowel aside, and they're moveable anyhow and they're pretty flexible and it wouldn't do much.

However, that same shot through the liver would cause a great deal of damage, because liver doesn't stretch very well, and, therefore, it would be damaged. And a lot of it has to do with how the body's—how the local anatomy and how the limitations of how tied down things are.

In automobile accidents, for instance, we know that if a person is hit very hard, say, with something in the abdomen and they have a full stomach, have just eaten, for instance, the stomach can burst from the hit. The temporary cavity does sort of the same thing. It pushes the tissue aside, and if you have a full stomach and got hit with a temporary cavity, you know, the organ could break or bowel or bladder or various full organs. Also, it depends if you—ordinarily, blood vessels are very moveable. It is extremely rare to see a blood vessel broken by—being hit by a temporary cavity. It's much more common to see a bone broken by a temporary cavity.

As a matter of fact, I testified in a case not too long ago, the second Menendez case, in which there were two bones broken by a short range shotgun blast in which the distance of fire was only about four feet and it acted like a single ball and the bone – the femur, a very large bone in the body, was not hit by the stock column, but it was broken by the cavitation. So you can get that.

Q. Ordinarily —

A. You don't get vessels broken by that because vessels tend to stretch aside, but in certain instances you will. While I was in Miami, we had one case, it was a handgun, and where the temporary cavity, you know, as I said, only the size of a large orange or a grapefruit, whereas some rifles can give cavities the size of a basketball, but anyhow, this is a shot right in the abdomen, hit the center portion of one vertebrae and it came between the right renal artery and the aorta. It didn't hit either one but it just about touched both of them and it tore. It tore between the right renal artery and the aorta it tore, because as the expansion went, there's no place to go. It was torn. I mean, it was held here. So if you get a temporary cavity and a place where a thing is held down and it can tear, whereas, if it's not held down, it's pushed aside.

So you basically have to take the basic wound profile and look at the intricacies of the local anatomy of where it went to figure out what it is going to do, but this is something that once you think about it, it is not really difficult.

Q. And it's apparently a matter of study and their calibrated —

A. Yes. Fortunately, today we have a great number of good cross-sectional anatomy books and these are very, very helpful. I have a skeleton at home and I have these cross-sectional anatomy books, because I can't keep in my mind the ribs going down and coming up again from where the, say, the fourth rib is in the midclavicular line, where another rib is. I have to, you know, take my skeleton and put a rod through it and then go to the cross-sectional anatomy books. Because they have now the computer tomography, the Cat scan which is very common in radiology, this is nothing but a series of cuts through the body. And because of that, I think it generated the addition of several—the publication of several very good cross-sectional anatomy books.

Q. So you can tell which organs it may have passed through by determining which bones it passed through?

A. Absolutely, and you can tell angles. If you have a particular angle, you can tell—or, for instance, I've had a case recently where an angle was described and at the autopsy, the—it was said that this went in through the back and went through the kidney and it went through the aorta. And if you take the cross-sectional anatomy at that same area, and you have two points, you have the kidney—actually, we had the entrance wound, too, but the bullet didn't exit. So putting a line, I mean, just take taking a ruler and draw it, and the angle is way off. You can get the angle from the cross-sectional anatomy. I'm not saying you get it exactly, but within, maybe, five degrees.

Q. Dr. Fackler, I have heard people say in autopsies where modern day weapons, projectiles, hit bone that it can cause radical changes in the trajectory. Is that—what is your experience about that?

A. In the trajectory of the projectile?

Q. Yes.

A. Well, it depends on the projectile. There are certain oddities and it tends to—in medicine, we tend to publish the very oddest things—like I said, we spend 95 percent of our time talking about the rarest one percent of what we see.

I recall in the *Journal of Academy of Forensic Sciences* having a case reported in which a bullet entered the head and entered at an angle and it bounced around the inside of the skull and came out the same hole. Now, that was published, because I don't think anybody has ever seen that before and it's extremely rare. That kind of thing can happen.

You see shots, especially a handgun, hitting the skull at any bit of an angle. There's a—the scalp is very thick and dense. The skull is hard, so you can get a bullet that will go in and stay—it will go in and stay in this plane, it will go around the skull rather than penetrate the bone. Now, you don't see that with a rifle bullet at 2,000 feet per second. This is limited to the lower speed handguns.

But as far as the change in direction—well, you see the change in direction in the bottom wound profile here. This is no bone. That's just the way it is in soft tissue. There are certain other profiles that I haven't shown up here that do have a marked change, most of these are replicas, but the handgun, typical handgun projectiles like the center one there, they tend to go pretty straight. If they hit a bone, I would say it is unusual to change direction more than 15 degrees, but you can predict. (Off the record.)

THE WITNESS: Yes. We have here—Mr. Haag has just provided me with two slices of gelatin from the recent shot. And one thing that I might show in here is they have a little BB in that gelatin. Now, that is an extremely important thing, a BB in the gelatin, because this gelatin is very tricky. If you don't make it just right, or if you don't shoot it at just the right temperature, it's not the same as other gelatin and we found this out after we developed it, but you can tell by shooting a BB at a known velocity, then you get the penetration of the BB and—

Q. So when you set this, you fired a BB into it?

A. Yes. Mr. Haag did this at home before he brought this in.

Q. You might step around and show them that so they can get a closer look at that.

A. Yes, I can. Here you can also see the powder residue, and a black powder weapon you see this very dark powder residue, and they go into the crack that forms in the cavitation, these crack and powder, black material right here. So that is and this is very useful technique.

Q. How far up the wound track was—is that—does that BB mark?

A. The BB generally goes about eight and a half to nine centimeters, which is a little over three inches and that's when it's shot at 600 feet per second. We shoot it with just a pump up BB gun. You get a pump up BB gun for $35 or so and it's very useful and you have to have a got to have a chronograph, of course, to measure the speed.

Q. At the site of the BB, that would be the track of the 68 caliber bullet at —

A. The BB—the only reason the BB is in here is to make sure the gelatin has been made right.

Q. So it doesn't go in the same distance every time?

A. No. Well, the BB does for a gelatin that's made right. That why we use the BB to make sure it goes in right, because when we first started this technique, we weren't calibrating gelatin. We were just starting and we made the gelatin just like the people said the directions on the box and we made the gelatin. And as a matter of fact, the directions say always start out with cold water. I thought everybody had the directions. Well, that wasn't true. They didn't, so I started getting reports from people that call in and say we followed your gelatin technique and we shot this particular projectile and you say you get 11 inches of penetration, we get 16 with the same projectile. I said well, send me some of your projectiles and I'll shoot them and see what I got, and I shoot them and I get the same thing that I do, 11.

So I said well, maybe there's some problems with your gelatin. How do you have make your gelatin? Well, they buy this gelatin from Time and Knox who sells the gelatin and there's no directions. They still—I don't think they put directions in it, there's no directions. You buy a little Jello at the grocery store and it will have directions. Well, these hundred pound boxes of gelatin and they don't have any directions.

Well, anyhow, people would go home and ask their wives well, how do you make gelatin? So she would go and look at the gelatin box and they would make gelatin that way. If you heat it too much, it destroys the integrity of it. It breaks down molecules and people were just heating the gelatin too much and then we had to do another paper and we had to publish this and because of that developed the calibration BB shot to make sure everyone, say, in the FBI lab and my lab and the Royal Canadian Mounted Police were all shooting the same—and Luke Haag's lab—were all shooting the same gelatin. Therefore, we can compare notes because we have a material that is the same. And without the BB shot you can't guarantee that..

GENERAL BAUGH: Questions from you, Mr. Tate?

MR. CORONER: Anybody have any questions?

GENERAL BAUGH: Dr. Fackler, I think may have questions for Mr. Haag. If you would stay up there, maybe both of y'all can handle those questions, if you don't mind.

LUCIEN HAAG

resumed the witness stand, and testified further as follows:

MR. HAAG: I'm not hooked up to mike, but when y'all came back, I shot a pattern at just cotton at six inches muzzle to cotton and you get some idea of carbonation material I talked about earlier.

We also had a fire to put out. There are two balls; one is in the gelatin that Dr. Fackler just showed you. That was two pieces that went end to end. The ball is intact. When you look at it, you can see the ramrod imprint. Those would be useful to a laboratory person to look at two guns to one gun, if we were so lucky to recover a ball.

This pattern was shot against a simple panel from a police type body armor. It clearly didn't go in. It simply deformed the ball ever so slightly, but you can still see these tool marks of the ramrod on it. So other than the fact the gun has very obviously been fired, if you wish to smell the gun, this will stink quite the room does at this point in time.

MR. CORONER: I think there's a question as to firing close —

EXAMINATION

BY MR. TURNBOW:

Q. I noticed when you shot the weapon pieces of cotton wad caught on fire. If Lewis was wearing a nightshirt, a cotton nightshirt, what is the probability that the nightshirt would have caught on fire? —

GENERAL BAUGH: His question was about the flammability of the nightshirt that Lewis may have been wearing.

THE WITNESS: This caught on fire. This is cotton. I reach down and got a handful of water and put it out. That's where the word powder burn came from. The patch burn because I failed to wet it, if it had been soaked in bear tallow, spit, it wouldn't have caught on fire. This one invariably, almost invariably will catch on fire the way of close range shot. This is interesting. If clothing is available to look at the scorching and burning or just simply a hole or a blast hole. And, of course, all of the clothing back then is going to be cotton or linen or some sort of animal skin, and linen will behave like cotton.

Q. If there's no evidence of any scorching on Lewis' nightshirt or on the bedding he was sleeping on, it's not written in any of the accounts, but does the absence of any kind of scorching or firing tell you anything about the closeness of which he was shot?

A. It is an enigma to us all, because thinking what we know today of what happened then, I view as two situations. If everyone came in and saw things they thought were obvious and, therefore, didn't report it, lots of soot in the wound, lots of scorching on clothes, and came to the conclusion that Mrs. Grinder did, that's her account, or these things weren't present and they weren't thinking in the analytical terms we do today. They didn't smell the gun, they didn't look at the clothing, they didn't really look at the wound. The record I'm aware of absolutely is silent on the sort of things I've shown you here today.

MR. CORONER: Any other questions?

GENERAL BAUGH: Thank you.

(WITNESS EXCUSED.)

GENERAL BAUGH: I think we're maybe at good point to stop if you want to recess for the day and come back tomorrow.

MR. CORONER: Recess today and come back in the morning.

GENERAL BAUGH: Probably have about three or four witnesses tomorrow.

THE CORONER'S INQUEST WAS ADJOURNED FOR THE DAY, AND SCHEDULED TO BEGIN AT 9:00, June 4, 1996.

I, Anita F. Polk, a Notary Public at Large, in and for the State of Tennessee, do hereby certify:
That the witness(es) in the foregoing proceedings named was/were present at the time and place therein specified; that the said proceedings were taken before me as a Notary Public at the said time and place and was taken down in shorthand writing by me; that the said proceeding was thereafter under my direction transcribed into computer-assisted transcription, and that the foregoing transcript constitutes a full, true and correct report of the proceedings which then and there took place;
That I am a disinterested person to the said action,
IN WITNESS THEREOF, I have hereto subscribed my hand and affixed my official seal this the 5th of July, 1996.

Anita F. Polk
Notary Public at Large
State of Tennessee

My commission expires: May 16, 1998.

Day Two: June 4, 1996

MR. CORONER: Come to order. We want to begin by doing a little housekeeping we need to do. The first thing we'd like to do today, it has come to our attention there are several descendents of Meriwether Lewis here with us today and yesterday. And we would like to recognize you and get your names and your connection and the town where you live so that we might have that a part of the record of this Inquiry. If you are a descendent of Meriwether Lewis would you please stand right now please?

So that the reporter can make this a part of our record, if you would begin right over here and give us your name and the town where you live and what your connection is, please.

MR. VAN STONE: My name is Keith Van Stone. I live in Hermitage, Tennessee right outside of Nashville and Meriwether Lewis was my great, great, great, great uncle.

MS. VAN STONE: I'm Annie Laurie Van Stone. I live in Nashville and I think that my—that Meriwether Lewis was my great, great, great—three greats or two?

MR. VAN STONE: Two

MS. VAN STONE: Great, great uncle. His sister was our grandmother, great, great grandmother.

MR. ANDERSON: I'm Dr. William Anderson. I live in Williamsburg, Virginia. Lewis' sister Jane was my great, great grandmother which makes me his great, great, great nephew.

MR. ANDERSON: I'm William from Alfredo, Georgia. This is my dad, so just add another great on there.

MR. CORONER: Thank you all very much, we appreciate you

coming. (Applause.) On behalf of this Jury let me say to you we appreciate very much you being here and thank you for—I know some of you have come quite a distance for being here and we thank you very much for being here. Is there any other housekeeping that we need to take care of?

GENERAL PHILLIPS: Just one announcement, Mr. Coroner and Members of the Jury, that is you have previously been submitted the typed copy of the letter of James Neely to Thomas Jefferson concerning the death of Governor Lewis, and you will note on the bottom of the second page, that is taken from the Donald Jackson work, *Letters of the Lewis and Clark Expedition.*

Professor Starrs does have a copy of the handwritten—what is taken to be the best handwritten version that is available, and it corresponds to this typed copy. He has that in his papers back at George Washington University, in addition to that you heard a good deal of testimony yesterday about writings of Governor Lewis and also writings of Major Russell. And we have submitted to the Jury this morning Xerox copies of what the document examiner yesterday was referring to; and also the document examiner today will make reference to the same documents.

We are going to request that Professor Starrs make a late exhibit to this proceeding of the handwritten version of the James Neely letter to Thomas Jefferson. If you could do that Professor Starrs.

(LATE FILED EXHIBIT NO. 2 ENTERED.)

GENERAL PHILLIPS: Mr. Coroner, are you ready for the next witness?

MR. CORONER: Yes.

GENERAL PHILLIPS: We call Dr. Dillon, Dr. Duayne Dillon. (Witness goes to Podium.)

GENERAL PHILLIPS: Ladies and gentlemen of the Jury, and Mr. Coroner, for the purposes of saving time I'd like to present to you the qualifications of Dr. Duayne Dillon. He is a graduate of the University of California, Berkeley, receiving their degrees of Bachelor of science Master's and Doctorate in Criminology. He as also done additional post graduate study at the University of Vienna, Austria as well as the office of Special Investigations of the United States Air Force.

During his professional career he as served in a number of positions including being Chief of the Criminalistic Laboratory of the Contra Costa County Sheriff's Department in California. He has been Criminalist and Acting Director of the Crime Laboratory of the San Francisco Police Department and he has served as a special agent of the Office of Special investigation of the United States Air Force.

He has held academic positions at the University of California at Berkeley, at JFK University and the University of Illinois. He has taught at a number of institutions including the FBI Academy at Quantico, Virginia. He has quite an extensive list of professional publications. We will be submitting his curriculum vitae to the Coroner's Jury, but at this time we submit to you Dr. Duayne Dillon and ask he be sworn to give expert testimony in this Inquiry.

DUAYNE DILLON, D. CRIM.

Having been first duly sworn was examined and testified as follows:

EXAMINATION

BY GENERAL PHILLIPS:

Q. Dr. Dillon, I will ask that you speak up since you are competing with a piece of heavy equipment just outside the building here. Dr. Dillon, are you presently working as a consultant; is that what your present position is?

A. Yes, presently I am a consultant in matters of questioned documents. I have been so for thirteen years since my retirement from government service.

Q. Where do you live, Dr. Dillon?

A. I live in Martinez, California.

Q. I have told the Coroner's Jury that you have extensive experience in public service laboratory work. Have you also had any involvement in controversies of a historical nature such as the subject matter of this Inquest.

A. Yes, I have. Since my retirement I have on occasion assisted authors on the authenticity of documents and in the comparison of documents relating to various historical events such as the Donner Party in Nevada, California; some early California land cases. And the first, including the first case in which handwriting went to the United States, Supreme Court and a number of other matters of that type.

Q. Dr. Dillon, as a document examiner have you had occasion to be accepted as an expert and give testimony in criminal cases?

A. Yes, I have.

Q. Have you done that on few or many occasions?

A. I have done it hundreds of occasions.

Q. Now would you tell us what work were you asked to do in this matter concerning the death of Meriwether Lewis.

A. I was asked to compare the handwriting which appeared on a variety of documents that I was provided, and I should clarify the statement of documents. I actually have seen nothing of which I would call a document in this matter. I have only seen copies and primarily copies of microfilm materials.

Q. And it is your understanding that's all you have seen because that is all that is available?

A. My understanding is I received what was obtained as the best copies available of these materials.

Q. What work were you asked to do this case?

A. I was asked to focus on three writings, the first writings, signatures of Gilbert Russell which appeared on several documents; to compare two signatures purported to be signatures of Jonathan Williams; and a series signatures in the name of Meriwether Lewis which appeared on a variety of documents most of which were letters.

Q. Now can you explain to the Jury what work you did and what conclusions you reached?

A. One of the things which I did because of the poor condition of the copies that I had, since many of them came from microfilm which is heavily scratched, I examined—I first scanned these images into a computer and removed the extraneous material that interfered with the signatures themselves and appearance of the signatures. So the slides I will show here today will represent signatures which have had the scratches and other extraneous marks which apparently were on the microfilm removed.

I first compared the signatures in the name of Gilbert Russell to determine the likelihood of the signatures having been written by one individual. I then compared the signatures in the names of Williams and finally intercompared all the signatures that were in the name that I was provided in the name of Meriwether Lewis.

I did not make an assumption that any particular signature was a known, valid signature of any of these three individuals. By simply intercomparing all of the signatures to see that signatures I could say were written by the same individual.

Q. Dr. Dillon, the Jury heard testimony yesterday from Mr. Gerald Richards, a retired FBI agent and former Chief of the FBI laboratories Documents Unit. You are aware of that?

A. Yes, I was here when he testified.

Q. And were your findings in your examination consistent with the findings that he also witnessed?

A. Yes, they were basically consistent in terms of which signatures could be attributed to a single writer and which signatures of that name were not written by the same person.

Q. And did you do your work independently of the work that former Agent Richards did?

A. Yes, I received materials in California and had no conversations with the other document examiner in this matter until two days go when we sat down and each of us presented our findings and found that we had reached substantially the same conclusion.

Q. Now Dr. Dillon, you have some slides with you that you could show the Jury concerning the work that you did?

A. Yes, I do. This shows an example of the condition that I received these documents in. It is a Meriwether Lewis signature and as one dated 4 January—excuse me. Meriwether Lewis signature simply to illustrate the scratches and other marks that are in the vicinity of the signature.

This is an intercomparison of signatures and I don't believe that is in focus, there we go. And the bottom three signatures were written in my opinion by the same individual while the top signature was written by a second individual. That is the signature which appears on the so-called Gilbert Russell statement that is supposedly given to Jonathan Williams.

Q. That's the statement where Gilbert Russell was telling the President about the circumstances of Meriwether Lewis' death.

A. Yes, that's correct. And it is my opinion that signature was not signed by the person that signed the remainder of the signatures. I did not intend in the presentation of these slides to go through all of the details, but there are significant differences including the exclusion of the middle initial of the name which is always in the Russell signatures that I have connected to both the first and last names.

(Next Slide.) This is the same document, the upper signature being a signature of Jonathan Williams in an unrelated matter from a Manuscript Collection and the bottom signature being the signature that appears at the bottom of the Russell statement with an accompanying explanation of the nature of that statement. That bottom signature if it is J. Williams as it appears to be simply an initial was not in my opinion written by the same person who wrote the James Williams Document of 1810.

Q. This is the same document that is the Major Russell Statement about the circumstances of Lewis' death?

A. It is. And both of these slides represent signatures which have had the scratches removed and represent the best representations I can obtain of those signatures. Though certainly the signatures that I looked at in both of the laser printouts and on the screen of the computer are somewhat better than the reproduction that is possible through projection of the slides.

Q. Would it then be a reasonable probability that if Major Russell made such a statement that was witnessed by Mr. Williams, that the copy of that which historians have relied upon was written by some third party, not by Russell and not by Williams?

A. Yes, that is a fair assumption.

Q. Go ahead.

(Next Slide.)

A. This is an example of the Gilbert Russell signatures as they were obtained from the documents. And you will notice all of those horizontal dark lines that go through there imply represent scratches on the microfilm and this is very common when dealing with archival material because this is the manner in which researchers are presented with this material, they use a microfilm viewer and over time the materials become exceedingly scratched and it is one for the purpose of preserving the original or copy of the document that is in the archives.

(Next Slide.) This is an example of a Meriwether Lewis signature showing in addition to the markings of—extraneous markings, which have occurred either over time through the folding of the document. The fact that if you will notice on this document that there appears to be faint vertical writing, that is the writing on the opposite side of the page. And we are not dealing with the original, so we don't know what is on the other side of the page. And when we say something is a letter, normally people think of a letter as something that has gone through the postal process.

At this time in American history letters, the envelope of the letter, the envelope and the letter were the same piece of paper. It was simply the manner in which the item was folded and it was addressed on one of the blank sides of any of the pages. And if we had originals of these, the problem of determining the origin of the document would be assisted in some fashion by the possibility of postal markings indicating the points of origin and points of receipt.

And even such information as the amount of money which was necessary for the postal process if they went through the Postal Service. This is approximately forty years before stamps were even used in this country. And this type of signature is the type of signature which I attempted just to show in greater detail by removing some of the material. And in this case it was not possible to remove the entire crease that goes through the name of Lewis.

Could I have the next one please? (Next Slide.) This is a comparison of all the Meriwether Lewis' signatures which I received. All of these signatures of various dates all agree internally while some variation is shown. The signatures dating from 1801 through shortly before Meriwether Lewis' death all agree.

My examination revealed no deterioration in these

signatures. If the signatures were undated there would be no manner in which anyone could organize these to show any progression of time with the signatures. They're essentially— they essentially vary with extreme—in extremely narrow range.

Q. Could I ask you a question about that slide? Does that slide now include the signature on the letter that he wrote to the President shortly—that he purportedly wrote to the President shortly before his death?

A. Which letter would that be?

Q. I'm referring to the letter that has sometimes been referred to as a rough draft?

A. Oh, yes. That does, see the letter of the 16th and that is the—on the right hand side of the screen and is the first of the two signatures on the right-hand side of the screen. Those are the last two dates of Meriwether Lewis' writings, the 16th and 22nd.

Q. The last two are the ones on the right?

A. Yes.

Q. And you see no degradation or deterioration of his signature shortly before his death?

A. No. Actually the quality of those signatures in the form we received these is actually superior. The definition is actually superior to many of the other signatures.

Q. I take it this display of Meriwether Lewis' signatures do not include the writing of Meriwether Lewis on the Will copy?

A. I did not assume that that was a Will. I assumed from what the documentation I had that that was a copy of something out of a clerk's book.

Q. Made by a clerk?

A. Yes.

Q. I want to make sure the Jury understands that this does not include the so-called signature on the so-called holographic Will?

A. Yes.

Q. You took the will to be a copy?

A. But it does include the signature in 1901 [sic] for the appointment of his attorney even though the remainder of that document was not written by his hand.

Q. You mean 1801?

A. 1801, yes.

MR. CORONER: May I ask a question right here? Is it your opinion that these seven signatures were signed by the same person?

THE WITNESS: Yes, it is.

MR. CORONER: All seven by the same person?

THE WITNESS: Yes, all are by the same person in my opinion.

BY GENERAL PHILLIPS:

Q. Okay, go ahead.

A. May I have the next slide?

(Next Slide.)

A. I spoke of lack of change of the signature. I also looked at the extended writing and rather than try to show paragraphs from the various letters I simply here have taken the closes that are used before the signatures in four locations. And we have the abbreviation "Obedient" used here in all of these, and the abbreviation for "Servant, Your Obedient Servant" and "Obedient and Very Humble Servant".

All of these for example were written in 1809, all represent documents dated in that year. And there is no observable variation in that writing throughout that period, and that includes the last two letters bearing the Meriwether Lewis' signatures.

Can we have the next slide? (Next Slide.) But I in the course of going through each of these, I compared that handwriting which made up the body of the letters to determine if there was anything within the body of the letters which would indicate any deterioration of the signatures, and anything which would indicate any difficulty on the part of writer in completing the writing. There is no change among the writings that I have that determined that all the signatures are by one person to indicate that in the body of the writing there is anything unusual about the writing.

Some authorities would attribute certain mental states to be reflected in writing. In order for anyone to make such a determination there has to be a change in the writing, and I find no change in the writing of these letters at all.

I have in the course of my work done experimental work and observed the work of individuals under the influence of alcohol for instance, which does markedly often affect writing, sometimes with not particularly high levels of alcohol. There is none of that type of change within any of this writing. The writing does not vary from letter to letter.

Now one of these letters does, the letter of the 16th does contain a number of corrections. But in reading the text of those letters, those corrections appear to be corrections to either clarify or more greatly emphasize the statements that are made in the sentences rather than to correct some error in the grammar or wording of the sentences.

Q. You are referring now to the letter from Governor Lewis to the President, James Madison?

A. Yes.

Q. There is nothing in that letter that you think indicates a mental or physical abnormality comparing it to his other writings from earlier time?

A. I don't purport to be able to diagnose mental state from handwriting, but if mental state can be diagnosed from handwriting the handwriting has to change. You have to have a change and be able to demonstrate some difference in the handwriting. And my examination does not indicate any differences in the handwriting throughout the period in which all of the signatures agree.

Q. Do you agree with the opinion expressed by the FBI Agent that that letter appears to be a rough draft?

A. It could very well be a rough draft. One however would have to—should have more writing of the writer during that period to find out what his habits were. But frequently people of position would have a clerk write the final draft of an important letter and simply sign it. And often—and we don't know frequently when we look at archival material if we're dealing with a letter that was actually mailed to the person it was addressed to or it was simply a file copy retained by the writer or it happened to be a draft that was made for a clerk to reproduce.

Q. Thank you. Go ahead. Dr. Dillon?

A. And I believe the last two are simply two more of these letters written, this is one written on 16 of September of 1909 {SIC}, it does have corrections.

Q. 1809?

A. Excuse me, 1809. 16 September of 1809, and it does have corrections. But again as I previously testified, these corrections are in the nature of either greater clarification or greater emphasis. And the final letter is the last letter in the series which does again show the same quality of writing, although this one has virtually no corrections in it.

Q. Is this also an 1809 letter?

A. Yes, that is one of 22 September of 18 0 9.

Q. This one was even later and closer to his death?

A. Yes, that's the last dated document that I was provided as a potential letter by Meriwether Lewis.

Q. You find this writing to be consistent with his earlier writings?

A. Yes, I do.

Q. No degradation or deterioration?

A. No significant changes at all during the writings throughout the period.

GENERAL PHILLIPS: Thank you. Dr. Dillon. Mr. Coroner?

EXAMINATION

BY MR. CORONER:

Q. The slide right before this, what was the date of that letter'

A. 16 September of 1809.

Q. That is the letter to James Madison?

A. Yes, that's correct, yes.

Q. Could we go back and look at that a second, back one slide. Is that bottom line where it say—it looks to me like it did say, "Your Obedient and Very Humble Servant," and "Very Humble" is marked out.

A. Yes, I believe on this next page has the closing on it with the signature. And I believe we are providing the copies I used to the Jury, is that correct.

Q. Yes, we have them.

MR. CORONER: Any other questions?

EXAMINATION

MR. TURNBOW:

Q. You ran a scan on these documents in your computer to remove lines that you thought were extraneous. Could any those lines be relative to determine whether or not Lewis executed the documents?

A. No, this is a routine procedure which I do. And if I feel there is any question about whether a mark or a line is actually related to the writing, if there is any question I leave it in. I only remove those where I can see the scratches going across the screen or some diagonal angle to the writing.

Q. I believe the documents we have are copies that were not scanned?

A. Yes, you have what I was originally provided with.

MR. TURNBOW: Okay.

EXAMINATION

BY MR. CORONER:

Q. Is it pretty well customary for two document examiners to work together like this—not together but with you on the same case?

A. It is not unusual to have more than one document examiner. I didn't know until I came here to testify that both document examiners in this matter had looked at the same material and would talk about the same material.

Q. So you have done this before as far as someone else working on the same case?

A. Yes.

Q. Is it unusual for you to agree as closely as you have?

A. No. It is not unusual to agree. Hopefully that would be the usual.

MR. CORONER: Any other questions? Thank you, Dr. Dillon.

WITNESS EXCUSED

GENERAL BAUGH: Our next witness will be Dr. Reimert T. Ravenholt.

REIMERT THOROLF RAVENHOLT, M.D.

Having been first duly sworn was examined and testified as follows:

EXAMINATION

GENERAL BAUGH:

Q. Mr. Tate, with your indulgence, and Members of the Jury with your indulgence, I'm trying to read you matters for expedience that have been provided to me about Dr. Ravenholt's background. He was born in Wisconsin. He received a medical degree from University of Minnesota, a Master's in Public Health Degree from the University of California. And has had extensive research, administrative and teaching experience in Epidemiology, Public Health, population and Family Planning.

He was an Epidemic Intelligence Service Officer, U.S. Public Health Service for Disease Control, Atlanta, 1952 to 1954. He was Director of Epidemiology and Communicable Disease Control, Seattle-King County Health Department, 1954-1961. He was an Epidemiology Consultant in Europe for the U.S. Public Health Service, American Embassy, Paris, France, 1961-1963; Associate Professor of Preventive Medicine, University of Washington, 1963-1966; Director Office of Population, U.S. Agency of International Development, Washington, DC, 1966-1980; Director of World Health Surveys, Centers for Disease Control, Rockville, Maryland, 1980-1982; Assistant Director for Research, National Institute on Drug Abuse, Rockville, Maryland, 1982-1984; Chief, Epidemiology Branch, U.S. Food and Drug Administration, Rockville, Maryland, 1984-1987; Director of World Health

Surveys, Seattle, Washington, 1987-1993; President currently of the Population Health Imperatives in Seattle, Washington.

He also researched extensively and published more than 150 scientific reports on epidemiology, preventive medicine, population and family planning. Smoking and health was also one of his topics. Publications include *Tobacco's Global Death March*; *Taking Contraceptives to the World's Poor*; *America's Battered Child Plague*; and *Triumph and Then Despair* which deals with the subject matter of your inquest.

For 14 years, Dr. Ravenholt directed the Global Population Program for the U.S. Agency of International Development. It was one of the world's foremost population programs, providing then half of all international population program assistance ($1.3 billion) during those years.

Notable honors received include distinguished Honor Award of the Agency for International Development "In Recognition of His Distinguished Leadership in the Development of Worldwide Assistance Programs to Deal with the Challenge of Excessive Population Growth"; the Hugh Moore Memorial Award from the Population Crisis Committee and the International Planned Parenthood Association Award for "Innovation and Vision in the Population Field"; and the Carl Schultz Award for the "Distinguished Service to the Field of Population and Family Planning."

Q. What is the particular area of expertise that you bring to this Inquest today, Dr. Ravenholt?

A. Well, let me first say, Professor Starrs and the District Attorney Joe Baugh and Paul Phillips, the Coroner Richard Tate, Members of the Jury and the descendents of Meriwether Lewis, I'm happy to be here in Tennessee. And I thank Professor Starrs for inviting me even though he came to somewhat different conclusions with respect to the death of Meriwether Lewis.

Q. Let me stop you just a second—has he sworn in?

A. Yes, I was sworn.

Q. Excuse me for interrupting.

A. Although we may differ somewhat with respect to the diagnosis, I agree very hardily we agree very hardily with his Voltaire "To the living we owe respect, but to the dead we owe only the truth". And it is in that quest for the truth we are gathered here in Tennessee close to where Meriwether Lewis died.

And I must say that when Professor Starrs invited me and said we would be staying close to his monument here in some little place along the Natchez Trace, I thought we might be staying in tents or something. But I am impressed that Hohenwald is a lovely community of more than three thousand people, and has offered us the most generous southern hospitality. With that said —

Q. I hope ABC News got that.

A. Let me return to your question, Mr. Baugh, which was —

Q. What is epidemiology?

A. What is epidemiology? Well epidemiology comes from the word epidemic which comes from the two Greek words, epi and demos meaning upon people. Something which descends upon people and historically it referred particularly to infectious diseases that swept through communities and these were epidemics and so forth. Epidemiology is the study of that.

But during my lifetime the application of Epidemiology has been enormously broadened to where now it is understood to be the study of the distributions and determinants of disease in human population. Disease of any kind, not just infectious but chronic, traumatic —

Q. What is the difference between infectious and chronic?

A. Sometimes they're the same. You can have a chronic infectious disease.

Q. Define those terms for me?

A. Pardon?

Q. Define those terms, what do you mean by infectious?

A. Infectious we refer to the entry of an organism which multiplies in the body. And as in tuberculosis and leprosy and quite a few diseases, this may cause a chronic disease but —

Q. Chronic being what?

A. Chronic means that it lasts a long time. And many of these such as in cardiovascular disease—for example, it may be chronic but not due to infection, though it can be.

Q. Epidemiology apparently includes both infectious disease and traumatic?

A. Yes, it is the whole matter of occurrence of diseases in human population. And let me say that I was fortunate following my internship in the Public Health in San Francisco, I entered the Epidemic Intelligence Service of the U.S. Public Health Service in Atlanta, Georgia which was then a rather embryonic organization but it has grown and it is a—the Center for disease control more commonly known as CDC is a preeminent organization of the world dealing with epidemiology and disease control. There is nothing to match it in the world. And much of that is done is with WHO and so forth is done actually by ex-EIS CDC personnel.

Q. Do you have an interest in Meriwether Lewis other than that generated by this particular Inquest or contact with Professor Starrs?

A. Well, my involvement has come somewhat accidentally but due to a combination of many things.

Q. Tell us about it.

A. I grew up in a farm in Wisconsin of Danish heritage. My four grandparents came to America My father's father came over as a Danish immigrant and he went to Montana to the gold fields in 1874-1876. And although he died long before I was born, my father used to tell me stories about him and his experiences in Montana.

That may have got me—in fact when my Grandfather left the gold fields in the summer of 1876, left Helena, he went to Fort Benton, the head of navigation. He was expecting to catch a steamboat there but there was no steamboat for the reason that this was the summer of Custer's Last Stand and General Crook and Miles and others had come in after that. And they were congregating a great Army force down on Yellowstone River and all the steamboats were diverted up the Yellowstone instead of the Missouri.

So my grandfather, a German and a Yankee, bought a row boat and went down from Fort Benton all the way down to Bismarck, North Dakota. So I used to hear stories about this from my father.

Q. Does part of the area of expertise you have in epidemiology deal with neurosyphilis?

A. It deals with it and —

Q. Tell us what it is.

A. Neurosyphilis is that disease caused by the invasion of the central nervous system by the syphilis spirochete, technically known as Treponema pallidum. It is kind of a little organism, sort of a cork screw like a microscopic organism.

Q. Is it single celled or multi-celled?

A. Yes, it is single organism, yes.

Q. And how is it transmitted normally?

A. It is ordinarily transmitted by sexual intercourse. And has of course been a great scourge in the history of civilization.

Q. Has there been some sort of controversy about the origin of syphilis, whether it is a North American disease or American Continent disease or an European disease?

A. Yes, there is usually controversy about just about everything and not just about that because it is has been such a historically disastrous disease. But I'm interested that Meriwether Lewis in his diaries came to an accurate observation when he was on the Continental Divide with the Shoshones saying that he had concluded then from the information he had obtained along the way and from the Shoshones that venereal disease, both Louis Veneri syphilis and gonorrhea were American diseases.

And that is actually true, that Europe did not know syphilis until March 1493 when Columbus and his sailors returned to the Iberian Peninsula. The captain of the Pinta was very seriously ill with syphilis when they arrived back and he died shortly thereafter. And the Court of Ferdinand and Isabella were indeed told this was a disease from the Indies as they called them, which was very prevalent there but not as severe there as it is among the Caucasians in Spain.

Q. So it is your opinion as a medical practitioner that this disease could have existed in North America long before it existed in Europe?

A. Yes.

Q. Were there strains of this disease which the Indians seemed more immune than Europeans?

A. To syphilis in general they were perhaps more resistant because the least resistant people had already died off from it.

Q. Are you familiar with the general works of Meriwether Lewis? I mean, the diaries, the historical record concerning Lewis?

A. Yes. Let me just say how I happened to get into this. In 1988 there was book published by David Lavender entitled *The Way to the Western Sea*. An interesting historical thing and I got a copy of that and read it considerably with interest. And that tells the story from especially from St. Louis to Astoria, Oregon and back again. But it ends just on the 23rd of September when they returned to St. Louis.

But it tells of the stories along tie way and I remember reflecting as I finished that book, well, my God, the biggest problem that the Corps of the Discovery had on this three year trip to Pacific and back was venereal disease. I was not thinking of Lewis at that time.

Q. What gave you that opinion?

A. Then a year later I happened to run across *A Biography of Meriwether Lewis* by Richard Dillon, an excellent biography, and I read that, and that biography does not stop when they get back to St. Louis but it tells what happened subsequently.

Especially what happened in his final weeks and days and hours. And as I read that it came through to me as clear as could be, this poor fellow died of neurosyphilis.

I have had very wide and diverse experience with all kinds of infections. I'm one of few perhaps that has diagnosed and treated diphtheria, typhoid, I have investigated smallpox in West Germany, Yorkshire, Wales, Stockholm, typhoid epidemics there and so forth, malaria, I have seen and all of these diseases. And syphilis too, I have diagnosed and treated.

Q. What are the symptoms of this disease, this infection that you would look for?

A. Well, syphilis has three phases. The first is what we call the primary phase. From the time of sexual intercourse to the occurrence of the lesion. And that lesion is ordinarily on the genitalia. And it is called a chancre. It is a sore; it is a fairly indolent long lasting sore. And it ordinarily takes at least ten days from sexual intercourse until the occurrence of the chancre. That is the first phase.

The second is the secondary phase which usually begins about a month after infection, and which afflicts especially the skin and mucous membranes. And this is the secondary syphilis.

And then the third phase is the attack of the spirochete upon the internal organs, upon the cardiovascular system, the central nervous system, the bones, the spirochete can attack any tissue in the human body. So it has always been a diagnostic puzzle for practicing physicians. Patient can come in complaining of almost anything and it may end up being syphilis.

But some forms are quite distinctive. The gumma, the occurrence of small tumors responding to the syphilitic organism, and cardiovascular disease. And to some extent the osseous disease and also the attack upon the central nervous system whether it be upon the spinal cord or upon the cerebrum. These are quite distinctive.

And I should just read what a person with syphilis, the

kind of disease, symptoms they may have. Because I went back to some of the old books, especially those published before penicillin.

Q. Let me ask a question before you start off with that. I'd like, if you see those symptoms, to correlate those with what you have read about the last six weeks of Lewis' life that may verify your diagnosis, if you don't mind?

A. Well, possibly I should leave it to then and come back to that.

Q. However you think would be best to present it?

A. Well let's talk about for the moment, let's say if he developed syphilis, where did he develop it. And just take it through that and then come to the more natural disease.

Q. That's fine?

A. As I said, it was in reading the biography by Richard Dillon with his details about the final days and hours, that it occurred to me this must be neurosyphilis, paresis is the specific term. This was 1990. And I told my wife, you know, I think I know what killed Meriwether Lewis and I am going to research it. I was busy remodeling and doing other things and it went along until 1993 but then I finally said if I'm ever going to do this, I better do it now.

I spent that winter researching. And fortunately there are many excellent books for this. There is of course the excellent general book published in 1814 on this to which Jefferson provided something. Then there are the books at the end of 19th century, especially the one by Professor Thwaites at Wisconsin in 1904. But the first biography really is the one by Richard Dillon in 1965.

But more recently there has been a tremendous effort to gather all the diaries together at the University of Nebraska, Gary Moulton and his staff have published a humongous collection of these diaries, there are now nine volumes and there are still going to be two more.

And I happened to get a hold of these and when I began

to, I bought a set of these and this enabled one to trace through the whole expedition of what preceded it and what went on and so I traced it and I would say that before the expedition, Meriwether Lewis lived at the White House with Thomas Jefferson for two years. And he was in apparent excellent health or he would not have been given the mission. And there was no hint of such disease when he went to St. Louis and there was no hint of it in the first year when they traveled up the Missouri River to Fort Mandan and wintered there.

We know there was syphilis at Fort Mandan because indeed Lewis and Clark mentioned this, and the sexual intercourse of the crew with the natives there but I don't think Lewis himself nor perhaps Clark had intercourse with the Indians at that time. They were very busy directing this and all kinds of activities and so forth.

Then in the spring of 1805 they proceeded up the Missouri and for four months they didn't meet another Indian. The only Indian was Sacagawea, the wife of Charbonneau, the interpreter for those four months. And they didn't meet until they got to the source of the Missouri on the Continental Divide, and just over it into Idaho when they met the Shoshones there.

And actually I spoke to the Lewis and Clark Trail Heritage Foundation at their annual encampment at Missoula, Montana two years ago in August of 1994. And indeed I met Mr. and Ms. Anderson, the relatives of Lewis there, that the Lewis and Clark buffs have such an encampment every summer, every August somewhere along the trail from St. Louis to Astoria, and it has been going on many years now.

And after that I went to Helena and then I went down and up the Jefferson and Beaverhead River to the Lemhi Pass and crossed over the Pass, the Lemhi River and along that to where Sacagawea was born. And I took some pictures and I will show those if I may.

(Slide Presentation).

Some of you will recall that when Lewis on the 12th of

August of 1805, he and his three companions were nearing the end of the Missouri —

Q. Where were those pictures made, Dr. Ravenholt?

A. These are made just short of the Summit, the seventy-three hundred foot summit of the Continental Divide. And I happened to be alone that day and had to set my camera to do it. And I did what McNeal did, I bestrode the Missouri River. There is the source of the Missouri River here between my legs. I think you can see that there, you see the beginning of the Missouri River.

Q. Right.

A. And the other two show the scenery. This sign post, "Sacagawea Memorial Camp, 12 miles, Lemhi Pass, 12 miles." This was 12 miles from the Lemhi Pass. And the Reservoir Lake Camp, that was actually Camp Fortunate —

Q. Is this where he met the Shoshone Indians?

A. I'll come to that.

Q. Let's kind of—we don't have a terrible amount of time, we need to kind of come to the point of your —

A. In the next one I will show you exactly where he met— which was the birth place of Sacagawea and the Shoshones. Here, actually here is on the top of the Lemhi Pass there is signs there. And this is looking south from there. Over here at the left, this is looking back from the Lemhi Pass back into Montana. And then down here we are—where the stone is, this is the Shoshone Meadows along the Lemhi Pass. It is a lovely meadow that stretches for a half a dozen miles along the Lemhi —

Q. Is this where Lewis met the Shoshone Indians?

A. This is where he very probably obtained his syphilis infection. This is the birth place of Sacagawea and the Shoshones, this as their traditional encampment on this meadow. And this is the Lemhi River which is a lovely mountain stream along there.

Q. What sort of symptoms did you first see after this meeting?

A. Yes, well I was interested where could he have gotten the syphilis, when could he have gotten it and so forth. And I saw no obvious source or place or likelihood until the nights of the 13th and 14th of August when he was staying—they had met the Shoshone Chief Cameahwait who is the brother of Sacagawea. And they established friendly relationships with the Shoshones to the extent that Chief Cameahwait sent one of his assistants ahead to setup the tent for, a buffalo hide tent for Meriwether Lewis.

Actually they only one leather tent right then because the Arikaras had attacked them the previous year and had taken or destroyed the rest of their tents. And that was no doubt pitched on this meadow along the Lemhi River there. Those two nights, the nights of the 13th and 14th, they were there, Lewis and his three companions were there. Clark and the rest of the Corps of Discovery were back at Camp Fortunate back on the Beaverhead River across the Pass. And Lewis mentions that there was partying going on and he made some very significant entries.

Q. So you think that was the time that he could have had contact with the women of the Shoshone Tribe?

A. Yes.

Q. And what symptoms did you see after that time?

A. Indeed I was very—actually this would have happened on the 13th and 14th of August. Significantly Lewis wrote several things just a few days later. On the 19th of August Lewis wrote as follows:

> The chastity of their women is not held in high estimation, and the husband will for a trifle barter the companion of his bed for a night or longer if he concedes the reward adequate. Though they are not so importunate that we should caress their women as the Sioux were, and some of their women appear to be held more sacred than in any Nation we have seen. I have requested the men to give them no cause

for jealousy by having connection with their women without their knowledge which with them strange as it may seem, is considered as disgraceful to the husband as clandestine connections as a similar kind are among most civilized nations. To prevent this mutual exchange of good offices altogether, I know it impossible to effect, particularly as on the part of our young men who some months abstinence have made very polite to this tawny damsels. I was anxious to learn whether these people had the venereal and made Inquiry through the interpreter and his wife, that is Sacagawea. The information was that they sometimes had it, but I could not learn their remedy. They most usually died with its effects, his seemed strong proof, these disorders; both gonorrhea and Louis Veneri are native disorders of America.

Q. So when did you see symptoms?

A. Then as I said ordinarily there is an incubation period of ten days before syphilis. But he was writing this just a few days after. Now if he or any of his three companions had developed gonorrhea, that could have triggered this sort of thing. But the first symptom suggestive of syphilis was an entry by his on the 19th of September, about a month, a little over a month later. When Lewis wrote that breakings out or eruptions of the skin have also been common with us for sometime.

This matter of cutaneous lesions, secondary lesions, I suspect that Lewis just when he wrote this, he didn't quite realize the full significance of that, that is the first. And then in succeeding weeks Lewis became very severely ill. For about two weeks he was having great difficulty. Clark wrote:

Captain Lewis scarcely able to ride on a gentle horse which was furnished by the Chief. Several men so unwell they're compelled to lie by the side of the road.

And on September 27th, he again said:

Captain Lewis very sick, nearly all the men sick.

And on October 4 he wrote:

Captain Lewis still sick but able to walk around
a little.

But then for three months Lewis stopped writing in the Diary. So his illness apparently continued, and Clark had to do all the writing and they never said why or they never said —

Q. How did they treat these illnesses on the trail?

A. The main treatment of syphilis at that time was Mercury. It was actually begun almost immediately after syphilis arrived in Europe in March of 1493.

Q. How was that treatment taken, carried out?

A. The first treatment with Mercury is as an ointment, to rub it on the secondary lesions. And because Mercury is so toxic, ordinarily if you rubbed it on secondary lesions, direct contact with the spirochete is, it would quite quickly cure the secondary the lesion would cease to fester.

But of course many of the lesions are internal and for this they took Mercury orally, and Mercury was the main treatment and they took large quantities of Mercury over a period of time. Ordinarily when they took a course of Mercury they would do so for a month or more. And they would take Mercury by mouth several times daily until it caused copious salivation, the sign they were getting too much was copious salivation, and then they would cut back. And Lewis had indeed taken substantial quantities of Mercury along on the voyage apparently anticipating something like this.

Q. There were other diseases that were epidemic out there, tuberculosis, influenza, malaria, how would you differentiate the symptoms of syphilis from those diseases?

A. Well, we don't know that there was any malaria there at that time. I looked particularly through the diaries. With malaria ordinarily it is a fairly recognizable disease because it causes

such acute attacks of chills followed by fever and followed by
sweats and this is on a periodic basis every third day or fourth
day and there is no suggestion of this in the diaries during the
trip. And I don't know about the tuberculosis. I didn't see any
indication of chronic coughing and all that on it and I don't
—

Q. What causes tuberculosis?

A. Well, the microbacterium tuberculosis is a bacteria that
causes tuberculosis.

Q. What causes malaria?

A. The plasmodium, the protozoan plasmodium, a number
of species like vivax, also falciparum. Falciparum and malaria
indeed does have a central nervous system phase where it is
quite deadly and it kills. But the progress of that, the episodic
kind of progress and the symptoms are quite different I think
from what we saw.

Q. Explain the differences?

A. Well, at least once that I became aware of during the years
that I was dealing with Africa and Asia and so forth, it does
not have the kind of capacity within my experience, one did
not see this curious craziness, insanity as a result. One saw
progressive neurological dysfunction leading to death in the
case of falciparum. But not this curious episodic attacks of
insanity which then tops and they occur later.

Q. Now you said that is a symptom of syphilis that you have
insanity and then it tops —

A. This is a symptom of neurosyphilis or paresis. And I must
say I have not gone as deeply into this until I got interested
in Meriwether Lewis and read a lot of the literature in this,
including the excellent text by Dr. Osler from 1892, who was
perhaps the most accomplished diagnostician at the time.

Q. What do you mean by paresis?

A. Paresis refers to the attack of the spirochete on the
cerebrum.

Q. What are the symptoms of the attack of the spirochete on

the cerebrum section of the brain?

A. Of course there are general symptoms of fever and general illness but it is, particularly this matter of progressive deterioration of the highest central nervous system function.

Q. Thought disorder?

A. Yes, thought disorder, and a very particular one is the increasing loss of judgment, of good judgment, which is a distinctive thing. I just want to read this because I went through some of these older books that had gave —

Q. While you are looking for that I believe that you have provided the Members of the jury with copies of the article that you wrote about that?

A. Uh-huh.

GENERAL BAUGH: And I'd like for you—we will make one of those, a copy, for our purposes in this hearing, in the Inquest, and we will also make a copy of your curriculum vitae, a copy, an exhibit rather to the Inquest.

(EXHIBIT NOS. 3 & 4 MARKED AND ENTERED.)

BY GENERAL BAUGH:

Q. Go ahead and read it to us.

A. Neurosyphilis is most frequently encountered among the higher intellectual types. Alcohol, mental exertion and emotional strain are mentioned as predisposing causes. The relation of the paretic, the person with the paresis, to the other members of society is almost diagnostic of the disease. There is often a loss of memory for recent events, although past events are fairly well recounted. There will be slight or even flaring mistakes in his business correspondence, subjects will creep in that have nothing to do with the business at hand. And letters will often take on a frivolous character where business itself is of a serious nature. Mistakes in business will have been found to crept into this man's dealings for quite a while before recognizable symptoms appear.

The depressed or introspective type in this type of paresis, the symptoms are apt to come on quite suddenly. The patient becomes melancholy and often has ideas of self destruction. In distinction to the other types he often realizes what his trouble is, and sees his vitality becoming less day by day. Unfortunately this realization of his condition stimulates his notion of self destruction. While these people are as a rule harmless to other members of society, they are quite often successful in doing damage to themselves.

It fits Lewis. I mean, William Clark and Thomas Jefferson commented on his depression. Well, if you had syphilis you would be pretty depressed too, especially if it were recurring and progressive.

Q. Let me ask you about this. Of course Lewis died 187 years ago. Would there be evidence in his skeletal remains that could confirm or verify your hypothesis about his infection?

A. To that I can't be completely definitive but I share very much with Professor Starrs the desire that a thorough look be taken. I think there are two things that might be discovered among the skeletal remains of Meriwether Lewis. The first thing that you look for would be is there any Mercury in the skeletal remains. Because if he were taking substantial quantities of Mercury late in his illness I would suspect some of this would remain and though leaching might have taken it out during the forty years before they put the monument on top.

Q. How are heavy metals carried in the body, simulated in the body, where are they?

A. Certainly, bone is one of the places depending on when they were taken and what they are.

Q. So there may be Mercury in the skeletal remains, the bones?

A. Pardon?

Q. There may be mercury in the bones itself, is that correct?

A. I would expect there may be some residual mercury.

Q. And what else?

A. The other is of course with modern technology and our

capacity to identify with great specificity whatsoever by the DNA. If Meriwether Lewis had substantial osteitis, meaning the spirochete was attacking the cartilage or bone in his latter, last part of his life, this would have stimulated inflammatory responses and perhaps new bone and so forth. And among that might very well be some treponema pallidum DNA.

If one finds that then of course that is highly specific indicating that he did at least have syphilis of the bone. And by inference he probably also did of the central nervous system in view of the symptoms.

GENERAL BAUGH: That is all the questions I have, Mr. Coroner.

MR. CORONER: Anyone of the Jury have any questions?

EXAMINATION

BY MR. BURKLOW:

Q. Would the large intake of mercury—could that not cause neurological results?

A. Yes, in recent decades we think more about because we are so familiar with some of the problems like Japanese from mercury exposure and so forth. But certainly in the old literature the treatment of syphilis, this seemed to be much less of a problem as far as a serious type of problem. It was a very common treatment; but there was not this awareness of the sort of the large side effects that might occur, because they really took it until copious salivation came, and this was on into the 20th Century that they did that.

Q. How would the mercury, in what form would it have been taken by mouth?

GENERAL BAUGH: His question was what form would mercury be taken—by mouth?

BY MR. BURKLOW:

Q. In other words not pure mercury itself?

A. They took of course a number of things. They took for example, Calamine is a mixture of a mercurous fluoride and they took that sometimes as a purgative. I didn't see just what the full composition of the mercury pill they took is. It no doubt was mixed with a variety of things, but I didn't see that in the diary. But they had Calamine too and what they called Galip, Pyorubin drug and they had Rush's Pills which may have much to do with the death of Sergeant Floyd in 1804, because if he had appendicitis and they gave him Rush's Pills, they probably insured that he would have a ruptured appendix.

EXAMINATION

BY MR. TURNBOW:

Q. You said one of the diseases was tuberculosis?

A. No, Mr. Baugh asked about it but I have no knowledge of tuberculosis among them at that time.

Q. But one of the symptoms of tuberculosis would be a cough, persistent cough?

A. Usually respiratory and usually there is chronic coughing and there is nothing in the diaries to indicate that.

Q. On page 376 of your report January 31st of 1806 Lewis says Bratton has an obstinate cough.

A. Okay, that may be but I don't know. But I was not impressed. Usually with tuberculosis and especially progressive tuberculosis, it gets worse and one didn't see that sort of thing. But I would not be surprised if some of them did have link to a tuberculosis infection. And I can't say that Bratton, even though his main complaints were referenced to his back and even though they were greatly benefited by a steam bath. I can not say with respect to the cough but no doubt they had coughs from a variety of causes.

Q. Would they have fever with tuberculosis?

A. Ordinarily, yes.

Q. And on May 24, 1806 it mentioned sweats, body sweats. I was curious—sometimes in epidemiology don't you try to determine a disease by disproving other diseases to show no way could they have had other diseases?

A. Yes, and of course in modern times in technological, competent circumstances one does many things. But you have to keep in mind the Lewis Expedition was a half a century before the advent of bacteriology, before Pasteur and the whole modern diagnostic measures and so forth.

Q. Can you rule out any other disease?

A. No, I'm sure they had—no, they had many diseases. And so I think one reason I come back to this, I have had such broad— for example Clark as they were ascending, they had repeated difficulties with boils and carbuncles, beyond the Great Falls, Clark would have gone forward with Lewis there on the 12th, at the end of the Missouri but he was laid up with at tumor of the ankles.

Well as it happens many years when I was in Seattle, I did extensive research first on hospital acquired staph infection that became epidemic during the fifties. But then I became aware there were non-human sources of staphylococcus disease and one summer I had a veterinary student help me and we did a study of staphylococcus infection among meat animals and meat workers and published on this. And in fact I think I have one in my briefcase.

And so I know I can recognize staphylococcus disease and boils and so forth, what they are. It would be very difficult I think for a young epidemiologist coming in who has not had experience with many different diseases to be able to sift out one set of symptoms and signs from the others.

Q. Is syphilis the only disease that could have produced these symptoms?

A. Let me say that one always—one is always aware that there are substantial overlaps between what various specific microorganisms can do. But Lewis' terminal illness and the course of the episodic febrile by attacks of the craziness and insanity is highly, to highly indicative of paresis, I think we can say that the nature of his illness was, pathognomonic is a medical term, pathognomonic. So highly characteristic one can make a strong presumptive diagnosis from it.

EXAMINATION

BY DR. BOULDIN:

Q. Isn't it true that syphilis has been known as the great imitator?

A. Right, this is what I mean. It could attack any tissue in the body and it did so. For centuries it was a huge problem until the advent of penicillin in the late forties.

EXAMINATION

BY MR. FLYNN:

Q. Doctor, we are going to make one assumption, in other words, we are saying Lewis didn't have any problems before he went on the expedition. It looked like he developed it on the expedition, or he was infected on the expedition, 1803 to 1806—somewhere along the line he was infected. But would you say that the disease evolve to that first stage where you go crazy in just six years to the time of his death?

A. Yes, there is still among the medical profession, many who think of neurosyphilis and paresis as being a late result of syphilis. And I had to go into this quite specifically and deeply because when I published this article in the *Journal of Epidemiology*, there were a couple of physicians that questioned that. And sent me back additionally to that and actually I published that as a follow-up to that, if I have it with me. And I can give you this, I can put it in the record.

But in fact what happened was that as soon as penicillin emerged in the forties and it was found to be remarkably effective against syphilis, every new case of primary or secondary or early or late syphilis received the penicillin treatment and that ordinarily with a cure as a result. But in the fifties and sixties and seventies, occasionally someone who had gotten infected in the twenties or thirties before penicillin and not received the treatment would

develop that.

And here again so many years have gone by and I have had so many experiences because in 1953 when from the Epidemic Intelligence Service, I was assigned to the Ohio Department of Health. The Ohio Department of Health was doing an intensive campaign against syphilis, and they recruited me one time to help them down in Gallipolis on the Ohio River.

I spent my time doing lumbar punctures to get samples of cerebral spinal fluid from people that had a positive Wassermann Test. They screened with Wassermann Test, blood test, and those are positive and then we did follow-up cerebral spinal fluid examinations and those received extensive penicillin treatment and I forgot about that until I did this.

But the thing is that the Center for Disease Control in recent years—just a year or three years ago—stated that the central nervous system syphilis can occur anytime after the initial infection. And I went back to read Dr. Osler's book from 1892, *The Principles and Practice of Medicine*, which is the most famous, and he says that it may occur within several months.

In other words there is not any compelling reason why neurosyphilis can not occur quite rapidly just as cardiovascular, it can hold for six years and stop in progressive things. It is the same thing with AIDS. AIDS has an average incubation period of ten years but some people have very rapid progress even through the central nervous system inversion with the HIV virus.

GENERAL BAUGH: Is this a good time to take a break, Mr. Tate?

MR. CORONER: Yes.

GENERAL BAUGH: Thank you. Dr. Ravenholt.

THE WITNESS: Just at the end, after the break, I would just like to read something in conclusion.

GENERAL BAUGH: I think he will want to take you before the break.

THE WITNESS: Let me just finish that then. In my conclusion I wrote as follows: The fabric of evidence that syphilis acquired during the explorative trip to the Pacific Coast was the underlying cause of Lewis' death includes these threads: (1) Lewis was in excellent health when he set forth up the Missouri River; (2) several Indian Tribes suffering from syphilis were encountered; (3) sexual intercourse with women of these tribes by Corps members was frequently urged by the Indians and was commonplace; (4) several corps members, probably at least eight, did develop syphilis; (5) when encountering the Shoshoni Tribe at the Continental Divide, Lewis had both a propitious opportunity and a compelling need for sexual intercourse; (6) a few weeks later he developed an illness which became severe and disabling for several months, but the nature of which was not described; (7) for some months in 1807 following his return from the expedition he was incapacitated by illness, the nature of which was not divulged; (8) during 1808-1809 he developed a progressive illness afflicting his central nervous system and diminishing his judgment faculties; (9) his terminal months were characterized by progressive, episodic, febrile illness, with severe mental and behavioral disorders highly characteristic of paresis; (11) Lewis himself recognized he was suffering from progressive disease likely to be fatal; (11) Thomas Jefferson and William Clark readily understood his death.

Just to talk a little about the last days as he came in, should I do that before we —

GENERAL BAUGH: I think if they don't have anymore questions, your time is about up.

THE WITNESS: Well, I think I must say as he came to Fort Pickering, leaving St. Louis on the 4th of September he proceeded by boat down the river. And on the 11th perhaps at Cape Girardeau or New Madrid he made out his Will. When he arrived at Fort Pickering, Chickasaw Bluffs or Memphis he was in very bad shape and crews said that he had attempted to commit suicide twice and they had restrained him.

He was in very bad mental shape for five days and then he recovered rather fully according to Captain Russell. And then he stayed there until the 29th of September and Captain Neely came there and Captain Neely took over from—Major Neely took over from Captain Russell and they proceeded southeast toward the Natchez Trace actually toward the Chickasaw Agency which was located between Tupelo and Houston.

They went there and they rested several days and then they proceeded North on the Natchez Trace to the Tennessee River. And though I have but I won't take the time, I have the slide, the key thing to this was the Colbert's Ferry along the Natchez Trace which had come into operation. And George Colbert was apparently a half breed and his brother Levi had an inn near the Colbert Ferry and they ferried over there on the 8th or 9th. They proceeded North to Dogwood Mudhole which is just eighteen miles south of the monument here and there they stopped there the night and in the morning two horses were loose.

Now some might say that this was just accidental but I'm an old farm boy and I do a lot with horses. And putting myself in Lewis' skin, Lewis as he came down the river realized they were keeping watch on him and at Fort Pickering they kept intensive watch. And Major Neely was keeping watch on him and how do I get Major Neely off my back, just slip a couple of the horses, particularly Major Neely's. And I suspect that Lewis may very well have done that to separate himself from Major Neely.

He then went on the 18 miles to Grinder's Stand and when he got there, he had asked—his servant came up and he asked him for powder. Apparently Major Neely had made sure his pistols were not loaded during that time, traveling, because indeed he was wary of him. But there was powder in the canister on Pernia's horse apparently. And he got that and during that evening he loaded his pistols and then he went on. He was acting very peculiar, walking up and down and talking to himself like a lawyer talking to —

GENERAL BAUGH: We all know how peculiar that is.

THE WITNESS: And then there were two cabins joined by a dogtrot there at Grinder's Stand. And Ms. Grinder put him up in one cabin and she bedded down with her two children in the other cabin which was the kitchen. She was nervous because of this peculiar acting person. And then about 3:00 a.m. she was halfway awake and she heard a gun report and a thud of something falling and then a little bit later another report. And then a little later, moans and groans and Lewis crawled up asking for help but she was terrified.

She was too terrified to go out and help him and he existed until morning. At dawn she sent her two children to the barn to get the two servants, Pernia and the other servant, and they came up and Lewis was still awake and still alive. And he commented that he had done the business and to get help, that he asked his servant for water. And he also asked him to shoot him and he died shortly after.

Now I say this in some detail because anybody who says this was murder has to say well Ms. Grinder was a liar and they also have to say that Pernier, Lewis' trusted servant who no doubt told—Major Neely came several hours later, told him about it as well as Ms. Grinder and went on with Major Neely to Nashville. They didn't know what was going on because Major Neely gave Pernia fifteen dollars and various things to take on to Thomas Jefferson.

And the servant who was the Mulatto, Lewis trusted free servant, went on then to Thomas Jefferson and no doubt gave Thomas Jefferson a detailed account of what he knew from that night including what Ms. Grinder had related. And following that Thomas Jefferson, William Clark, Lewis' mother, Lucy Marks, all of them were fully accepting that this was suicide. There was never any indication that they faltered in the knowledge this was suicide.

In conclusion I would say that I'm not a Virginian but I side fully with the Virginians in this matter, Thomas Jefferson, William Clark, Lucy Marks, Lewis brother Ruben, who was a physician, and also with Ms. Grinder and Captain Neely and Alexander Wilson that this was a case of suicide.

And to say otherwise I think brings unnecessary dishonor upon Ms. Grinder. The chance of her being able to concoct the story such as she told out of the full cloth, I think it is absurd, you know, in the middle of the night in a little cabin, how are you going to concoct a story like that and have it verified by Pernia and everything else.

I conclude wholeheartedly that it was a sad case of suicide. But understandably the thing was until you put syphilis in the equation it is not quite understandable because Lewis was an extraordinarily able, well directed person, why did he commit suicide.

EXAMINATION

BY GENERAL BAUGH:

Q. Dr. Ravenholt, do you have any statistics on the number of people that suffer from tertiary syphilis, who end their lives by suicide?

A. Not really, of course it is a long time ago. And since penicillin there is not very many.

Q. Now I understand it would not be many?

A. But it was common during the 19th century.

Q. Do you have any statistics on how many people say with immune deficiency, AIDS, end their lives by suicide?

A. No, I don't think it is as common in AIDS. The cerebral component of HIV infection is not as prominent in AIDS as it was in Syphilis.

Q. You think that —

A. Let me say this —

Q. You think that judgment, that reduction in their judgment ability with syphilis added to the increased likelihood that you would have suicide?

A. Yes, and let me say this. I learned additionally as I have researched this, it has to do with, you know, insanity in the United States. In the 19th century, in the first half of the 20th Century every principal population in the United States, be it county or city, had an insane asylum where they put people who were insane. Then in the 1950's mysteriously the population in the institutions for the insane went rapidly down in the U. S. And this is fully understandable because a large portion of those in the institution for the insane were syphilitics. And they were—some of them went through a more protracted course and somebody had to take care of them.

In fact I would say this, our legal definition of insanity and how someone might be absolved from crime because they were insane was really based on syphilis. Because when somebody got syphilis, spirochetes destroying the brain, they didn't just go slightly insane, they went fully insane. They went crazy; they really could not take care of their selves. Now the lawyers I would submit —

Q. If we don't conclude now I think that they're going to think we are insane so —

A. No, if —

Q. If you could go ahead and conclude now, we need to go to a break?

A. In recent decades, you know, in every—in many, many trials somebody imparts a definition of insanity which is far and far removed from what actually was at play when this was put into law.

GENERAL BAUGH: Any other questions? Thank you, Dr. Ravenholt.

WITNESS EXCUSED
(WHEREUPON, A RECESS WAS TAKEN.)

WILLIAM M. BASS, III

GENERAL PHILLIPS: Mr. Coroner and Members of the Jury, I will ask Dr. Bass to step up to the podium. Again, in the interest of time I have the privilege to present to you Dr. William M. Bass, III. His curriculum vitae will be presented to you and it goes on for some 21 pages. He is a graduate of the University of Virginia, the University of Kentucky and University of Pennsylvania, holding, B.A., M.S. and Ph.D. degrees.

He is board certified in forensic anthropology. And he has as you might imagine extensive teaching experience. I might say that I realize that most of you are familiar with Dr. Bass given the fact that he has done forensic work in Tennessee for many years, including work in Lewis county and Hickman county and counties in this area, including recent cases.

But in his teaching experience he has taught at the University of Pennsylvania, the University of Nebraska, the University of Kansas and of course culminating in his Professorship at the University of Tennessee where he was head of the Department of Anthropology from June of 1971 until his semi-retirement in May of 1992. We have no intention of allowing Dr. Bass to retire completely.

He is now of course Professor Emeritus and Director of the Forensic Anthropology Center at the University of Tennessee. He has extensive research experience having done research for the Smithsonian Institution, the University of Nebraska, the National Science Foundation, and the National Geographic Society among others.

He has received extensive grants and fellowships from among others, the University of Pennsylvania, the University of Nebraska, University of Kansas, National Park Service, National Science Foundation and again the National Geographic Society.

Members of the Jury and Mr. Coroner, Dr. Bass has been honored extensively. He received the Outstanding Teacher

Award from the University of Kansas during his tenure there. At the University of Tennessee he was the Alumni Distinguished Professor in 1978. He was the Macebearer at the University of Tennessee in 1985-86 which is the highest honor that the University of Tennessee confers on any faculty member.

He has received the American Academy of Forensic Science Physical Anthropology Award; he was National Professor of the Year named by the Council for the Advancement and Support of Education in 1985. As you will recall he was honored at a Joint Session of the Senate and House of Representatives of Tennessee in 1986 for his outstanding contribution to Higher Education and Forensic Science. He received the Distinguished Lecture Award of the National College of District Attorneys; he has been a distinguished Visiting Professor at the University of Iowa and Jacksonville State University.

You will recall that he received the Alexander prize from the University of Tennessee in 1993. And he received the highest award given by the American Academy of Forensic Science in 1994, which is the Distinguished Fellow Award. I might say that is the same award that Professor Starrs has received, although Professor Bass received his first.

He has had a book dedicated to him dealing with skeletal biology. He has had an issue of the *Journal of Forensic Sciences* dedicated to him. He has been a consultant to the Medical Examiners of the State since 1971. A consultant to both the Law Enforcement Academy of Tennessee and the TBI since 1973. He has been a consultant to both the United States Air Force and United States Army. He is a veteran having entered service in 1951 and being discharged in 1953. He is presently on the Editorial Board of the *American Journal for Forensic Anthropology*, the *Journal of Forensic Science*, and the *Forensic Science Review*. He is on the Ethics Committee of the American Academy of Forensic Sciences.

Members of the Jury, he is widely credited by forensic scientists with being the Father of Forensic Anthropology in the United States. Many of, or most of the outstanding forensic anthropologists of the country have been trained by Dr. Bass. His publications will be submitted to you, there are a hundred and ninety-four entries in his list of published articles dealing with forensic anthropology. I submit to you to take an oath and render expert testimony in this case, Dr. William Bass.

WILLIAM M. BASS, III

Having been first duly sworn was examined and testified as follows:

DIRECT EXAMINATION

BY GENERAL PHILLIPS:

Q. Dr. Bass, it is true is it not that your heart is a big orange?

A. Yes, since 1971 that's correct.

Q. Now Dr. Bass in your work as a forensic anthropologist have you had the occasion to examine skeletal remains which have been buried for long periods of time before now?

A. Yes, sir. I have had extensive experience in the excavation and analysis of prehistoric skeletal remains.

Q. You have heard the recommendation of the geologist to you that the site of the Meriwether Lewis Monument and the assumed burial site is favorable in general from the standpoint of a geologist for there being remains that you could examine; you are aware of his opinion?

A. Yes, I participated in the ground penetrating radar research that was done there in 1992 with the geologist, Dr. Stephens.

Q. Do you agree from the standpoint of your perspective as an anthropologist and archaeologist, it is a favorable site?

A. Yes, it is a favorable site. Not only—well, it is a favorable site because of the building of the monument. And in the 1930's, the increase of dirt that was put around the monument. As far as protecting of the skeletal remains, if you're looking at it logically, you would expect that the skeleton would be in a fairly good state of preservation.

Q. If the skeleton was to become available for a forensic anthropology examination, could that be conducted near the site with a field laboratory; could that be done?

A. It could. It would be better if it were done in a standard laboratory like the one we have in Knoxville. However it can be done in the field, I have done this many times.

Q. Would the lab of the University of Tennessee be available for examination if that should become appropriate?

A. Yes, it would.

Q. But should the Park Service stipulate that the examination be done closer to the site, it could be done in a field laboratory?

A. Yes, it can be done in a field laboratory. I think what you are asking, not only the analysis of the skeletal remains but you certainly want to x-ray all the material as Dr. Ravenholt was talking about. If there were mercury taken by Lewis, there should be evidence of this either in the bone or as the body decays, as soft tissue decays, there should be evidence of this in the dirt underneath the body. So you would want to take careful samples if you did it in the field, this certainly can be done.

Q. It could be done by forensic scientist in the field if that should be needed?

A. If that is a stipulation, that is really no problem.

Q. Now Dr. Bass you understand that the primary issue and controversy here is the manner of death of Meriwether Lewis?

A. Yes.

Q. I take it you would be concerned as an anthropologist with the identity of the remains as well; would you not?

A. Well, we have a situation in which we assume that Meriwether Lewis is buried under the monument or near the monument, but there are also other burials there also. I think, you know, in science you want to be accurate. You want to be exact, and I think the first thing that you would want to do if you found a skeleton under or near the monument, you would want to make sure it was indeed Meriwether Lewis. You would not want to do all this analysis and then somebody down the road say hey, they dug up the wrong individual.

Q. Could you determine the age of the person —

A. Yes.

Q. — represented by the skeleton?

A. Yes. What you would do in a situation like this, you have a skeleton and the police ask me to do this all the time, age, sex and race, what is the stature, what you determine as the individual that would allow me to make an identification and also allow you to determine the manner of death. And this can be done.

In Meriwether Lewis' case he was a thirty-five year old individual. You would look at such things as all the maturity indicators would be complete, the teeth, the enclosure of epiphyses, the long bones, in other words, he is now a mature adult. And some of you are not going to like this, you really in biology reach your peak at about age 21 and any of you older than 21, it is all down hill from there on.

And so what you are doing then is you are looking at degenerative changes. You are looking at osteoarthritic changes, build up of bone around joint surfaces. And you should be able to certainly identify him on the basis of age.

On the basis of sex the best area to the look at is the pelvis. Most of you have noted that females have broader hips than do males. If you have not, and you want to notice this, you can do it now in the name of science, but women are called upon to bear the young of the species and they have broader hips. And in Meriwether Lewis' case there should be fairly narrow hips.

The skull should have muscle markings as should the long bones. He had just returned from a long two year trip to the Pacific Coast where he walked or rode most of the way. And he would be in good physical condition. This should be evident in the skeleton.

The ancestry or race of the individual can be told from two different areas. From the skull, particularly the face, he should have a narrow nose, should have a face that comes to a point along the midline. He should have dental characteristics that would indicate he is Caucasian or white. The distal end of the femur, the knee, recently I had a doctoral student who has been able to determine with ninety percent accuracy if we had only the distal end of the knee, we can tell if he was Caucasian or not. All of those things I think you would do as a standard examination.

Q. You could determine a lot of circumstantial evidence then as to whether or not this was Meriwether Lewis?

A. Yes, I feel confident about that. This is something we do all the time.

Q. What can you tell us about the practicality of excavation at this site. You have examined the monument, you are familiar with the methods of anthropologist and archaeologist, can this site be excavated in such a way to exhume and examine the remains and not damage the monument. And return to its—to the condition that it is now?

A. Yes, I think this could be done. I won't say fairly easily but certainly I don't think it raises any major problems. I think what you would do in a situation like this you could come in from the side with a tunnel. Most of the time you see graves that have been excavated, you look at a view looking down on the grave. Actually this is not the best way to excavate the grave.

A better way is particularly if your grave is fragile, if the bones are fragile, beginning to decay away, if you come down on top of the grave, you have the dirt, you are removing the dirt, and that dirt tends to fall back on the bones and you keep sweeping or taking a paint brush and removing the dirt.

One of the better ways of course if you went in from the side, this would put you coming into the burial from the side of the burial and this would give you a place to pull your dirt down and away from the skeleton without damaging the skeletal remains. I think it is something that can be done, has been done and is certainly a feasible project.

Q. You think it is very feasible?

A. Yes, sir.

Q. Now Dr. Bass, you said that you would expect from your examination of the site, you would expect bones of the— probability is that bones would be in good enough condition for examination, is that correct?

A. Well, we hope so. You never know until you look. As a matter of fact you and I have sat here the last day and a half listening to all of this information, and I hope that you feel somewhat like I do, that I felt like clapping after every one of these experts gave their testimony. You have listened to some very, very good information. Something that you really could not get to read, but we were able to put together here to look at this situation.

You would assume given Tennessee, given the amount of water and given the PH of the soil, you would assume that there would be bones remaining there because he was buried for about thirty-nine years before the monument was built on top of him. Building the monument over the grave really is not only a good thing for the general public, but was an excellent means of protecting the skeleton from further decay that you would get from a normal cemetery situation in Tennessee.

Then of course in 1930's the WPA or CCC comes along and adds dirt to the area, this again is protecting the bones. The skeleton is my understanding of reading the literature, looking at the monument, when the monument was built the skeleton was opened and there is no indication that there was any major deterioration to the material. And given the two events that occurred since that time, I think the material if you are looking at it logically which is what you have to do at this stage of the game, you would assume that the skeleton should be there and we hope in good enough condition to answer many of the questions or all of the questions that have been raised at this

Inquest.

Q. Do you think that you and other forensic scientists could answer a lot of these questions if the skeleton is in good condition?

A. I think we could, yes. Having dealt with prehistoric material that covered this range in the early 1880's and so forth, I think you could certainly tell if the skull had been impacted by bullet. You could tell the direction the bullet was going, if it is true that there was a grazing wound and the brain was exposed, this certainly should be there on the skeletal remains. If there was a shot through the chest, ribs don't hold up as well as the bones of the skull because they are not as dense but it should be there. Entrance and exit wounds should be something that would not be too difficult to interpret.

X-ray, you are being shot in this case with a lead ball. As lead goes through bones we get what is called lead wipe. You get this even today with people being shot. You always x-ray the material and you can see the lead wipe going through there. The possibility of a lead ball still being there is excellent. There was no indication in the early literature that these balls go through, they may, the one through here probably did. But, you know, certainly the evidence of the lead wipe would be there.

Q. Does even syphilis show up on the bones?

A. Syphilis will show up on the bones. I'm not sure it will show up in the four to five year period that Dr. Ravenholt is talking about, but it is a possibility. Syphilis appears on bones in two different areas. If your tibia which is the bone between your knee and ankle, what is known as a saber shin, is very common with people in advanced stages of syphilis.

Dr. Ravenholt was talking a little bit ago, maybe of the attitude of the individual would indicate that there may be some inflammation to the brain. Well, this inflammation probably also would attack the bone. So what you would get on the inside of the skull or maybe on the outside, but more likely inside, you would get areas on the bone that would show this inflammation. The attack of bone by the spirochete that causes syphilis, so yes, that should be there.

Q. So there are many things that could be told if the skeleton is in good condition?

A. As a matter of fact I think the ultimate of all of this is, if you don't look at the skeleton, now this is assuming if you look at and decide there is only dust, which I doubt there is only dust, but if you don't look at the skeleton you are not going to answer the questions that have been brought up.

Q. As a forensic anthropologist do you recommend excavation?

A. Absolutely, this is the only way to solve the problem we have is to excavate and look at it.

GENERAL PHILLIPS: Mr. Coroner, do you or members of the Jury have questions?

EXAMINATION

BY MR. CORONER:

Q. You're talking about tunneling in from the side to get to the grave site. In the examination of the cemeteries there at the monument what was the closet grave to what is believed to be Meriwether Lewis' grave site, do you remember on that?

A. General recollection, don't put this in concrete.

Q. I understand?

A. I think there is a grave of a woman who is identified only about six to ten feet away from the edge of monument. There may be another one there. I'm going back four years now and trying to tell you what is there. The ground penetrating radar which goes down and you have the base of the monument is bigger than what you see there because essentially three or four feet of dirt was added on the mound. I think Professor Starrs showed a picture of the mound earlier.

Q. Right?

A. But to the best of our ability ground penetrating radar

shows something underneath the mound. You don't know if it is a vault or whether it is a burial but it tends to be something there.

Q. I guess what I'm asking is, is there a probability that you are going to have to disturb any other graves?

A. I don't think so. We know from the ground penetrating radar where the other burials are and I don't think you have to go through—you would not have to go through any of those to get in under the monument.

MR. CORONER: Other questions?

EXAMINATION

BY MR. TURNBOW:

Q. Can you answer the question of what would have to be done to protect the monument itself from any movement or shifting or damage during the excavation process?

A. Well, you are getting—the question was could I comment on what would have to be done to keep the monument from shifting and so forth. I'm not an engineer, since I will probably be the individual going down there, I hope they do a good job of holding the thing up. I don't want to end up under that thing permanently. I don't think that you need a great big— you don't need a highway through there to get underneath the thing. I think you could get into it, be able to work in a space that you would not materially alter the monument. I would much rather talk to an engineer who knows more about that than I do but I have gotten down in tunnels and things before, we didn't disturb what was above us.

MR. CORONER: Any other questions?
(No response.)
MR. CORONER: Thank you. Dr. Bass.
WITNESS EXCUSED

CONCLUSION

GENERAL BAUGH: Mr. Coroner, I understand we have two people, Mr. Starrs and Dr. Guice that want to address the Jury. We made that known to you and you said that you do want to hear them. And they understand the time constraints that you have, so Mr. Starrs?

MR. STARRS: I did want to point out even though I'm from big city, the outskirts of a big city, and my manners have left me, I should have thanked everyone and I want to take this very short opportunity to do so. I want to thank everyone here assembled and indeed all of those who are touched by being here and by reporting to them what you have heard and seen. Where are my manners when I point this out. The cordiality, the warmth, the courtesy, we have all been shown is something that I will take back to Virginia with me.

But in addition to that I want to point out the fact I want to thank the relatives who have taken the time and interest to be here representing not only themselves but so many other relatives that are overwhelmingly in support of my position that there is need through scientific means to resolve this dispute over the death of Meriwether Lewis.

I don't want to let the opportunity pass to let it be known that my first order of business in any exhumation is to consult with the relatives. If the relatives had in any way, shape or form had disagreed with my proposal or my point of view or my attitude that we could not get a concurrence with, I would not be here today. I would not be doing this at all. And that is a matter that occurred in the past in the Lizzie Borden attempts and the relatives said no, and I said, no.

These relatives are informatively and almost unanimously in support of this project. In addition I would not be going forward if this were only a project for the purpose of the analysis of remains. By the analysis of remains we are preserving the remains. These remains, yes, I consider to be in sufficient condition for analysis today. But they will not always be in that condition. It is important to recognize that the heritage of Meriwether Lewis is such that we must preserve not only the dignity of the person of Meriwether Lewis but the remains of Meriwether Lewis.

And therefore after the analysis, carefully, and in a dignified way conducted, we would then put him into a vault that would remain intact, impermeable to the weather for centuries to come. You would be preserving him for the erosion that is going on now on a day-to-day basis. This is something therefore that has a two-fold objective, not only for the analysis but or the preservation of what we see.

In addition to that I want to point out everything we would do would be highly dignified. We do not intrude on other remains and everything we do is entirely dignified. We do not allow scurrilous publicity and otherwise. Of course, we would observe anything and everything that the National Park Service would require of us. I'm sure their requirements might not even reach the requirements of our own individual scientific requirements. I thank you very much.

GENERAL BAUGH: Dr. Guice, would you like to come forward?

DR. GUICE: Thank you, can you hear me? My brief remarks will be something anticlimactic, after that wonderful statement by Professor Starrs. Indeed after hearing Dr. Bass' calm and marvelous testimony I started not to stand up again. However, I realize today that we have press available who were not here yesterday. And as I listen to Dr. Ravenholt's wonderful presentation because he is a man who is very powerful in his conviction and a good speaker, I felt compelled to read to you a just a few words and I won't take but a minute or two of your time.

These words were written in the summer of 1994, they're from an article of mine published last summer. And it is the portion of my article that deals with his article and as you recall, right before he sat down, he took a piece of paper out and he read to you a summation of the article which I also have in my article. And I want to read to you the last five or six assertions that he makes and I want to read to you about two sentences from my article and then I'm going to sit down.

I don't want to wear the Jury out. I have taught some ten thousand students in my life and I have never had students listen to me as attentively as these people are doing today, and it has been a thrill. I am reading my summation of his article.

For some months after 1807 after his return, he was incapacitated, incapacitated by illness. In 1809, 1808-1809 he developed a progressive affliction of the central nervous system; (9) during his last moments of 1809 he suffered during his last months, months of 1809. He suffered from a progressive, these are his words, a progressive, episodic, febrile illness with severe mental behavior disorder highly characteristic of paresis; (10) he recognized he was suffering from a fatal illness; (11) Thomas Jefferson and William Clark understood when he killed himself. I'm still quoting. Ravenholt concludes his article with a summation of my reviews of suicide against people that died from syphilis.

Many of Ravenholt's assertions are highly speculative, I'm speaking now, highly speculative, and I say this for the benefit of the relatives here. I don't think we have any conclusive evidence of the type of behavior that Dr. Ravenholt asserts in his article. Many of Ravenholt's assertions are highly speculative and not sustained by medical evidence. Many causes other than syphilis could account for the symptoms cataloged by Ravenholt from the Journal of Lewis and Clark. And even if one concedes that Lewis was infected with syphilis, it is highly unlikely although it is indeed possible, highly unlikely that the disease would have advanced as quickly as Ravenholt contends. I want to thank you for being such wonderful listeners. I want to thank the people for their hospitality and thank you again for this brief moment to respond.

GENERAL BAUGH: Thank you, Dr. Guice. Mr. Coroner, I believe that concludes our proceedings as far as the evidence is concerned.

MR. CORONER: This Jury has expressed to me they're very appreciative of the attendance of the relatives of Meriwether Lewis and at this time would like to give any of them that might like to make a statement to this Jury an opportunity to do so. If there are any of the relatives of Meriwether Lewis that has a statement they'd like to make to the Jury at this time, we would ask you to make yourself known so we might be able to hear that. Dr. Anderson.

GENERAL BAUGH: Dr. Anderson, raise your right hand. (Witness Sworn.)

DR. ANDERSON: I'd just like to first thank the Jury and the attorneys and everyone who has come to this inquest. And the State also, I have never seen any event go off so well and according to plan. And I think that shows an awful lot of expert planning on the part of Professor Starrs and many others.
I have heard about Uncle Meriwether ever since I was four or five years old. But I think I have learned at least as much as I already knew from this Inquest. I'm delighted that so many people here are interested in the cause of death. And I as a physician have been twice as interested as any of the rest of you are. I love facts, I love truth. I don't like speculation. I don't like conjecture and I can't see any other way to do it to get the facts than to examine the bones.

I was trained in pathology too. I have done many, I know about what you can find. And I'm all for it and I again want to thank you for giving me the chance to be here and to speak to you.

MR. CORONER: Is there anyone else from the family?
(No response.)

MR. CORONER: General Baugh and General Phillips, on behalf of this Jury I would also like to add to the statements that were made by Dr. Starrs, I think that this has been a very informative event. I have to be totally honest in telling you in the beginning I was not at all sure what I was in for the previous two days. I have been intrigued by those that have come to testify. On behalf of this Jury I would like to thank the District Attorney's Office for your help in carrying out these proceedings. You have been very helpful.

And I would like to make a comment to the Press. It has been—I have had some previous dealings with the Press and I guess what I want to say today is thank you for your courtesy. The Press has been very courteous in every move they have made and I really appreciate that. We have had numerous telephone calls, even last night the press was calling and every single reporter that I myself or anybody on this Jury has talked to has been very courteous and we thank you for that. Usually you will find a bad apple somewhere and I know he is out there, we just have not found him yet. Thank you very much for your courtesy.

Also we need to say thank you to the National Guard Armory for allowing us to use this facility in that our local courthouse was occupied the last couple of days and we were not able to use that facility. They have made us very comfortable, they have lent their help and we thank you for doing that. And also our local police and Sheriff's Department that has been here with us guarding us and protecting us from all you bad people, and we thank them very much for doing that. They didn't have to do that and I do remind you that everybody that is involved here, there is no one here being paid, so we thank them very much for doing that.

And also I myself personally I would like to say thank you for the Jury, for giving their time and for the hours that are ahead of us in deliberation. I know there has been a lot of careful consideration already given and there is going to be in the deliberation process.

General Baugh, at this time the Jury will go to the Jury room and we will take some thirty minutes and then report back to you as to what our next step is going to be.

GENERAL BAUGH: Very well, Mr. Coroner.
(Jury Deliberations began at 11:42.)
(WHEREUPON, A RECESS WAS TAKEN.)

GENERAL BAUGH: The Jury has informed me they are going to recess an hour and come back in an hour and go into further deliberations.
(WHEREUPON, A RECESS WAS TAKEN.)

GENERAL BAUGH: We have a verdict.

THE VERDICT

(Whereupon the jury rendered its verdict in open Court at 1:36 p.m., and the following proceedings were held.)

MR. CORONER: After deliberation this Jury has submitted the following report to myself as Coroner of Lewis County. I would first of all like to read to you the report of the Jury and act accordingly: The report reads: To the Coroner of Lewis County this 4th day of June 1996; This decision was rendered by Jury convened into the matter of the death of Meriwether Lewis.

Whereas the following decisions were made by unanimous agreement.

Number One: There is very little tangible evidence for this Jury to base a credible ruling as to the matter of murder or suicide.

Number 2: Because of the importance of the person in question, to the history of Lewis County, we feel exhumation is necessary for closure in this matter.

Number 3: We further request that it be taken into consideration that exhumation be carried out with an examination being done on-site. And that the remains of Meriwether Lewis not leave the site of Meriwether Lewis Park.

Number 4: That the remains be returned in a timely manner to the same grave site for which they were exhumed.

This is the Jury's Verdict. As far as their deliberation, as Coroner, I have received this verdict and I have accepted it and so order it to be.

(WHEREUPON THE PROCEEDINGS WERE ADJOURNED.)

CERTIFICATE

I, DONNA BUFORD, Court Reporter and Notary Public at Large, do hereby certify that the foregoing proceedings were transcribed by me at the time and place set out in the caption hereto and I certify that the foregoing is a true record of the testimony given by the witness at that time.

I do further certify that I am neither of kin, counsel, nor interest to any party hereto.

Date _____

_____

Donna F. Buford, Court Reporter, and Notary Public at Large, State of s

My Commission Expires: July 14, 1997

Part Two

The Evidence:
Documents & Photos

Introduction

The 20 documents in this section form the basic record of what is known about the last days of Meriwether Lewis's life and the events surrounding his death—yet most are second-hand or even third-hand accounts. They are a mixture of truth, lies, rumors and outright forgery. Two hundred years have passed, and this is all the evidence that has been found, except for a few scattered accounts by others which are variations of Mrs. Grinder's stories.

Did Meriwether Lewis commit suicide or was he assassinated, and are some of the documents part of a cover up? The November 26, 1811 Russell Statement (document 15, p. 254) often cited as evidence of suicide was neither written nor signed by either Gilbert C. Russell or Jonathan Williams whose signatures appear on it.

Documents examiner Jerry Richards has certifed that the "Russell Statement" is written in the same handwriting as that found in a 12 page court brief in the Jonathan Williams Archives at the Lilly Library at the University of Indiana (See Appendix A). The so called "Russell Statement" and this court brief written about one month earlier were included among papers relating to General Wilkinson's court martial held at Frederick -Town, Maryland. It is most likely that the two documents were written by Wilkinson's clerk.

There was no federal investigation of Lewis's death, and no attempt was made to arrange for a Christian reburial in the family graveyard in Charlottesville, Virginia. His body remained in a lonesome, solitary grave near the place where he died. Meriwether Lewis was Governor of Louisiana Territory, one of the highest ranking officials in the federal government, and a national hero—why did this happen?

There was a local coroner's inquest in 1809, but the records have been lost. Tradition has it that the jurors were afraid to name Robert Grinder as his murderer, fearing the consequences. Grinder was the owner of the roadside inn and tavern on the Natchez Trace where Lewis met his death on October 11, 1809. Supposedly he was away from home that night.

Mrs. Grinder's Three Different Versions

The accounts of Lewis's death rely on three different versions told by Priscilla Grinder to other people. Grinder's wife never claimed to have seen the shooting—only to have heard either two, or three, gun shots.

As for what she claims to have seen afterwards, John Guice, who testified at the 1996 Coroner's Inquest, has since published an essay in *By His Own Hand? The Mysterious Death of Meriwether Lewis*, which adds new evidence to the scene of the shooting. On the night of October 10-11, 1809 it was one day past a new moon, and in the densely forested Natchez Trace, Mrs. Grinder could not have seen anything; it was pitch black. Her story of seeing Lewis crawling or staggering around the yard was not possible. Mrs. Grinder was undoubtedly lying, but did parts of her stories contain some truth?

Grinder's Inn consisted of two one room cabins, joined together by a common roof with a central passageway or "dog trot" in between the cabins. (See page 272 for a photo of the reconstructed building, which is not really typical of the dog trot construction.) There was a kitchen out-building, "only a few paces from the house," and a horse barn 200 yards away. The family lived in one cabin, and travelers stayed in the other one. In two accounts, Mrs. Grinder had decided to sleep in the kitchen building with her children rather than in the cabin. The two servants accompanying Lewis slept in the horse barn. In all three accounts the gun shots happened in the middle of the night, in the early hours of October 11th.

One account mentions the presence of children. Alexander Wilson wrote that Mrs. Grinder told him she sent two of her children at daybreak to wake the servants in the barn. The most unlikely aspect of all these stories is the inability of the servants to hear gun shots at a distance of 200 yards. In the Neelly account, after hearing gun shots about 3 A. M. she goes herself to wake the servants. In the last account she is surprised the servants have not slept in the cabin with Lewis, but have instead slept in the horse stables, and they appear at her door at daybreak.

The first account (#4, p. 234) is the letter written by Indian Agent James Neelly, who was acting as Lewis's escort on the Natchez Trace en route to Nashville, Tennessee. Major Neelly—like Robert Grinder—was supposedly not present on the night of Lewis's death. He showed up after daylight and arranged for Lewis to be buried near the place where he died. This site is the location of the Meriwether Lewis Gravesite & National Monument on the Natchez Trace Parkway near Hohenwald, Tennessee.

The second account (#14, p. 251) was written by a friend of Lewis's, the ornithologist Alexander Wilson who was traveling through the South sketching birds. He had planned to visit Lewis in St. Louis, but instead had the unhappy duty of visiting his friend's gravesite six months after his death, where he interviewed Mrs. Grinder and paid for a fence to be erected.

The third account (#18, p. 260) was published in a newspaper in 1845 and represents the story as told by a third person, a "teacher of the Cherokee Nation," who interviewed Mrs. Grinder in 1838. Again, there was a new version of her story— this time told after her husband's death.

This version included a visit by "two or three other men." When they arrived at dusk, Meriwether Lewis immediately "drew a brace of pistols, stepped towards them and challenged them to fight a duel." The men rode off. She said that Lewis's body was found in old clothes after his death, and that his servant Pernier was wearing the same clothes Lewis wore when he arrived at the Inn and was carrying his gold watch.

It seems likely that Pernier was going to act as a decoy when he rode off the next morning. John Pernier was a free mulatto, half French, half African-American. He had been a servant in the White House in 1804-05, and had come with Lewis to St. Louis to serve as his personal valet. He has been accused of participating in the assassination. Lewis's mother, Lucy Marks, thought so. Pernier brought the news of Lewis's death to Lewis's mother, Thomas Jefferson and President James Madison. Six months later he was dead. (#13, p. 249).

Lewis's gold watch and his brace of pistols—along apparently with his money—came into the possession of James Neelly, who refused to give them up. Lewis's step brother John Marks visited Neelly's home in 1811, but was unsuccessful in retrieving them, though he retrieved his rifle and his horse.

The Reaction of Thomas Jefferson

Thomas Jefferson wrote almost nothing on the subject until he was asked by the publisher of the *Lewis and Clark Journals* in 1813 to contribute a biographical essay on Meriwether Lewis (#16, p. 257). Even though the former president accepted his friend's death as a suicide, his words are contradictory and his famous words of praise for Lewis have much more meaning:

> "Of courage undaunted, possessing a firmness and perseverance of purpose which nothing but impossibilities could divert from its direction."

He must have terribly regretted the loss of his friend and protege, and yet it was not in the national interest to say that his death was an assassination. Particularly if the assassination had any connection with General James Wilkinson, the commanding general of the United States Army—who to the mystification of many observers—was supported by Jefferson throughout much of his career. The circumstances surrounding Lewis's death are dealt with in Part Three of this book, where the complicated politics of this time period are discussed.

The Reaction of William Clark

Three letters of William Clark are included here. They were written to his brother Jonathan in the weeks immediately following Lewis's death. The last letter (#9, p. 242) reveals the machinations of General James Wilkinson because Clark is responding to information contained in letters he believes were written by Captain Gilbert Russell, the commander of Fort Pickering where Lewis spent some of his last days. Their reported content—suicide attempts, mental derangement—is similar to the content of document #15 (p. 254), now proven to be a forgery which was most likely composed by Wilkinson under Russell's name two years later. It may be assumed that the letters Clark received were also forgeries created by the General for the purpose of misleading Lewis's best friend. These letters have never been found, so the handwriting cannot be analyzed.

The letters cleverly contained news of a "second will" written at Fort Pickering—which most likely was said to have given the Lewis and Clark expedition journals and papers to Clark. Though Clark searched for it, he never found this second will. He took over the project anyway. The letters he received have not been found, so an examination of the handwriting is not possible. But since Russell did not mention attempted suicides, mental derangement or the writing of a second will, in either of his two letters to Thomas Jefferson written in January, 1810 it indicates that other forgeries were written in his name.

General Wilkinson's Forged Document

It is highly likely that General James Wilkinson created the forged Gilbert Russell statement concerning the death of Meriwether Lewis dated November 26, 1811 (#15, p. 254). The handwriting has been identified by documents examiner Jerry Richards as matching the handwriting of another document concerning the General's court martial taking place at that time. It was most likely written by his clerk. Historians agree that the General used forged documents to destroy the career of General George Rogers Clark, the older brother of William Clark, and other forgeries by the General have also been suspected.

The "Russell Statement" aroused the suspicions of several historians—most notably Vardis Fisher, the author of *Suicide or Murder? The Strange Death of Meriwether Lewis*. It is the second most important document supporting the suicide story—the first being Neelly's letter to Jefferson. The "Russell Statement" claims that Lewis made "two attempts to kill himself" while traveling to the fort and was in a state of mental derangement for 6 days while at the fort. The "Russell Statement" and the other document in the same handwriting are found in the papers of Colonel Jonathan Williams, an old friend of Wilkinson's, who was the first Superintendent of the West Point Academy. Colonel Williams served as an associate judge in the General's court martial, which took place at Frederick-Town, Maryland from September through December, 1811.

The General was standing trial on two matters not related to Lewis's death: (1) that he was receiving pay as an double agent from the Spanish government; and (2) that his neglect of duty had resulted in the death and desertion of nearly half the soldiers under his command at Terre aux Boeufs in 1809. (Gayarre in his *History of Louisiana* states that out of 1953 regular soldiers, 795 died and 166 deserted. Terre aux Boeufs is the area of St. Bernard's Parish east of New Orleans where Hurricane Katrina did so much damage in 2005.) Though the charges were actually true, Wilkinson was acquitted and returned to active duty. The General is known as:

> "The General who never won a battle, and who
> never lost a court martial."

Captain Russell did testify at Wilkinson's court martial on November 26th. His brief testimony concerned the character of Thomas Power, a known Spanish agent and associate of Wilkinson's. He stated that he did not know him, but he knew of his reputation. That was it. Did Gilbert Russell know anything about the forged statement written in his name? It doesn't seem likely. His own letters to Thomas Jefferson (#s 10-12, pp. 243-249) are honest and sincere, and are essential in providing any understanding of the real circumstances surrounding Lewis's death. His presence at the trial most likely inspired the General to create a new piece of evidence in his name (assuming the letters Clark received from Russell were earlier forgeries of his).

Some of the most loathsome words imaginable are found in this 1811 statement, words attributed to Captain Russell, who is supposedly reporting the last words of Meriwether Lewis:

> ". . .he lay down and died with the declaration to the Boy that he had killed himself to deprive his enemies of the pleasure and honor of doing it."

The implications are two fold—that the General felt the need to create some supporting evidence of prior suicidal intentions, indicating he was worried he might be charged with Lewis's death and that he took "pleasure and honor" in killing Meriwether Lewis!

The court martial he was undergoing had absolutely nothing to do with Meriwether Lewis's death. Which is exactly the reason I was curious about seeing a copy of the "Russell Statement" and examining the other Wilkinson materials in the Jonathan Williams Archives. Why was it found here? Why had it never surfaced before Donald Jackson published it in the *Letters of the Lewis and Clark Expedition*? The answer most likely is that Wilkinson had Williams keep it as an "insurance policy" in case he was ever charged with Lewis's murder.

The letters written by Captain Russell to Thomas Jefferson in January, 1810 have never been published in their entirety

(#s10-12). They are first hand accounts, and they are known to be written by the Captain. They provide a very different picture of Lewis's last days and should be taken as a starting point in any reexamination of the historical record.

What would an exhumation settle?

Professor Starrs has not taken a position on the cause of Meriwether Lewis's death. I, on the other hand, believe it was an assassination. An exhumation of his remains could possibly settle the matter of whether it was suicide or murder, depending on what is found. In two previous examinations of his gravesite, it has been strongly suggested by those involved that they found evidence of assassination.

In 1848, when a Monument Committee appointed by the Tennessee State Legislature opened his grave, they stated that though it was commonly believed that Lewis committed suicide, "it seems to be more probable that he died at the hands of an assassin." (#19, p. 262)

In 1924, when the Meriwether Lewis Memorial Association successfully petitioned President Calvin Coolidge to make the gravesite a National Monument, they stated "Investigations have satisfied the public that he was murdered presumably for the purposes of robbery." (#20, p. 265)

In 1928, the Monument was refurbished and it was said that the Superintendent remarked "Isn't it interesting that a man who killed himself shot himself in the back of the head?" This information is reported as local lore in *Lewis County, Tennessee*, p. 13 (Turner Pub., Paducah, KY, 1995).

In each of these situations, the primary purpose was not to establish the truth concerning Meriwether Lewis's death, but rather to honor him or to care for his gravesite. What is needed is an official exhumation of his remains to settle the matter, if it is possible to do so.

(1) Lewis to President James Madison

This is the letter that has been said to indicate suicidal tendencies because of the poor quality of the handwriting. See pages 126-140 for an analysis by Gerald B. Richards. The cost of printing the *Territorial Laws* was one of the items that the government was refusing to pay. Fort Pickering was located on Chickasaw Bluffs, the site of present day Memphis, Tennessee.

Chickasaw Bluffs, September 16, 1809

Dear Sir,

I arrived here (yesterday—inserted) about (2 Ock—crossed out) P.M. (yesterday—inserted) very much exhausted from the heat of the climate, but having (taken—inserted) medicine feel much better this morning. My apprehension from the heat of the lower country and my fear of the original papers of the voyage falling onto the hands of the British has induced me to change my rout and proceed by land through the state of Tennisee to the city of washington. I bring with me duplicates of my vouchers for public expenditures &c. which when fully explained, or rather the general view of the circumstances under which they were made I flatter myself (that—inserted) they (will—inserted) receive both (sanction &—inserted) approbation (and—crossed out) sanction.

Provided my health permits no time shall be lost in reaching Washington. My anxiety to pursue and to fulfill the duties incedent to (the—inserted) internal arrangements incident to the government of Louisiana has prevented my wri (t—inserted) ing you (as—crossed out) (more—inserted) frequently. (Mr. Bates is left in charge.—crossed out) Inclosed I herewith transmit you a copy of the laws of the territory of Louisiana. I have the honour to be with the most sincere esteem your Obt. (and very humble—crossed out) Obt. and very humble servt.

Meriwether Lewis

James Madison Esq.
President U States

(2) Lewis to Amos Stoddard

Major Amos Stoddard was an old friend. In this letter, Lewis asked him to repay $200 he had loaned him, and send it either to Washington before the end of December; or to St. Louis after that, indicating Lewis's intention to return to St. Louis. However, Captain James House reports in a letter dated September 28th that Major Stoddard was in Nashville, and has heard rumors of Lewis attempting suicide and being mentally deranged.

Fort Pickering, Chickesaw Bluffs,
September 22nd 09

Dear Majr,

I must acknowledge myself remiss in not writing to you in answer to several friendly epistles which I have received from you since my return from the Pacific Ocean. Continued occupation in the immediate discharge of the duties of a public station will I trust in some measure plead my apology.

I am now on my way to the City of Washington and had contemplated taking Fort Adams and Orlianes in my rout, but my indisposition has induced me to change my rout and shall now pass through Tennessee and Virginia. The protest of some bills which I have drawn on public account form the principal inducement for my going forward at this moment. An explaneation is all that is necessary I am sensible to put all matters right.

In the mean time the protest of a draught however just, has drawn upon me at one moment all my private debts which have excessively embarrassed me. I hope you will therefore pardon me for asking you to remit as soon as convenient the sum of $200. which you have informed me you hold for me. I calculated on having the pleasure to see you at Fort Adams as I passed, but am informed by Capt. Russel the commanding officer of this place that you are stationed on the West side of the Mississippi.

You will direct to me at the City of Washington untill the last of December after which I expect I shall be on my return to St. Louis. Your sincere friend & Obt. Servt.

Meriwether Lewis

(3) James House to Frederick Bates

This letter, written before Lewis even left Fort Pickering, is the first evidence of a widespread conspiracy. Captain House says he met a person who said that he prevented Lewis from committing suicide en route to the Fort. It is interesting that House doesn't give his name. The story is contradicted by the letters James Neely and Captain Russell wrote to President Jefferson (#s 4,10-12). (*Courtesy of Missouri History Museum, Frederick Bates Collection*)

Nashville, Sept. 28, 1809

Dr Sir

I arrived here two days ago on my way to Maryland—yesterday Maj^r Stoddart of the army arrived here from Fort Adams, and informs me that in his passage through the indian nation, in the vincinity of Chickasaw Bluffs he saw a person, immediately from the Bluffs who informed him, that Governor Lewis had arrived there (some time previous to his leaving it) in a state of mental derangement, that he had made several attempts to put an end to his own existence, which this person had prevented, and that Capt. Russell, the commanding officer at the Bluffs had taken him into his own quarters where he was obliged to keep a strict watch over him to prevent his committing violence on himself and has caused his boat to be unloaded and the key to be secured in his stores.

I am in hopes that this account will prove exaggerated tho' I fear there is too much truth in it—As the post leaves this tomorrow I have thought it would not be improper to communicate these circumstances as I have heard them, to you.

I have the Honor to be, Sir with much esteem & respect Y^r ob^e Serv.

JAS. HOUSE

Fred^k Bates Esq
Secy of the Territory U Louisiana

(4) James Neelly to Thomas Jefferson

This letter is the primary source for the story that Lewis committed suicide. Notice that Neelly makes no mention of two other versions of the story: that Lewis attempted suicide twice while en route to Fort Pickering; and that after shooting himself twice, Lewis began cutting himself with his razor.

James Neelly was the newly appointed Indian Agent to the Chickasaw Nation. His headquarters were located in the Chickasaw Towns at Pontotoc near today's Tupelo, Mississippi. Neelly arrived at Fort Pickering "on or about" September 18th, 3 days after Lewis's arrival. He stayed there for 11 days—for no apparent reason, until leaving with Lewis on September 29th.

Neelly owed his appointment as Indian Agent to General James Wilkinson, who was in charge of developing the Natchez Trace as a military road in 1801-03. Wilkinson was the highest ranking General in the U. S. Army, heaquartered in New Orleans; and Lewis's predecessor in office as the Governor of Louisiana Territory.

Nashville Tennessee, 18th Octr. 1809

Sir,
It is with extreme pain that I have to inform you of the death of His Excellency Meriwether Lewis, Governor of upper Louisiana who died on the morning of the 11th Instant and I am sorry to say by Suicide.

I arrived at the Chickesaw Bluffs on or about the 18th of September, where I found the Governor (who had reached there two days before me from St. Louis) in very bad health. It appears that his first intention was to go around by water to the City of Washington; but his thinking a war with England probable, & that his valuable papers might be in dainger of falling into the hands of the British, he was thereby induced to Change his route, and to come through the Chickasaw nation by land; I furnished him with a horse to pack his trucks &c. on, and a man to attend to them; having recovered his health in some degree at the Chickasaw Bluffs, we set out together and on our arrival at the Chickasaw nation I discovered that he appeared at times deranged in mind. We rested there two days & came on. One days Journey after crossing Tennessee River & where we encamped we lost two of our horses. I remained behind to hunt them & the Governor proceeded on, with a promise to wait for me at the first houses he came to that was inhabited by white people; he reached the house of a Mr. Grinder about sun set, the man of the house being from home, and no person there but a woman who discovering the governor to be deranged gave him up the house & slept herself in one near it. His servant and mine slept in the stable loft some distance from the other houses. The woman reports that about three o'clock she heard two pistols fire off in the Governors Room: the servants being awakined by her, came in too late to save him. He had shot himself in the head with one pistol & a little below the Breast with the other. when his servant came in he says; I have done the business my good servant give me some water. He gave him some water, he survived but a short time. I came up some time after, & had him as decently Buried as I could in that place. if there is any thing wished by his friends to be done to his grave I will attend to their Instructions.

I have got in my possession his two trunks of papers (amongst which is said to be his travels to the pacific ocean) and probably some Vouchers for expenditures of Public Money for a Bill which he said had been protested by the Secy. Of War, and of which act to his death, he repeatedly complained. I have also in my Care his Rifle, Silver watch, Brace of Pistols, dirk & tomahawk: one of the Governors horses was lost in the wilderness which I will endeavour to regain, the other I have sent on by his servant who expressed a desire to go to the governors Mothers & to Montic[e]llo: I have furnished him with fifteen Dollars to Defray his expenses to Charlottsville; Some days previous to the Governors death he requested of me in case any accident happened to him, to send his trunks with the papers therein to the President, but I think it very probable he meant to you. I wish to be informed what arrangements may be considered best in sending on his trunks &c. I have the honor to be with great respect Yr. Ob. Sert.

James Neelly
U.S. agent to the Chickasaw Nation

The Governor left two of his trunks in the care of Gilbert C. Russell, commanding officer, & was to write to him from Nashville what to do with them.

(5) Memorandum of Lewis's Personal Effects

After Lewis's death, Thomas Freeman, a close associate of General Wilkinson, brought Lewis's possessions to Washington. In 1798, Freeman was fired from his assistant surveyor's job by Andrew Ellicott, who surveyed the boundary line between Spanish Florida and U. S. Territory. Ellicott called Freeman "An idle, lying, troublesome, discontented, mischief-making man." (Google books: *Andrew Ellicott: His Life and Letters* by Catherine Van Cortlandt Matthews (1908), p. 160) Subsequently Freeman was employed by Wilkinson. He was the leader of the Freeman-Custis Expedition which explored the Red River in 1806.

Isaac A. Coles was Jefferson's last private secretary, and stayed on in the capacity under President James Madison. Note that among Lewis's papers and journals, there was a bundle of papers on the lead mines to be delivered to President Madison: "P. U. S. One do. papers relative to the Mines." (P. U. S. is President of the United States; "do" means ditto, or in this case "bundle.") Did these papers reach the President? See the next entry, stating they arrived "badly assorted" when Cole took possession of them, and that he had to sort them into bundles again, with no mention of their contents.

[23 November 1809]   (5)

Memorandum of Articles Contained in two Trunks the property of Governor Lewis of Upper Louisiana Left in care of William C. Anderson Near Nashville Tennessee and taken charge by Thomas Freeman to be safe Conveyed to Washington City—Nashville 23rd Novr. 1809.
Taken in presence of Captn. Boote U. States Army—Captn. Brahan—Thomas Freeman & Wm. C. Anderson

*One old Port folio containing
  a few papers of no consequence
*One Tomahawk—
  handsomely moun[te]d

I.A.C.   One ½ pint silver Tumbbler

	*One pair of red slippers
forwarded to Richmond	One Black broadcloth coat
forwarded do.	Two striped summer coats
forwarded do.	Five vests
	*Two Pair Nankeen Panteloons
forwarded do.	One pr. Black silk Breeches
	*Two Cotton shirts—one Flanl. Do.
forwarded do.	One pr. Old flannel Drawers
	*Six pr. of short stockings
	*Two pr. cotton stockings
	*Three pr. of silk stockings
	*One Cambrick Handkerchiff
forwarded	One cotton do. two Ba —old. Do.
	*One small bundle Medecin
Depts.	One small bundle of Letters & Vouchers of consequence
Dept. War	One Plan & View of Fort Madison
	Two Books of Laws of Upper Louisana
W.C.	One Book an Estimate of the western Indians
	*One old Razor case— No Razors
I.A.C.	One Horizontal silver Watch
T. Jefferson	One small Package containing the last will and Testament of Govr. Lewis Deceas'd & one check on the Bank of New Orleans for 99 58/100 dollars
forwarded to Richmond	One Round Portmteau Trunk
W.C.	One Handsome dressed Sea Otter skin
I.A.C.	One Ladies Pocket Book
Th. Jefferson	One Memorandum Book
W.C.	Two small bundles containing silk for dresses —for Mr. Clark
Pret. U.S.	A transcript of Records &c.
W.C.	Nine Memorandum Books
W.C.	Sixteen Note Books bound in red morocco with clasps
Th. Jefferson	One bundle of Misceleans. paprs.
War Dept.	No. 2 Returns of Militia—

	papers not acted on
Th. Jefferson	One bundle papers indorsed —"From the Drawer of my Poligt. [polygraph]
P.U.S.	One do. papers relative to the Mines
War Dept.	One do. Public Vouchers
Th. Jefferson	One do. "Taken from the drawer of my Poligraft
W.C.	Six note books unbound
Th. J.	One bundle of Indorsed Letters &c.
War Dept.	One do. Of McFarlane's acct. for the outfit of Salt Petre expend.
War Dept.	One journal of do.
W.C.	One bundle of Maps &c.
W.C.	One do. "Ideas on the Western expedition
War Dept.	One bundle of Musterrolls
State Dept.	One do. Vouchers for Expendrs. Dept. State
W.C.	One do. Vocabulary
W.C.	One do. Maps & Charts
War Dept.	One do. Vouchers for expenditures in the War Departmt.
Th. Jefferson	One bundle of papers marked A
W.C.	One Sketch of the River St. Francis with a small Letter Book
Th. Jefferson	One do. Containg. Commissn. and Diploma
P.U.S.	One do. Sketches for the President of the U. States

N. Those articles marked in the Memorandum with a Star are left in a square black Trunk (the property of Govr. Lewis) in care of Wm. C. Anderson—the trunk not being of convenient shape & size for Packing.

Thos. Freeman

(6) Isaac A. Coles Receipt of Personal Effects

Washington Jany. 10. 1810

The bundles of Papers referred to in the above memorandum were so badly assorted, that no idea could be given them by any terms of general description. Many of the bundles containing at once, Papers of a public nature—Papers intirely private, some important & some otherwise, with accts. Receipts. &c. They were all carefully looked over, & put up in separate bundles. Every thing public has been given to the President or proper dept. Every thing relating to the expedition to Genl. Clarke, & all that remained has been sent to Mr. Jefferson to be delivered to Mr. Meriwether, to the care of Mr. Geo. Jefferson the following articles, viz.

In a Small Trunk contained in the larger one	In the large Trunk a Pistol case—containing a Pocket Pistol—3 Knives &c. &c.
1. Broadcloth Coat	
2. Summer Do.	8 Tin Canisters containing
5. Waistcoats	a variety of small articles
1. Pair black Silk Breeches	of little value.
4. Handkerchiefs	
3. Old flannel _____ .	A Sword, Tomahawk, Pike Blade & part of the Handle

A very small Trunk

I. A. Coles

[In margin] N. B. The trunk will be sent by the first vessel to Richmond, addressed to Wm. Meriwether to the care of Rob. Gordon mercht. of that place.

I. A. C.

(7-9) William Clark to Jonathan Clark

William Clark and his family traveled from St. Louis to the East Coast a few weeks after Lewis's departure. They visited his brother Jonathan and other family members in Louisville, Kentucky and then went on to Fincastle, Virginia, where Julia and their 10 month old son Meriwether Lewis Clark stayed with her parents while Clark continued onto Washington.

In these three letters to Jonathan, we have almost the only reactions to Lewis's death that William Clark ever committed to paper. In assembling these documents for publication, I realized the letters Clark received from Captain Russell (referred to in his letter of November 26th—#9) were almost certainly other forgeries created by Wilkinson.

Compare their reported contents with the following two letters that we know were written by Captain Russell in January, 1810 to Thomas Jefferson (#s 10-12) and the known forgery (#15). In the authentic letters written by Russell there is no mention of attempted suicide before Lewis arrived at Fort Pickering; no "15 days in a state of derangement," and no second will. The 1811 forgery declares there were two attempted suicides, but backs off from the claim of 15 days in a state of mental derangement.

The "letters from Capt. Russell" Clark received were well crafted, because the mention of a second will made at Chickasaw Bluffs —perhaps said to be assigning the expedition papers to Clark—would seem logical and give credibility to the other statements. Though Clark searched diligently for a second will, it was never found. It almost certainly never existed. The "letters from Capt. Russell" have also never been found.

The letter that Lewis wrote to Clark from New Madrid—that Clark was anxious to obtain from his brother—may have concerned the disposition of the expedition papers. Lewis wrote his will of record at New Madrid, Missouri on September 9, 1809 while en route to Fort Pickering. He was ill from malarial fevers, and rested a few days before continuing to travel. He wrote the will in his memorandum book, a small notebook, leaving everything to his mother, and had it witnessed.

(Reprinted with the permission of the Filson Historical Society of Louisville, Kentucky, from *Dear Brother: Letters of William Clark to Jonathan Clark*, by James J. Holmberg. Yale University Press, 2002).

(7) William Clark to Jonathan Clark

Lexington Octr. 30 1809

Dear Brother

We arrived here this evening all in the Same State of health we were when we parted with you, but not in the Same State of mind, I have herd of the Certainty of the death of Govr. Lewis which givs us much uneasiness. I have wrote to judge Overton of Nashville about his papers,—[I] have Some expctation of their falling into the Care of the Indian agent who is Said to have Come on imediately after his death &c.—I wish much to get the letter I receved of Govr. Lewis from N. madrid, which you Saw it will be of great Service to me. prey Send it to Fincastle as Soon as possible, I wish I had Some conversation with our about our Book. [and] the plans of [the] Govr. write me to fincastle if you please.

we Shall Set out at Sun rise tomorrow and proced on Slowly—
our love to Sister & nany &
acup [it for] your Self [also]
Wm Clark

Julia requst John to bring on 12 pockons* for her & more if Convenent.

* Holmberg says that "pockons" are puccoons. Puccoon, or bloodroot, was a plant used both as a red dye and as a medicinal herb. Modern research shows that it has many important disease fighting constituents.

(8) William Clark to Jonathan Clark

Beens [Bean] Station Wednesday 8th oct. [Nov.] 1809.

Dear Brother,

We arrived here this evening much fatigued, all quit [e] as well as when we parted with you. Lewis [their son] has a verry bad Cobld which does not decrease. The leathers which Support be [the] body of our Carrage broke on the way which detained us half a day, and the rain of last Friday was So constant and Cold that we lay by at Rickastle that day which is every [crossed out] all the detention we have had—The roads are verry bad thro' the wilderness and more perticularly on the Turn pike of Clinch mountain, we have been all day Comeing 16 miles, over what they Call a turnpiek road, whor [for] which pleasent traveling I payed 162 $^1/_2$ cents—

You have heard of that unfortunate end of Govr. Lewis and probably more than I have heard. I was in hopes of hearing more perticular [s] at this place, but have not—I wrote from Lexington to Wm. P. Anderson, to Send the Govrs/ paipers to me if they were yet in his part of the Conntry—

I am at a loss to know what to be at his death is a turble Stroke to me, in every repsect. I wish I could talk a little with you just now.

John Allen talked a little to me about filling his [Lewis's] place, when at Frankfort and injoined it on me to write him on the Subject which I must do tomorrow, and what must I say?—to have a green pompous new englandr* imedieately over my head will not do for me—!—

We Shall leave this in the morning and proceed on without loss of time.

Julia joins me in love to all and beleve me to be yr. Afft. Bro.

Wm Clark

* Clark is referring to William Eustis, the Secretary of War who was denying payment of expenses to government officials. Eustis was forced to resign in 1813.

(9) William Clark to Jonathan Clark

Colonel Hancocks November 26 1809

Dear Brother,

We arrived her on the 22nd. on a Cold and Snowey day without any material accidents. Col. H. met us about forty miles from this and Came down with us and on our arrival and Sense much job have been apperent in the Countenacs of all, Lewis is much broke out in Sores, but Continues helthy otherwise.

I expect to leave this [place] for washington on Sunday morning I have delayed this week expectig to receive Govr. Lewis papers by Mr. Whitesids, a Senator from Tennessee, whome I am in formed by Mr. W. P. Anderson, will take Charge of thoese papers for me and bring them on—I have just receved letters from Capt. Russell who Commands at the Chickasaw Bluffs that Govr.

Lewis was there detain by him 15 days in a State of Derangement most of the time and that he had attempted to kill himself before he got there—his Servent reports that [ ] "on his way to nashvill, he would frequently "Conceipt [conceive] that he herd me Co-meing on, and Said that he was certain [I would] over take him, that I had herd of his Situation and would Come to his releaf"— [ ] Capt. rusell Sais [ ] he made his will at the Bluffs and left Wm. Merrewether & myself Execeters and derected that I Should dis-poses of his papers &c. as I wished—pore fellow, what a number of Conjecturral reports we hear mostly unfavourable to him. I have to Contredict maney of them—I do not know what I Shall do about the publication of the Book, it will require funds which I have not at present. perhaps I may precure them—I have just herd that one of my Bills drawn on the Secty. of War for the quar-terly pay of Docr. Robinson a Sub Indiana Agent of the Osage apt. by Govr. Lewis have been protested for $160 which alarms me verry much. if this Should be the Only one I shall be easy, as I am convenced that explanation will Cause the Secty. to pay this Bill which was drawn previous to the late arragemt. made by the Secty. in respect to those appts.—

Maj. Preston Doct. Floyd and maney others in this quarter have got the Louisiana fever verry hot and will vesit that Country next Spring—Crops are fine about here but below the Blue ridge I am told are very bad—I hope to See John [Hite Clark] this week before I Set out, as he had expectations of getting here about this time—The Small Change [purse] which I thought had been left at your house was found Since we Came here among our Clothes—

Julia joins me in love to yourself Sister nancy Bro Edmund & Isaac acpt of our preyer for the helth and hapiness of you all

Yr

Wm Clark

(10-12) Gilbert C. Russell to Thomas Jefferson

(Captain Russell was promoted to Major on May 9, 1809. For unknown reasons, he continued to be addressed and to refer to himself as Captain during this time.)

Captain Gilbert Christian Russell of the Fifth Infantry was the commander of Fort Pickering. Some of his bills for govern-ment expenses had also been refused and he wanted to go with

Lewis to Washington on the same mission—to straighten out matters with government bureaucrats. After Lewis recovered his health, he waited 6 to 8 days for Russell to receive permission from General James Wilkinson to travel with him; but permission was denied and instead James Neelly accompanied Lewis on his fateful journey.

Captain Russell must have made his request to Wilkinson for permission to travel prior to Lewis's arrival, as the General was in New Orleans in September. It is 640 river miles from Memphis to New Orleans on today's river. A post rider made at most 50 miles a day, indicating that 3-4 weeks was a more likely estimate combining river and overland travel. Governor Lewis's travel down river was a subject of news stories, and Russell may well have anticipated his arrival, or his own request may have simply been a coincidence.

These letters indicate that Russell was careful of facts, and if Lewis had attempted suicide, been in a state of mental derangement, or written a second will at Fort Pickering, he would have reported it to Thomas Jefferson. In the letter of January 31, 1810 Russell condemns the character of James Neelly and writes that, if instead, he had been allowed to accompany Lewis, or send one of his own men with him, Lewis's death would not have taken place. He writes:

"Unfortunately for him this arrangement did not take place, or I hesitate not to say he would this day be living."

The pistols were never recovered from Neelly, despite the attempts of Meriwether Lewis's stepbrother, John Marks, to retrieve them when he visited Tennessee in 1811. An undated note by John Marks in the Lewis-Marks Collection at the University of Virginia Library states that Major James Neely still had Meriwether Lewis's gold watch and pistols.

Russell believed the suicide story, and blamed Neelly for encouraging Lewis's drinking. He also believed that Lewis's servant, Pernier may have been involved, from something he has heard. Perhaps he heard the story of Pernier dressing in Lewis's clothes, as reported in document #18.

Lewis was not a drinker. Frederick Bates, the Secretary of the Territory—a jealous and spiteful man who quarreled with Lewis—never accused him of either alcoholism or depression. Lewis had suffered from malaria for years. He was worried and being escorted by a man whom he most likely did not trust, as the following analysis of the memorandum indicates.

Concerning Lewis's Memorandum

The memorandum on the care of his trunks, a package and a case, and the trunks of Captain House, is an important one that has never received the attention it deserves. (#11, pp. 247-48)

> "M. Lewis would thank Capt. R. to be particular to whom he confides these trunks &c. a Mr. Cabboni of St. Louis may be expected to pass this place in the course of the next month, to him they may be safely confided."

Lewis would <u>thank</u> Captain Russell to only give these trunks &c. to either Jean-Pierre Cabanne, a wealthy St. Louis fur trader to be delivered to Lewis's friend, Will Carr, the United States Land Agent; or to await further instructions <u>by letter</u> from Lewis after he has arrived at Nashville.

Instead, Captain Russell responds to a verbal message delivered by an unnamed messenger, after Lewis has left the fort to "keep them until I shall hear from him again." It was an early foreshadowing of the death of Lewis. Someone wanted to examine the contents of those trunks. It appears likely there was incriminating evidence in them. Another implication is that Lewis was uncertain as to whether he would reach Nashville alive. If he did, he would write with further instructions. The obvious arrangement would be to send them to Washington.

Benjamin Wilkinson, the General's nephew, was at Fort Pickering on September 29th, and he took possession of Captain House's trunks. He was going to New Orleans to travel by ship to Baltimore. He died on board ship in February, 1810 of an unknown cause. Captain House was in Nashville, where he wrote his letter of September 28th to Bates (#3).

(10) Gilbert C. Russell to Thomas Jefferson

Fort Pickering, Chickesaw Bluffs,
January 4th 1810

Sir,

Conceiving it a duty incumbant upon me to give the friends of the late Meriwether Lewis such information relative to his arrival here, his stay and departure, and also of his pecuniary matters as came within my knowledge which they otherwise might not obtain, and presuming that as you were once his patron, you still remain'd his friend, I beg leave to communicate it to you and thro' you to his mother and such other of his friends as may be interested.

He came here on the 15th September last from whence he set off intending to go to Washington by way of New Orleans. His situation that rendered it necessary that he should be stoped until he would recover, which I done & in a short time by proper attention a change was perceptible and in about six days he was perfectly restored in every respect & able to travel. Being placed then myself in a similar situation with him by having Bills protested to a considerable amount I had made application to the General & expected leave of absence every day to go to Washington on the same business with Governor Lewis. In consequence of which he waited six or eight days expecting I would go on with him, but in this we were disappointed & he set off with a Major Neely who was going to Nashville.

At the request of Governor Lewis I enclosed the land warrant granted to him in consideration of his services to the Pacific Ocean to Bowling Robinson Esq Sec'y of the T'y [Treasury] of Orleans with instructions to dispose of it at any price above two dollars per acre & to lodge the money in the Bank of the United States or any of the branch banks subject to his order.

He left me with two Trunks a case and a bundle which will now remain here subject at any time subject to your order or that of his legal representatives. Enclosed is his memo respecting them but before the Boat in which he directed they might be sent got to this place I rec'd a verbal message from him after he left here to keep them until I should hear from him again.

He set off with two Trunks which contain'd all his papers relative to his expedition to the Pacific Ocean, Gen'l Clark's Land Warrant, a Port-Folio, pocket Book, and Note Book together with many other papers of both a public & private nature, two horses, two saddles & bridles, a Rifle, gun, pistols, pipe, tomahawk & dirks, all ellegant & perhaps about two hundred & twenty dollars, of which $99.58 was a Treasury Check on the U. S. branch Bank of Orleans endorsed by me. The horses, one saddle, and the check I let him have. Where or what has become of his effects I do not know but presume they must be in the care of Major Neely near Nashville.

As an individual I verry much regret the untimely death of Governor Lewis whose loss will be great to his country & surely felt by his friends. When he left I felt much satisfaction for indeed I tho't I had also been the means of preserving the life of this valuable man, and as it has turned out I shall have the consolation that I discharged those obligations towards him that man is bound to do to his fellows.

It is probable that I shall go to the City of Washington in a few weeks also. I shall give you a call and give any further information you may require that has come within my knowledge.
Having had the pleasure of knowing Mr. Wm. Randolph, I pray you to tender my respects to him.
I remain Sir with the utmost veneration and respect your Ob't Servant.

Gilbert C. Russell

Thomas Jefferson Esq.

(11) Lewis Memorandum for Gilbert Russell

Fort Pickering, Chickesaw Bluffs,
September 28th 1809

Capt. Russell will much oblige his friend Meriwether Lewis by forwarding to the care of William Brown Collector of the port of New Orleans, a Trunk belonging to Capt. James House addressed to McDonald and Ridgely Merchants in Baltimore. Mr. Brown will be requested to forward this trunk to its place of destination.

Capt. R. will also send two trunks a package and a case addressed to Mr. William C. Carr of St. Louis unless otherwise instructed by M. L. by letter from Nashville.

M. Lewis would thank Capt. R. to be particular to whom he confides these trunks &c. a Mr. Cabboni of St. Louis may be expected to pass this place in the course of the next month, to him they may be safely confided.

[On reverse side of Lewis Memo to Russell]
Memorandum
Sent Capt. Hous's Trunk by Benjamin Wilkinson on the 29th Sept. 1809

                                            Russell
Gov'r Lewis left here on the morning of the 29th Sept.

(12) Gilbert C. Russell to Thomas Jefferson

Fort Pickering, Chickesaw Bluffs,
31st January 1810

Sir,
I have lately been informed that James Neely the Agt. to the Chickasaws with whom Govr Lewis set off from this place has detained his pistols & perhaps some other of his effects for some claim he pretends to have upon his estate. He can have no just claim for any thing more than the expenses of his interment unless he makes a charge for packing his two Trunks from the nation. And for that he cannot have the audacity to make a charge after tendering the use of a loose horse or two which he said he had to take from the nation & also the aid of his servant. He seem'd happy to have it in his power to serve the Govr & but for making the offer which I accepted I should have employ'd the man who packed the trunk to the Nation to have them taken to Nashville & accompany the Govr. Unfortunately for him this arrangement did not take place, or I hesitate not to say he would this day be living. The fact is which you may yet be ignorant of that his untimely death may be attributed solely to the free use of liquor which he acknowledged verry candidly to me after he recovered & expressed a firm determination to never drink any more spirits or use snuff again both of which I deprived him of for several days & confined him to claret & a little white wine. But after leaving this

place by some means or other his resolution left him & this Agt. being extremely fond of liquor, instead of preventing the Govr from drinking or keeping him under any restraint advised him to it & from every thing I can learn gave the man every chance to seek an opportunity to destroy himself. Also from the statement of Grinder's wife where he killed himself I cannot help to believe that Purney was rather aiding & abeting in the murder than otherwise.

    This Neely also says he lent the Govr money which cannot be so as he had none himself & the Govr had more than one hund. $ in notes & specie besides a check I let him have of 99.58 none of which it is said could be found. I have wrote to the Cashier of the branch bank of Orleans as whom the check was drawn in favor of myself or order to stop payt. when presented. I have this day authorized a gentleman to pay the pretended claim of Neely & take the pistols which will be held sacred to the order of any of the friends of M. Lewis free from encumbrance.
I am Sir with great respect your Obt Servt.

Gilbert C. Russell

Tho. Jefferson Esq.

(13) On the Death of John Pernier

Julian Boyd, the editor of *The Papers of Thomas Jefferson*, found several letters to Thomas Jefferson regarding Meriwether Lewis's servant John Pernier's request for the back pay of $240 owed him by the Lewis Estate; and the subsequent attempts by his friend John Christopher Sueverman to claim the money after Pernier's death. Dr. Boyd passed them on to Donald Jackson who published them in an article entitled "On the Death of Meriwether Lewis's Servant" in 1964. Jackson discovered that Pernier had been employed as a servant in the White House by Thomas Jefferson for parts of 1804 and 1805, and found a pay record for Sueverman in 1803.

    Jefferson in a letter supporting Sueverman's claim wrote:

"Suverman was a servant of mine, a very honest man. He has since become blind, and gets his living by keeping a few groceries which he buys and sells from hand to mouth. He is miserably poor."

So this letter was not written by Sueverman, who was blind, but was written for him. William Clark, the administrator of Lewis's estate, did not think Sueverman's claim on Pernier's estate was justified and refused to pay it. John Pernier was a free mulatto, of French and African American ancestry. He accompanied Lewis to St. Louis in 1807 and served as his personal valet and servant. He was present at the scene of Meriwether Lewis's death. Lucy Marks, Lewis's mother, believed Pernier had participated in the murder of her son. Perhaps, like Russell, she may have been reacting to the story of Pernier dressed in Lewis's clothes. (See #18, p. 262). Reprinted from *The William and Mary Quarterly* (3rd Ser., 21:3, July, 1964, pp. 445-448) by permission of the Omohundro Institute of Early American History and Culture.

---

(13)

City of Washington 5th May 1810

Sir,

Respectfully I wish to inform you of the Unhappy exit of Mr. Pirny. He boarded, and lodged, with us ever since his return from the Western Country. The principal part of the time he has been confined by Sickness, I believe ariseing from uneasyness of mind, not having recd. anything for his late services to Govr. Lewis. He was wretchedly poor and destitute. Every service in our power was rendered him to make him confortable, not doubting but the moment he had it in his power he would thankfully and honestly pay us.

Last Week the poor Man appeared considerably better, I believe in some respects contrary to his wishes, for unfortunately Saturday last he procured himself a quantity of Laudenam. On Sunday Morning under the pretence of not being so well went upstairs to lay on the bed, in which situation he was found dead, with the bottle by his Side that had contained the Laudanam. Our distress was great but it was to late to render him any assistance. He was buried neat and decent the very next day which in addition to his former expences, fall very heavy upon us, whose circumstances you are well with acquainted with, cannot bear it without suffering considerably, and hope you will be so oblidgeing as [to] assist us as Soon as it is possible to recover anything on behalf of the poor Man.

I am with great Respect Sir your Obedt. H'ble Servt.

John Christoper Sueverman

(14) Alexander Wilson's Account of Lewis's Death

The great bird artist Alexander Wilson was a personal friend of Lewis's. When Lewis came to Philadelphia in 1807, he gave Wilson the bird specimens he had collected on the expedition, and drawings of these birds were included in the second volume of Wilson's *American Ornithology*.

Wilson was as hardy and tough as Lewis; he was accustomed to traveling hundreds of miles on foot and horseback, in pursuit of both birds and of subscribers to his multi-volume publication, which eventually reached nine volumes. When he traveled south in the spring of 1810, he visited Grinder's Inn on May 6, 1810.

(This account describing his visit to Lewis's gravesite is taken from a long letter recording his travels on the Natchez Trace.)

Natchez, Mississippi Territory

18 May 1810   (14)

To Alexander Lawson,

...Next morning (Sunday) I rode six miles to a man's of the name of Grinder, where our poor friend Lewis perished. In the same room where he expired, I took down from Mrs. Grinder the particulars of that melancholy event, which affected me extremely. This house or cabin is seventy-two miles from Nashville, and is the last white man's as you enter the Indian country. Governor Lewis, she said, came hither about sunset, alone, and inquired if he could stay for the night; and, alighting, brought the saddle into the house. He was dressed in a loose gown, white, striped with blue. On being asked if he came alone, he replied that there were two servants behind, who would soon be up. He called for some spirits, and drank a very little. When the servants arrived, one of whom was a negro, he inquired for his powder, saying he was sure he had some powder in a canister. The servant gave no distinct reply, and Lewis, in the meanwhile, walked backwards and forwards before the door talking to himself. Sometimes, she said, he would seem as if he were walking up to her; and would suddenly wheel round, and walk back as fast as he could. Supper being ready he sat down, but had eaten only a few mouthfuls when he started up, speaking to himself in a violent manner. At these times, she says, she observed his face to flush as if it had come on him in a fit. He lighted his pipe, and drawing a chair to the door sat down, saying to Mrs. Grinder, in a kind tone of voice, "Madame this is a very pleasant evening." He smoked for some time, but quitted his seat and traversed the yard as before. He again sat down to his pipe, seemed again composed, and casting his eyes wistfully towards the west, observed what a sweet evening it was. Mrs. Grinder was preparing a bed for him; but he said he would sleep on the floor, and desired the servant to bring the bearskins and buffalo robe, which were immediately spread out for him; and it being now dusk, the woman went off to the kitchen, and the two men to the barn, which stands about two hundred yards off. The kitchen is only a few paces from the room where Lewis was, and the woman being considerably alarmed by the behaviour of her guest could not sleep, but listened to him walking backwards and forwards, she thinks, for several hours, and talking aloud, as she said, "like a lawyer." She then heard the report of a pistol, and something fall heavily on the floor, and the words—"O Lord!" Immediately afterwards she heard another pistol, and in a few minutes she heard him at her door calling out "O madam! Give me some water, and heal my wounds." The logs being open, and unplastered, she saw him stagger back and fall against a stump that stands between the kitchen and room. He crawled for some distance, and raised himself by the side of a tree, where he sat about a minute. He once more got to the room; afterwards he came to the kitchen-door, but did not speak; she then heard him scraping the bucket with a gourd for water; but it soon appeared that this cooling element was denied the dying man! As soon as the day broke and not before—the terror of the woman having permitted him to remain country which their sons are destined to fill with arts, with science, with freedom & happiness.

he uncovered his side, and showed them where the bullet had entered; a piece of the forehead had blown off, and had exposed the brains, without having bled much. He begged they would take his rifle and blow out his brains, and he would give them all the money he had in his trunk. He often said, "I am no coward; but I am so strong, so hard to die." He begged the servant not to be afraid of him, for that he would not hurt him. He expired in about two hours, or just as the sun rose above the trees. He lies buried close by the common path, with a few loose rails thrown over his grave. I gave Grinder money to put a post fence round it to shelter it from the hogs, and from the wolves; and he gave me his written promise he would do it. I left this place in a very melancholy mood, which was not much allayed by the prospect of the gloomy and savage wilderness which I was just entering alone. . . .

Alexander Wilson

(15) Statement of Gilbert Russell (1811)

This document was found in the papers of Colonel Jonathan Williams at the Lilly Library, University of Indiana. The two document examiners, Gerald B. Richards and Duayne Dillon agree that it was neither written nor signed by either of the two men whose names are on the document—Gilbert C. Russell and Jonathan Williams. (See pp. 126-140, 164-175, 256.)

It was first published by Donald Jackson in his *Letters of the Lewis and Clark Expedition* in 1962. Because it was published without the two letters written by Captain Russell to President Jefferson in January, 1810, it's authenticity was never questioned by scholars. Though Vardis Fisher in his 1962 book, *Suicide or Murder?: The Strange Death of Meriwether Lewis* wrote:

"But for us there is something strangely unl'   -ell
in his manner of writing this account of Le
In his two letters to Jefferson his friend'
feeling for Lewis shone through at ever'
he says that Lewis killed himself in '

desperate and Barbarian-like manner'—strange words from an army man whose profession was killing with guns."

Upon my [Kira Gale] discovery of a second document in the Williams Archives in the same handwriting—a 12 page court brief for Wilkinson, supposedly signed by him—this new document was examined by Jerry Richards in December, 2008. He has certified that both documents were written by an unknown person. (See Appendix A and illustrations on p. 256.) It is likely they were both dictated to a subordinate by General Wilkinson. The court brief was simply Wilkinson's defense of his conduct and career in preparation for the court martial he was undergoing. The language and the references of the 1811 "Russell statement" bear little relationship to Russell's letters of January 4 and January 31, 1810. (See discussion on pp. 227-230 and 243-246; and documents 10-12 on pp. 246-249.)

---

(15)

[Russell Statement, 26 November 1811]

Governor Lewis left St. Louis late in August, or early in September 1809, intending to go by the route of the Mississippi and the Ocean, to the City of Washington, taking with him all the papers relative to his expedition to the pacific Ocean, for the purpose of preparing and putting them to the press, and to have some drafts paid which had been drawn by him on the Government and protested. On the morning of the 15th of September, the Boat in which he was a passenger landed him at Fort pickering in a state of mental derangement, which appeared to have been produced as much by indisposition as other causes. The Subscriber being then the Commanding Officer of the Fort on discovering from the crew that he had made two attempts to Kill himself, in one of which he had nearly succeeded, resolved at once to take possession of him and his papers, and detain them there untill he recovered, or some friend might arrive in whose hands he could depart in Safety.

In this condition he continued without any material change for five days, during which time the most proper and efficatious means that could be devised to restore him was administered, and on the sixth or seventh day all symptoms of derangement disappeared and he was completely in his senses and thus continued for ten or twelve days. On the 29th of the same month he left Bluffs, with the Chickasaw agent the interpreter and some of the Chiefs, intending to proceed the usual route thro' the Indian Country, Tennessee and Virginia to his place of distination, with his papers well secured and packed on horses. By much severe depletion during his illness he had been considerably reduced and debilitated, from which he had not entirely recovered when he set off, and the weather in that country being yet excessively hot and the exercise of traveling too severe for him; in three or four days he was again affected with the same mental disease. He had no person with him who could manage or controul him in his propensities and he daily grew worse untill he arrived at the house of a Mr. Grinder within the Jurisdiction of Tennissee and only Seventy miles from Nashville, where in the apprehension of being destroyed by enemies which had no existence but in his wild immagination, he destroyed himself, in the most cool desperate and Barbarian-like manner, having been left in the house intirely to himself. The night preceeding this one of his Horses and one of the Chickasaw agents with whom he was traveling Strayed off from the Camp and in the Morning could not be found. The agent with some of the Indians stayed to search for the horses, and Governor Lewis with their two servants and the baggage horses proceeded to Mr. Grinders where he was to halt untill the agent got up.

After he arrived there and refreshed himself with a little Meal & drink he went to bed in a cabin by himself and ordered the servants to go to the stables and take care of the Horses, least they might loose some that night; Some time in the night he got his pistols which he loaded, after every body had retired in a Separate Building and discharged one against his forehead not making much effect—the ball not penetrating the skull but only making a furrow over it. He then discharged the other against his breast where the ball entered and passing downward thro' his body came out low down near his back bone. After some time he got up and went to the house where Mrs. Grinder and her children were lying and asked for water, but her husband being absent and having heard the report of the pistols she was greatly allarmed and made him no answer. He then in returning got his razors from a port folio which happened to contain them and Seting up in his bed was found about day light, by one of the Servants, busily engaged in cutting himself from head to foot. He again beged for water, death was greatly lamented. And that a fame so dearly earned as his should be clouded by such an act of desperation was to his friends still greater cause of regret.

(Signed) Gilbert Russell

The above was received by me from Major Gilbert Russell of the [blank] Regiment of Infantry U. S. on Tuesday the 26th of November 1811 at Fredericktown in Maryland.

J. Williams

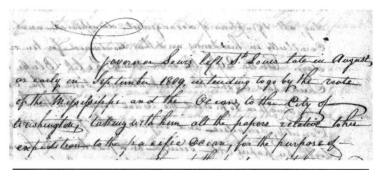

November 26, 1811 Statement—Some old documents experience bleed through from the reverse side of the page, as seen here. The contrast has been increased so that the distinctive long "t bars" are seen clearly.

An undated brief of 12 pages hand written and bearing the name of James Wilkinson as its author regarding his court martial (circa October, 1811). However, it is not in the handwriting of General Wilkinson.

(16) Thomas Jefferson to Paul Allen

These three excerpts are taken from a biographical essay of Meriwether Lewis which Thomas Jefferson was asked to provide for the publication of the *Lewis and Clark Journals* in 1814. Paul Allen was the publisher. The former president wrote at length about Lewis's ancestors; his own early attempts to send someone to explore the Pacific Northwest; the two years Lewis spent living and working in the White House as Jefferson's private secretary; and the expedition itself. The passages relating to Lewis's character, mental depression, and praise for his accomplishments are reprinted here.

---

(16)

Monticello, Aug. 18, 1813
Sir
(first excerpt)
. . . Captain Lewis who had then been near two years with me as private secretary, immediately renewed his sollicitations to have the direction of the party. I had now had opportunities of knowing him intimately. Of courage undaunted, possessing a firmness & perseverance of purpose which nothing but impossibilities could divert from it's direction, careful as a father committed to his charge, yet steady in the maintenance of discipline & order, intimate with the Indian character, customs & principles, habituated to the hunting life, guarded by exact observation of the vegetables & animals of his own country, against losing time in the description of objects already possessed, honest, disinterested, liberal, of sound understanding and a fidelity to truth so scrupulous that whatever he should report would be as certain as if seen by ourselves, with all these qualifications as if selected and implanted by nature in one body, for this express purpose, I could have no hesitation in confiding the enterprise to him. To fill up the measure desired, he wanted nothing but a greater familiarity with the technical language of the natural sciences, and readiness in the astronomical observations necessary for the geography of his route.

(second excerpt)

. . . It was the middle of Feb. 1807 before Capt. Lewis with his companion Clarke reached the city of Washington where Congress was then in session. That body granted to the two chiefs and their followers, the donation of lands which they had been encouraged to expect in reward of their toils & dangers. Capt. Lewis was soon after appointed Governor of Louisiana, and Capt. Clarke a General of it's militia and agent of the U. S. for Indian affairs in that department.

A considerable time intervened before the Governor's arrival at St. Louis. He found the territory distracted by feuds & contentions among the officers of the government, & the people themselves divided by these into factions & parties. He determined at once, to take no side with either; but to use every endeavor to conciliate & harmonize them. The even-handed justice he administered to all soon established a respect for his person & authority, and perseverance & time wore down animosities and reunited the citizens again into one family.

Governor Lewis had from early life been subjet to hypochondrial affections. It was a constitutional disposition in all the nearer branches of the family of his name & was more immediately inherited by him from his father. They had not however been so strong as to give uneasiness to his family. While he had lived with me in Washington, I observed at times sensible depressions of mind, but not knowing their constitutional source, I estimated their course by what I had seen in the family. During his Western expedition the constant exertion which that required of all the faculties of body & mind, suspended these distressing affections; but after his establishment at St. Louis in sedentary occupations they returned upon him with redoubled vigor, and began seriously to alarm his friends. He was in a porxysm of one of these when he affairs rendered it necessary for him to go to Washington.

(third excerpt)

...About 3 oclock in the night he did the deed which plunged his friends into affliction and deprived his country of one of her most valued citizens whose valour & intelligence would have been now imployed in avenging the wrongs of his country and in emulating by land the splendid deeds which have honored her arms on the ocean. It lost too the nation the benefit of recieving from his own hand the Narrative now offered them of his sufferings & successes in endeavoring to extend for them the boundaries of science, and to present to their knoledge that vast & fertile

To this melancholy close of the life of one whom posterity will declare not to lave lived in vain I have only to add that all facts I have stated are either known to myself, or communicated by his family or others whose truth I have no hiesitation to make [myself] responsible; and I conclude with tendering you the assurances of my respect & consideration.

Th: Jefferson

(17) On the fate of Seaman, the dog

This entry was found in *A Collection of American Epitaphs and Inscriptions with Occasional Notes by Rev. Timothy Alden* (1814). It relates the sad fate of Meriwether Lewis's dog, a Newfoundland dog named Seaman. The collar has been lost to history. This is the only mention that has ever been found, and there is no reason to doubt it. Reverend Alden founded Allegheny College in western Pennsylvania. James Holmberg of the Filson Historical Society located this reference.

Entry 916   (17)

"The greatest traveller of my species. My name is SEAMAN, the dog of captain Meriwether Lewis, whom I accompanied to the Pacifick ocean through the interior of the continent of North America."

The foregoing was copied from the collar, in the Alexandria Museum, which the late gov. Lewis's dog wore after his return from the western coast of America. The fidelity and attachment of this animal were remarkable. After the melancholy exit of gov. Lewis, his dog would not depart for a moment from his lifeless remains; and when they were deposited in the earth no gentle means could draw him from the spot of interment. He refused to take every kind of food, which was offered him, and actually pined away and died with grief upon his master's grave!

(18) 1845 Newspaper Account
of Lewis's Death

Robert Evans Griner/Grinder died in 1827. It is thought that after his death, Priscilla Grinder felt free to tell another version of the story of Lewis's death, which found its way into this newspaper account in 1845.

The family name is Griner, but they are more commonly known as Grinder. After Lewis's death it is said they came into a large sum of money and moved to Hickman County, TN.

Despite the local tradition of Grinder murdering Lewis, it appears likely that he was part of a wider conspiracy. (The document is found in the Draper Manuscript Collection, Wisconsin Historical Society, 29 CC 33.)

DISPATCH   (18)
New-York, February 1, 1845
Published on the first of every month by
B. H. Day and J. G. Wilson

Singular Fate of a Distinguished Man

We find in the *North Arkansas*, a paper published at Batesville, Ark., a communication stating some singular and not generally known facts concerning the mysterious death of Capt. George M. Lewis, one of the two persons employed by the U. S. Government to conduct the celebrated Expedition of Lewis and Clark, in exploring the region West of the Rocky Mountains. The writer is at present a teacher in the Cherokee Nation, and says that he is personally acquainted with the circumstances which he relates. The expedition, consisting of seventy or eighty persons, under the guidance of Lewis and Clark, was commenced in 1803 or 1804, and completed in about three years. The writer says the remains of Captain Lewis are "deposited in the southwest corner of Maury county, Tennessee, near Grinder's old stand, on the Natchez trace where Lawrence, Maury, and Hickman counties corner together." He visited the grave in 1838, found it almost concealed by brambles, without a stone or monument of any kind, and several miles from any house. An old tavern stand, known as Grinder's, once stood near by, but was long since burned. The writer gave the following narrative of the incidents attending the death of Capt. Lewis, as he received them from Mrs. Grinder, the landlady of the house where he died in so savage a manner.

She said that Mr. Lewis was on his way to the city of Washington, accompanied by a Mr. Pyrna and a servant belonging to a Mr. Neely. One evening, a little before sundown, Mr. Lewis called at her house and asked for lodgings. Mr. Grinder not being at home, she hesitated to take him in. Mr. Lewis informed her two other men would be along presently, who also wished to spend the night at her house, and as they were all civil men, he did not think there would be any impropriety in her giving them accommodations for the night. Mr. Lewis dismounted, fastened his horses, took a seat by the side of the house, and appeared quite sociable. In a few minutes Mr. Pyrna and the servants rode up, and seeing Mr. Lewis, they also dismounted and put up their horses. About dark two or three other men rode up and called for lodging. Mr. Lewis immediately drew a brace of pistols, stepped towards them and challenged them to fight a duel. They not liking this salutation, rode on to the next house, five miles. This alarmed Mrs. Grinder. Supper, however, was ready in a few minutes. Mr. Lewis ate but little. He would stop eating, and sit as if in a deep study, and several times exclaimed, "If they do prove any thing on me, they will have to do it by letter." Supper being over, and Mrs. Grinder seeing that Mr. Lewis was mentally deranged, requested Mr. Pyrna to get his pistols from him. Mr. P. replied, "He has no ammunition, and if he does any mischief it will be to himself, and not to you or any body else." In a short time all retired to bed; the travellers in one room as Mrs. G. thought, and she and her children in another.

Two or three hours before day, Mrs. G. was alarmed by the report of a pistol, and quickly after two other reports, in the room where the travellers were. At the report of the third, she heard some one fall and exclaim, "O Lord! Congress relieve me!" In a few minutes she heard some person at the door of the room where she lay. She inquired,, "Who is there?" Mr. Lewis spoke and said, "Dear Madam, be so good as to give me a little water." Being afraid to open the door, she did not give him any. Presently she heard him fall, and soon after, looking through a crack in the wall, she saw him scrambling across the road on his hands and knees.

After daylight Mr. Pyrna and the servant made their appearance, and it appeared they had not slept in the house, but in the

stable. Mr. P. had on the clothes Mr. L. wore when they came to
Mrs. Grinder's the evening before, and Mr. L.'s gold watch in his
pocket. Mrs. G. asked what he was doing with Mr. L.'s clothes on;
Mr. P. replied "He gave them to me." Mr. P. and the servant then
searched for Mr. L., found him and brought him to the house, and
though he had on a full suit of clothes, they were old and tattered,
and not the same as he had on the evening before, and though
Mr. P. had said that Lewis had no ammunition, Mrs. G. found
several balls and a considerable quantity of powder scattered over
the floor of the room occupied by Lewis; also a canister with several pounds in it.

(19) Report of the Lewis Monument Committee (1850)

In 1848 the State of Tennessee appropriated $500 to erect a
monument to Meriwether Lewis. In the process of identifying
his gravesite, the remains of Meriwether Lewis were exhumed.
Dr. Samuel B. Moore was a member of the monument committee who examined the "upper portion of the skeleton." Later in
the report, the committee states, that though it was commonly
believed that Meriwether Lewis committed suicide, "it seems
to be more probable that he died by the hands of an assassin."

****

(19)

To the General Assembly of the State of Tennessee:
    By the 9th section of an act, passed at the last session of the
General Assembly on this State, entitled an act to establish the
County of Lewis the sum of $500 was appropriated, or so much
thereof as might be necessary, to preserve the place of interment
where the remains of GEN. MERIWETHER LEWIS were deposited; and the undersigned were appointed the agents of the
General Assembly to carry into execution the provisions of the
act, and report to the present General Assembly.
Looking upon the object to be accomplished to be one highly
honorable to the State, the undersigned entered upon the duties
assigned them cheerfully and with as little delay as possible. They
consulted with the most eminent artists and practical mechanics

as to the kind of monument to be erected, and a plan being agreed upon, they employed Mr. Lemuel W. Kirby, of Columbia, to execute it for the sum of five hundred dollars.

The entire monument is twenty and a half feet high. The design is simple but is intended to express the difficulties, successes, and violent termination of a life which was marked by bold enterprise, by manly courage and by devoted patriotism.

The base of the monument is of rough, unhewn stone, eight feet high and nine feet square where it rises to the surface of the ground. On this rests a plinth of cut stone, four feet square and eighteen inches in thickness, on which are the inscriptions given below. On this plinth stands a broken column eleven feet high, two and a half feet in diameter for the base, and a few inches smaller at the top. The top is broken to denote the violent and untimely end of a bright and glorious career. The base is composed of a species of sandstone found in the neighborhood of the grave. The plinth and shaft, or column, are made of a fine limestone, commonly known as Tennessee marble. Around the monument is erected a handsome wrought iron rail fence.

Great care was taken to identify the grave. George Nixon, Esq., an old Surveyor, had become very early acquainted with its locality. He pointed out the place; but to make assurance doubly sure the grave was re-opened and the upper portion of the skeleton examined, and such evidence found as to leave no doubt as to the place of internment. Witnesses were called and their certificate, with that of the Surveyor, prove the fact beyond dispute. The inscription upon the plinth was furnished by Professor Nathaniel Cross of the University of Nashville. It is beautiful and appropriate. It is placed on the different sides of the plinth, and is as follows:

MERIWETHER LEWIS
BORN NEAR CHARLOTTESVILLE, VIRGINIA,
AUGUST 18, 1774
DIED OCTOBER 11, 1809; AGED 35 YEARS;
An Officer of the Regular Army – Private Secretary to President Jefferson –
Commander of the Expedition To The Oregon in 1803–1806
–
Governor of the Territory of Louisiana – His Melancholy Death OccurredWhere This Monument Now Stands, And Under Which Rests His Mortal Remains.

In the language of Mr. Jefferson:

"His Courage Was Undaunted; His Firmness and Perseverance
Yielded To Nothing But Impossibilities;
A Rigid Disciplinarian, Yet Tender As A Father
To Those Committed To His Charge;
Honest, Disinterested, Liberal, With A Sound Understanding,
And A Scrupulous Fidelity To Truth.

Immaturus Obi; Sed Tu Felicior Annos
Vive Meos, Bona Republica! Vive Tuos.
ERECTED BY THE LEGISLATURE OF TENNESSEE,
A. D., 1848.

In the Latin diatich, many of your honorable body will no
doubt recognize as the affecting epitaph on the tomb of a young
wife, in which by a prosopopocia, after alluding to an immature
death, she prays that her happier husband may live out her years
and his own.

Immaturus pari: sed tu felicior annos.
Vive meos, conjux optime! Vive tuos.

Under the same figure, the deceased is represented in the Latin
diatich as altered, after alluding to his early death, as uttering as
a patriot a similar prayer, that the republic may fulfill her high
destiny, and that her years may equal those of time. As the diatich
now stands, the figure may be made to apply either to the whole
Union, or to Tennessee, that has honored his memory by the erection of a monument.

The impression has long prevailed that under the influence of disease of body and mind – of hopes based upon long and valuable
services – not merely deferred, but wholly disappointed – Governor Lewis perished by his own hands. It seems to be more probable that he died by the hands of an assassin. The place at which he
was killed is even yet a lonely spot. It was then wild and solitary,
and on the borders of the Indian Nation. Maj. M. L. Clark, a son
of Governor Clark of Missouri; in a letter to the Rev. Mr. Cressey
of Maury County says:

"Have you ever heard of the report that Gov. Lewis
did not destroy his own life, but was murdered by his
servant, a Frenchman, who stole his money and horses,
returned to Natchez, and was never afterwards heard

of? This is an important matter in connection with the erection of a monument to his memory, as it clearly removes from my mind at least, the only stigma upon the fair name I have the honor to bear."

The undersigned would suggest to the General Assembly, the propriety of having an acre of ground, or some other reasonable quantity, around the grave secured against the entry of private persons. This can be done, either by reserving the title in the State, or by directing a grant to be issued in the name of the Governor and by his successors. The first mode would perhaps be the best.

All of which is respectfully submitted,

EDMUND DILLAHUNTY,
BARCLAY MARTIN,
ROBERT A. SMITH,
SAMUEL B. MOORE.

Citation: Meriwether Lewis Memorial Association Papers 1880-1931, Tennessee State Archives: Accession # 93-001; Microfilm # 1374, Legislative Documents, Tennessee General Assembly, 1850

(20) Meriwether Lewis Memorial Association to President Calvin Coolidge

John Trotwood Moore, Tennessee State Historian, and P. E. Cox, Tennessee State Archeologist, presented a petition to President Calvin Coolidge in October, 1924 from the Meriwether Lewis Memorial Association requesting that the gravesite become a National Monument. It was declared a National Monument on February 6, 1925. Dedication ceremonies were held on August 18, 1925, the birthday of Meriwether Lewis, when a crowd estimated at between 7,000 to 10,000 attended the event. The monument is now part of the Natchez Trace Parkway system administered by the National Park Service.

(*An excerpt from the petition*)   (20)

Congress in recognition of Capt. Lewis' services granted him large areas of land. March, 1807 Capt. Lewis was appointed Governor of Louisiana Territory and proceeded to St. Louis; he rendered faithful, effective and satisfactory service to the Nation; the record of the Oregon expedition had not been prepared by him, and at the request of President Jefferson to report in Washington for the purpose of completing this work, he started overland on horseback reaching Chickasaw Bluffs, now Memphis, Tennessee; he then proceeded along the Indian trails to the Tennessee River above Muscle Shoals, where he crossed this river, reaching the ancient road known as the Natchez Trace; pursuing his journey, on October 11, 1809 he arrived at Grinders Stand on the edge of Indian country, where he intended to spend the night. In this wilderness and alone, on this night, he died. Investigations have satisfied the public that he was murdered presumably for the purposes of robbery.

Members of the National Monument Movement seen here at the dedication ceremonies are: P. E. Cox, State Archeologist; John Trotwood Moore, State Historian; Governor Austin Peay, and Dr. J. N. Block. *Courtesy of the Tennessee State Library and Archives.*

Portrait of Meriwether Lewis by Charles Saint-Memin, who used a "physiognotrace" to create an accurate profile. Drawn in chalk, the drawing was
created either in 1803 or 1807. William Clark owned a small engraving of
this portrait and said it was the best likeness of his friend.
Courtesty of the Missouri History Museum

Sheheke-Shote—the Mandan Indian Chief also known
as Big White Chief—sat for a black and white chalk portrait by Charles Saint-Memin in Philadelphia in 1807.

Courtesy of the American Philosophical Society, FAP 144

Meriwether Lewis wax figure at Peale's Museum above Independence Hall by Charles Saint-Memin. The mannikin is wearing the fur cape of 140 ermine skins, presented to Lewis by Sacagawea's brother, the Shoshone Chief, Cameahwait.

Courtesy of the New-York Historical Society, accession # 1971.125

Portrait of General James Wilkinson by John Wesley Jarvis.
The original is on display at the Filson Historical Society in
Louisville, Kentucky. The general wore uniforms of his own
design covered with gold braid and used gold stirrups and
spurs and a leopard skin saddlecloth with dangling leopard
claws for riding.
Courtesy of the Filson Historical Society, Louisville, Kentucky.

The Natchez Trace Parkway near the Meriwether Lewis Gravesite &
National Monument, located near milepost 389.5 on the Parkway

The road that leads to the cabin from Highway 20

Photos by Tony Turnbow

Replica of Grinder's Inn at the Meriwether Lewis Gravesite &
National Monument near Hohenwald, Tennessee

A free campground run by the National Park Service, several miles
of hiking trails, and a section of the Old Trace are located here.

Photos by Tony Turnbow

National Guard Armory in Hohenwald, where the Lewis County
Coroner's Inquest into the death of Meriwether Lewis was held in 1996

Hohenwald, Tennessee
(population 3,788) is
located 60 miles south-
west of Nashville.

*Photos by Tony Turnbow and
Hohenwald Chamber of Commerce*

Family and friends gather at the Lewis family graveyard in Albemarle County, Virginia for a Locust Hill Graveyard Foundation
meeting. The foundation does not want to have the remains of
Meriwether Lewis reburied at Locust Hill; but they have requested
that if an exhumation of the remains occurs, they want to have a
Christian reburial at the National Monument gravesite.

Family photos courtesy of Thomas McSwain, Jr.

Howell Lewis Bowen, Jane Lewis Henley, Anne Tufts (President of the Home Front Chapter of the Lewis and Clark Trail Heritage Foundation) and Thomas C. McSwain, Jr. (President of the Locust Hill Graveyard Foundation) at the unveiling of the Meriwether Lewis bust in the Old Hall of the Virginia House of Delegates on August 18, 2008.

Family members shown here are Dr. Alden Scott Anderson, Jr. (L.) his daughter Sara Lewis Anderson Vines and grandson Nicholas Vines. Dr. William Morris Anderson (R.), his brother, attended the Coroner's Inquest hearings in Hohenwald in 1996.

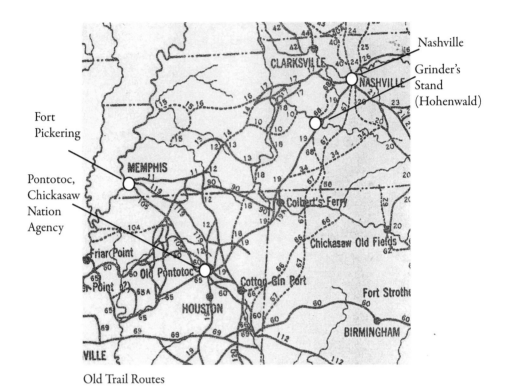

Fort
Pickering

Pontotoc,
Chickasaw
Nation
Agency

Nashville

Grinder's
Stand
(Hohenwald)

Old Trail Routes

Governor Lewis and James Neely traveled approximately 105 miles south from Chickasaw Bluffs (Memphis TN) to Old Pontotoc, the site of the Chickasaw Villages and Neely's Indian Agency before heading north to Nashville, their destination.

Using a modern map program it is :
    101 miles—Memphis TN to Pontotoc MS
    151 miles—Pontotoc to Hohenwald TN
    82 miles—Hohenwald to Nashville TN

    258 miles—Memphis to Nashville via route US-64 and the Natchez Trace Parkway

From the map "The Trail System of the Southeastern United States in the Early Colonial Period" by W. E. Myer, 1923; *Natchez Trace Parkway Survey* (1941): 76th Congress; 3rd Session, Doc. #148

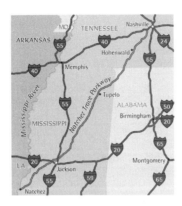

16 Destinations along the Natchez Trace Parkway from *Lewis and Clark Road Trips* by Kira Gale. The book features over 800 destinations along the Lewis and Clark Trail; 43 are located in Region 10, which covers the area from New Orleans, Louisiana to New Madrid, Missouri.

Links to all the destination websites are found on the Trip Planner at www.deathofMeriwetherLewis.com

20 Emerald Mound
21 Mount Locust
22 Sunken Trace
23 Mississippi Museum of Natural Science
24 Mississippi Crafts Center
25 Cypress Swamp Walking Trail
26 Kosciusko Museum & Visitor Center
   (Oprah Winfrey's hometown)
27 French Camp
28 Chickasaw Village Site
29 Natchez Trace Parkway Visitor Center
30 Elvis Presley birthplace home & museum
31 Tupelo Buffalo Park & Zoo
32 Colbert Ferry
33 Florence Mound & Museum
34 Meriwether Lewis Gravesite & National
   Monument
35 Old Trace
36 Gordon House & Ferry

NEW ORLEANS

The Cabildo

The Louisiana State Museum is located in the Cabildo, where the Louisiana Purchase transfer took place on December 20, 1803.

Lafitte's Blacksmith Shop & Bar

The oldest bar in the U. S. is located on Bourbon Street. The famous pirate Lafitte Brothers who were heroes of the Battle of New Orleans used to hang out here. It is still a neighborhood bar.

Jackson Square

The Cabildo and other historic buildings are located on Jackson Square. Across the street, the Cafe du Monde offers New Orleans's famous coffee and beignets, the sugared French doughnuts.

New Orleans street scene

It is easy to imagine life in the early 1800's when you visit New Orleans.

NATCHEZ TO NASHVILLE

Grand Village of the Natchez Indians, National Park Service Natchez, Mississippi

Historic Jefferson College in Washington, Mississippi, established in 1802, was the site of Aaron Burr's trial.

Andrew Ellicott's house Natchez, Mississippi. He taught Meriwether Lewis surveying skills in Lancaster, Pennsylvania.

Bale of cotton at Kosciusko Visitor Center & Museum (Oprah Winfrey's hometown)

One of the largest Indian mounds in North America, covering 8 acres, Emerald Mound was the site of a ceremonial temple of the Natchez Indians. It is located on the Natchez Trace Parkway.

Andrew Jackson's grand estate, The Hermitage, in Nashville, Tennessee is a National Historic Landmark

FROM MEMPHIS TO NEW MADRID

Fort Pickering was located on the Chickasaw Bluffs, a few miles south of Mud Island, where I-55 crosses the river.

Monorail to Mud Island River Park, Memphis TN

Mississippi River Museum on Mud Island

The Mud Island River Park walking path replica of the Mississippi River is 5 blocks long

The Museum in New Madrid, Missouri has a 24 hour seismograph machine recording earthquake tremors. The town was the epicenter of America's largest earthquakes in 1811-12. New Madrid's motto is "It's our fault!"

Photos by Kira Gale; and courtesy of the
Mississippi River Museum and The Hermitage

Part Three

The Case for Murder

by

Kira Gale

Meriwether Lewis (1774-1809)

William Clark (1770-1838)

Meriwether Lewis and William Clark portraits
by Charles Willson Peale
Independence National Historical Park

Introduction
to The Case for Murder

by

Kira Gale

S tephen Ambrose made the case for Meriwether Lewis having committed suicide in *Undaunted Courage*, his biography of Lewis published in 1996. Because his popular book was the cornerstone of the 2004-2006 Lewis and Clark Bicentennial Commemoration, it is now a widely held belief that the famed explorer committed suicide. But through the years many historians have questioned this.

In 1988, Ambrose himself appears to have endorsed the murder theory. He wrote a foreword for a new edition of Richard Dillon's 1965 biography, *Meriwether Lewis*, in which Dillon stated about Lewis's death, "Yes it was murder." Ambrose wrote in his foreword:

> "The only reason I have not written his biography [Lewis's] is that Richard Dillon did it first, and his is such a model biography there is no need for another one."

Why did Ambrose use the words "Undaunted Courage" in his title and why did President Jefferson describe his friend as being "of courage undaunted . . . which nothing but impossibilities could divert from its direction" if indeed they thought Meriwether Lewis had committed suicide? It is a contradiction—a person commiting suicide is not "undaunted."

The answer may be they believed that Lewis had "undaunted courage," and that they wished to honor the memory of Meriwether Lewis as a true hero, and leave it to future historians to unravel the cause of his death. It is a mystery, and the only real answer may lie in the exhumation of the famed explorer's remains.

THE CASE FOR THE MURDER OF MERIWETHER LEWIS is made in this last section. It incorporates the new evidence discovered in preparing this book for publication—the identification of General James Wilkinson as being associated with the forgery of the November 26, 1811 document, which is often cited as proof of Meriwether Lewis's suicidal intentions. In the preceeding sections you have read the testimony of expert crime scene investigators and historians and examined the documetary evidence. But, if it was a case of murder—whether or not an exhumation takes place, or the evidence is conclusive—the question remains, for what reason?

The story of the Lewis and Clark Expedition will always endure as a great, exciting adventure story, but it took place against a backdrop of power politics that has yet to be explored. In this account of the last three years of Meriwether Lewis's life, the world in which he lived is revealed, and a case is made for Wilkinson and others as conspirators in Lewis's assassination.

Returning Home
in the Summer of 1806

RETURNING HOME IN THE SUMMER OF 1806, Captains Meriwether Lewis and William Clark and the other members of the Lewis and Clark Expedition were bringing great news—they had explored the vast continent; held councils with over a dozen Indian tribes; and, most importantly, they had reached the mouth of the Columbia River on the Pacific Ocean coast. The official name of the Lewis and Clark Expedition was the "Corps of Volunteers for Northwestern Discovery."

They were an elite, hand-picked, army unit of 27 soldiers and two commanding officers whose mission was to reinforce the American claim to Oregon Country. In 1792, the American ship captain Robert Gray had discovered the mouth of the Columbia on the Pacific Coast. He had sailed up it and named it for his ship *The Columbia*. In 1805-06, expedition members were reinforcing America's claim by keeping travel journals, branding trees, carving their names in rocks, and building Fort Clatsop—all signs of occupying the land, which was the second step in establishing a legal claim to ownership according to international law.

The "Doctrine of Discovery" meant land could be claimed in a "new country" by discovering the mouth of a river, which then entitled the discovering nation to all the land drained by that river. The "Graveyard of the Pacific," the treacherous area at the mouth of the Columbia, had prevented its discovery by British and Russian sailing ships. The Columbia, the largest river in the Pacific Northwest, was the gateway to the lucrative Chinese overseas market for furs and a global trading network for the United States.

Four nations all had vested interests in the Pacific Northwest. The Spanish colonial empire stretched southward from the San Francisco Bay area to the tip of South America. The Russians, who were making enormous profits in the seal and otter skin trade, established a colony in the San Francisco Bay area in 1812. Great Britain, of course, had a colonial empire in Canada, and was challenging the United States for control of the border area from the Great Lakes to Oregon Country. The 49th parallel boundary line, which was settled by a treaty in 1846, finally ended their dispute over the Pacific Northwest.

JEFFERSON'S GOAL OF AN AMERICAN TRANS CONTINENTAL EMPIRE depended upon two things—reinforcing America's legal claim to the Pacific Northwest, and gaining control of the fur trade of the Northern Great Plains. The British had a strong presence in the region. British traders were active in the Pacific Northwest, and they controlled the fur trade through their allies the Blackfeet Indians. If America was going to stretch from "sea to shining sea," the United States had to take control from Britain for the land and commerce on both sides of the Rocky Mountains.

It was up to Meriwether Lewis to inform the Blackfeet that their days of unquestioned dominance over the buffalo plains and beaver streams east of the Rockies were over. Americans were going to supply their enemies with guns and ammunition, and Americans were going to trade for furs with any and all Indian tribes. Most decisively, the Americans planned to build a trading post in the heart of Blackfeet territory at the junction of the Marias and Missouri Rivers.

After crossing the Rocky Mountains, Lewis and Clark had split up to explore the tributaries of the Missouri River. It was the single most dangerous move of the entire expedition. Clark took one group to explore the Yellowstone River, which was the second largest tributary of the Missouri, and Lewis and three companions headed north to explore the Marias River. Lewis wanted to see if he could push the boundary line claim of the United States further north by following the river to its headwaters. At "Camp Disappointment" near Browning, Montana he realized that the headwaters of the Marias lay south of the 49th parallel.

The Marias was in the heart of Blackfeet Indian territory. British Canadian traders on the Saskatchewan River in Canada had been supplying the three Blackfeet tribes with arms and ammunition since the 1750's. The other tribes of the region— the Shoshone, Flathead and Nez Perce—had only a handful of guns. When they hunted buffalo on the plains of Montana east of the Rocky Mountains, they traveled in groups for protection against the Blackfeet.

For thousands of years the Blackfeet had controlled the Northern Great Plains; the Shoshone and Flatheads had lived in the mountain valleys of western Montana; and the Nez Perce had lived west of the mountains in Idaho. The plains were filled with tens of millions of buffalo during their annual migration, covering the landscape as far as the eye could see. When Lewis and Clark met with these rival tribal leaders they promised the American government would supply them with arms and ammunition so that they could safely hunt for food and defend themselves against the Blackfeet.

CAPTAIN LEWIS MET THE BLACKFEET near the Two Medicine River, a tributary of the Marias on July 26th. A party of eight young Piegan, or Blackfeet, Indians had been out on a horse stealing raid. Over the evening campfire he informed them that an American trading post would be established at the junction of the Marias and Missouri Rivers. He wrote that he told them:

> "I had been to the great waters where the sun sets and had seen a great many nations all of whom I had invited to come and trade with me on this side of the mountains."

[also] ". . . that I had come in surch of them in order

to prevail upon them to be at peace with their neighbors particularly those on the West side of the mountains and to engage them to come and trade with me when the establishment is made at the entrance of this river."

The next morning, when the young men attempted to steal the Americans' guns and horses, two of them were killed. Lewis, who had given a peace medal to one of them the night before, wrote that he:

> "left the medal about the neck of the dead man that they might be informed who we were."

To escape pursuit by the Blackfeet, the four men rode as fast as they could for the Missouri River. They rode through immense herds of buffalo for hours, continuing on into the night under stormy moonlit skies. Lewis praised the quality of his Indian horse and estimated they covered 100 miles before they ended their ride at 2 A. M. They awoke at daybreak, and Lewis and the others were so sore they could scarcely stand. But he warned them that:

> "our own lives as well as those of our friends and fellow travelers depended upon our exertions of this moment."

They thought they heard gunfire when they arrived at the Missouri, and after traveling along the river's edge for some miles, they had "the unspeakable satisfaction" to find other members of the expedition bringing down the white pirogue and five smaller canoes. Reunited, they proceeded on to their rendezvous site with Clark and the others at the junction of the Missouri and Yellowstone Rivers.

THE TWO BLACKFEET WHO WERE KILLED by Meriwether Lewis and Reuben Field marked the beginning of more than a quarter of a century of warfare between the Blackfeet and American fur trappers. At least two members of the Lewis and Clark expedition, who returned to trap beaver in

Montana, lost their lives to the Blackfeet: John Potts in 1808 and George Drouillard in 1810. John Colter, Potts's companion, only escaped death by making his famous run for his life.

Over twenty American trappers were killed by the Blackfeet in 1808 alone. The Blackfeet not only wanted to kill them, they were after their beaver pelts, which often represented sizable fortunes, and were traded for ammunition and alcohol with the British traders on the Saskatchewan. The artist Alfred Jacob Miller who traveled in the Far West in 1837 said that the Blackfeet still attacked 40-50 trappers per season.

> "They are the sworn enemies of all—Indians and white men alike. . .Undoubtedly the Blackfeet have the worst reputation for war and aggression of all the Indians of the North-West. Their very name is a terror to most of the Indian tribes."

When Meriwether Lewis ventured into Blackfeet territory he was directly challenging British control of the Northern Plains through their Blackfeet proxies—just as establishing Fort Clatsop on the Pacific Coast challenged the British claim to the Oregon Country. Within a few years, the United States and Great Britain would be at war with each other. The arming of Indians by the British and the encouraging of attacks on Americans was a direct cause of the War of 1812.

MERIWETHER LEWIS WAS SHOT himself while out elk hunting with Pierre Cruzatte on August 11th, 1806. He wrote in his journal:

> "I instantly supposed that Cruzatte had shot me in mistake for an Elk as I was dressed in brown leather and he cannot see very well; under this impression I called out to him, damn you you have shot me"

Lewis spent an uncomfortable month recovering from his wounds, as the rifle ball had passed through both his left thigh and right posterior. He was lucky in that it didn't penetrate the sciatic nerve of his left leg, which would have crippled him for life. The next day Lewis wrote:

> "my wounds felt very stiff and soar this morning but gave me no considerable pain. there was much less inflammation that I had reason to apprehend there would be. I had last evening applied a poltice of peruvian barks."

Two hunters from Illinois were encountered the next day on August 12th; they were the first white men they had seen since leaving the Mandan-Hidatsa Villages in the spring of 1805. Joseph Dixon and Forrest Hancock, who had left the Illinois Country in the summer of 1804, were on their way to Montana to trap beaver. Lewis gave them advice as to the best beaver stream locations, and a "file and a couple of pounds of powder with some lead" before hurrying on to meet up with Clark at the the junction of the Yellowstone and Missouri, their designated rendezvous.

Lewis then wrote his last words on the journey:

> "at 1 P. M. I overtook Capt. Clark and party and had the pleasure of finding them all well. as wrighting in my present situation is extremely painfull to me I shall desist until I recover and leave to my Capt. C. the continuation of our journal."

Clark's journal notes reveal that Dixon and Hancock turned around and returned to the Mandan Villages for a longer visit with them. Private John Colter, an expert hunter, received special permission to leave the expedition and went back west with the two hunters.

The seven Mandan-Hidatsa Villages on the Knife River in today's North Dakota were a prosperous center of trade, with several British traders living there, and a population of about 3,000. It was the home of Sacagawea and her husband Toussaint Charbonneau. After leaving the villages, William Clark realized that he missed their little son, Pompey, tremendously, and he wrote a letter a few days later asking the Charbonneaus to allow him to raise and educate him. He called Pompey "my little danceing boy" and asked them to bring their son, who was then 18 months old, to St. Louis, and requested they stay with him there until he was old enough to leave his mother.

THE MANDAN CHIEF SHEHEKE accompanied the expedition for the rest of their journey. His entourage consisted of his wife and son; and a French-Canadian interpreter, Rene Jessaume, with his Mandan wife and two children. The Mandan Chief had been invited to visit President Jefferson in Washington. The families traveled in two dugout canoes, lashed together with poles, for speed and stability. The Captains called Sheheke, "Big White Chief." He was six feet, ten inches tall and fair skinned. Sheheke means "White Coyote" in the Mandan language. (His portrait appears on page 268.)

The Mandan Indians were a subject of great curiosity around the world—they were thought to be "White Indians," descended from the Welsh Prince Madoc and his followers who—according to legend—had come to Mobile Bay on the Gulf Coast in 1170 A. D. and gradually migrated north along the Mississippi and Missouri Rivers. In the time of Lewis and Clark this was a very popular subject.

Lewis and Clark carried a copy of a map made by John Evans, a Welshman who had traveled to the Mandan Villages in 1796 to see if the Mandans were, indeed, descended from the Welsh. Evans concluded they were not, but his objectivity was questionable because he received money from, and lived as a guest of, the Spanish governor in New Orleans after he returned from his travels. He had originally been sent to investigate the matter by a Welsh nationalist group in England.

"Welsh Indians" had been a hot topic since the time of Queen Elizabeth I. The Queen and her advisors promoted the idea of Welsh Indians in order to make a claim under the Doctrine of Discovery for legal possession of the New World by the English rather than the Spanish. Regardless of whether they were—or were not—of Welsh descent, President Jefferson would have been eager to meet the Mandans. Both he and Meriwether Lewis were of Welsh descent.

William Clark grew up in Louisville hearing about the Welsh Indians. It was a local tradition that the White Indians had lost a major battle with the Red Indians at the Falls of the Ohio, where thousands of human bones had been found on an old battlefield. His brother George Rogers Clark was the leading expert in the west on prehistoric Indians and other studies in the natural sciences. Today, the Falls of the Ohio Interpretive Center has an exhibit displaying ancient armor and coins found in the area of the Falls.

The artist George Catlin visited the Mandan Villages in 1832. In *North American Indians* Letter #13 he wrote extensively about them and stated:

> "Governor Clarke told me before I started for this place that I would find the Mandans a strange people and half white."

The French explorer Verendrye and others also commented on their white appearance. Perhaps DNA testing will reveal some answers. It is interesting that Lewis and Clark kept their opinions to themselves about White Indians—other than referring to Sheheke as "Big White Chief."

THEY FINALLY HEARD NEWS FROM HOME on September 2nd, when they encountered the trader James Aird coming up river. He told them of the "maney Changes & misfortunes" that had occurred since they left the Illinois Country in the spring of 1804. Their friend Pierre Chouteau had lost his house in a fire, and there were a couple of international incidents involving American ships and sailors, but the news that would have the most impact on their lives was this:

> "General Wilkinson was the governor of the Louisiana and at St. Louis 300 of the american Troops had been Contuned on the Missouri a few miles above its mouth. Some disturbance with the Spaniards in the Nackatosh

Country is the Cause of Their being Called down to that Country. . . and that Mr. Burr and Genl. Hambleton fought a Duel, the latter was killed &c. &c."

The news must have been too much to be absorbed. What Meriwether Lewis didn't realize was that for the rest of his all too short life—for the next three years—he would be dealing with these matters. He was 32 years old, and within a few months President Jefferson would appoint him to the post of Governor of Louisiana Territory, replacing General Wilkinson who still remained in command of the United States Army.

It seemed from the news they received that war with Spain might have started on the borderland area of the Sabine River between New Spain (Texas) and the Arroyo Hondo near Natchitoches, Louisiana. ("Nack-a-tosh" is how locals still prounce the name.) But the news wasn't all bad—James Aird generously gave every man on the expedition who smoked enough tobacco to last until they reached St. Louis. He also gave them a barrel of flour which they hadn't tasted in many months, and they gave him six barrels of corn to take up river.

They were near the Big Sioux River and the gravesite of Sergeant Charles Floyd, the only man to die on the expedition. They paid a visit to his grave on the top of the high hill where they had buried him, and found that his grave had been opened. They refilled the grave, and continued on.

THEY WERE ALMOST CAPTURED BY THE SPANISH as they neared the mouth of the Platte River. The Spanish government in New Spain had sent out three previous expeditions to capture "Captain Merry Weather," as they called him—all ending in failure. But their last attempt almost succeeded, as Spanish troops were only 4-5 days march away when the Lewis and Clark Expedition passed the Platte on September 10th.

General Wilkinson had written to the Spanish in March, 1804 proposing that they arrest Lewis and Clark. It was shortly after he presided over official ceremonies taking possession of the Louisiana Purchase for the United States at New Orleans on December 20, 1803. The General—who had been in the pay of Spain since 1787—received $12,000 for a secret report entitled "Reflections on Louisiana'" informing them of the expedition's goal to reach the Pacific Ocean.

The Pawnee Indians stopped the fourth and last attempt by the Spanish to capture "Captain Merry" in late August or early September. When a Spanish military force of about 360 men, headed by Lieutenant Facundo Melgares, arrived at their village on the Republican River near today's Kansas-Nebraska border, they refused to allow him and his troops to continue on with their march to the Missouri River. Yet a few weeks later, when Zebulon Pike arrived with an expedition of about 25 men, they allowed them to continue on their journey west towards Sante Fe. Pike and his men spent almost two weeks at the village, from September 25-October 7th, and learned from French traders who arrived there on October 4th that the Lewis and Clark Expedition was on its way home.

LEWIS AND CLARK WERE MAKING FAST TIME, traveling 78 miles in one day, as they reached the mouth of the Platte River. Clark wrote that everyone was "extremely anxious" to get home to their friends and Country. And he was pleased to report that his "worthy friend can walk and even run nearly as well as ever he Could." The next day, September 10th, they met another trader on the river, who gave them a bottle of whiskey, and told them the news that General Wilkinson and his troops had descended the Mississippi; and that an expedition had set out for the southwest on the Arkansas River under the leadership of Captain Zebulon Pike and Wilkinson's son, Lieutenant James B. Wilkinson.

Now they were meeting trading parties going up river almost every day and continuing to receive gifts of whiskey. Near Leavenworth, Kansas, Clark wrote "Sung Songs until 11 oClock at night in the greatest harmony." Though they were finding it hard going on the Missouri—between the humidity and warm weather they were no longer accustomed to, the mosquitoes, and the sandbars and snags—they were very excited and happy to be arriving home.

CAPTAIN JOHN McCLELLAN was encountered near the Grand River on September 17th. (A few days earlier Lewis and Clark had met an old friend from army days, the trader Robert McClellan.) They stayed up talking "until near mid night." McClellan said they had long ago been given up for dead and were almost forgotten; but that the President had not yet given up hope for their safe return.

He told them that he had recently resigned from the army and was on a "speculative venture" to New Spain. McClellan was, in fact, a business partner of General Wilkinson, and they were going into trade together. He described his intentions as—first, the building of a trading post at the mouth of the Platte; then, the making of friends with the Pawnee and Otoe Indians; and finally using their influence to set up a successful trade with Sante Fe to obtain the "Silver & gold of which those people abound."

For reasons unknown, none of this happened. His real destination may always have been the fur country of the Northwest. Historians believe that McClellan's party went on to become the mysterious group of Americans known to history as the "James Roseman, Zachary Perch/Jeremy Pinch" party who were present in Montana in 1807-1810. It is probably no coincidence that "Zachary Perch" appears to be a word play on the name "Zebulon Pike." None of these names are found in military records, so the signature of Zachary Perch could also have been misread as Jeremy Pinch.

In any event, these names were the aliases of Americans who sent letters to the British trader David Thompson warning him that the region was under American control. Thompson was establishing a trading house for the Northwest Company near Banff, Canada in 1807, when he received two threatening letters, delivered by Indian messengers, dated "Fort Lewis,

Yellow River, Columbia, July 10, 1807" and "Poltitopalton Lake, September 29, 1807." The men were apparently somewhere in the vicinity of Missoula, Montana in the Bitterroot Mountain Valley. The letters charged Thompson with not acknowledging "the authority of Congress over these Countries." The first letter contained regulations governing commerce with the Indians under American rules, written in language very similiar to the language in documents Zebulon Pike was carrying on his expedition to the Southwest. Thompson responded to the second letter saying he had no authority to discuss these matters.

Copies of the letters were found by Hudson Bay Company historians in 1938. It is thought that all the men associated with the mystery group—42 men or more—were killed by Blackfeet Indians in the next few years. Dr. Gary Moulton, the editor of the *Lewis and Clark Journals,* says that three members of the Lewis and Clark Expedition who returned to Montana, are believed to have joined the McClellan party and were later killed. They are Pierre Cruzatte, Joseph Field(s) and John B. Thompson.

THEY WERE CONTENT TO EAT PAWPAWS, a native tree fruit, tasting somewhat like bananas, as they sped home. They still had a few biscuits, and didn't want to waste any time hunting. Clark wrote that when they saw some cows on the bank everyone cheered. That night, on September 20th, they reached the little French village of La Charette, and fired off their guns in a salute—a salute which was returned by the five trading boats docked at the village. The next day they arrived in St. Charles, where they enjoyed a day of feasting and hospitality. On September 22, they visited Fort Belle Fontaine for the first time; the military cantonment on the banks of the Missouri had been established the previous year during their absence. The next morning they took the Chief to the commissary store at the fort and outfitted him with some new clothes.

THEY RECEIVED A "HARTY WELCOM" and were met by "all the village" of St. Louis when they arrived at noon on September 23rd. A letter to a newspaper described them as looking like "Robinson Crusoes." Lewis and Clark were hosted by Pierre Chouteau and his family, and after a short round of visits, they sat down to write letters to be sent off with the waiting post rider. Lewis wrote to the President, and Clark wrote to his brother Jonathan in Louisville, announcing their safe arrival back in St. Louis.

They had survived the perils of the wilderness—would they be able to survive the political perils of the new republic?

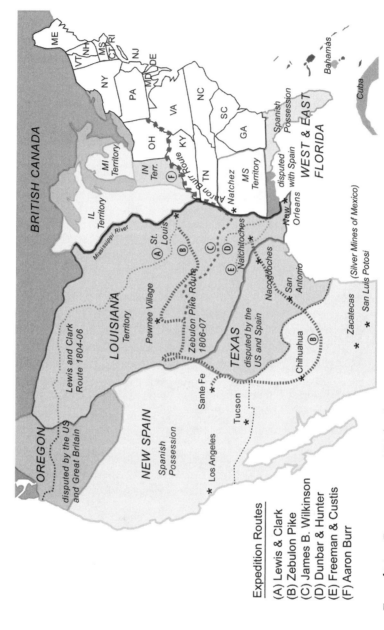

Expedition Routes

Expedition Routes, circa 1804-06

(A) Lewis & Clark
(B) Zebulon Pike
(C) James B. Wilkinson
(D) Dunbar & Hunter
(E) Freeman & Custis
(F) Aaron Burr

The Burr-Wilkinson
Conspiracy

CONSPIRACIES ARE NOT EASILY UNDERSTOOD, and—by their very nature—they are not meant to be. The last three years of Meriwether Lewis's life were often involved with the conspiracies of Aaron Burr and James Wilkinson, and so they will be discussed in this chapter. Lewis must have known the two conspirators rather well. When Burr was the Vice President of the United States, Lewis was President Jefferson's private secretary; and Lewis served as a career army officer on the frontier under General James Wilkinson.

Burr and Wilkinson were always interested in the Spanish territories bordering the United States as a source of riches and power. Their conspiracies may have played a role in two of the great dramas of the early republic—the closely contested presidential election of 1800, and Burr's duel with Hamilton in 1804. It seems likely they were planning to invade Mexico in 1801 if Burr had won the presidency. In 1804, Burr may have killed Hamilton to prevent his rival from competing with him to lead a new invasion scheme with General Wilkinson—the one that became known as the "Burr Conspiracy" or the "Burr-Wilkinson Conspiracy."

THE BURR-WILKINSON CONSPIRACY dominated the news in 1807—far eclipsing news of the return of the Lewis and Clark Expedition. The conspiracy was reaching its final stages as Lewis and Clark were returning home in September of 1806. Burr and Wilkinson were planning to invade Spanish territories in the event of war with Spain and to take possession of the Spanish lands of West and East Florida, Texas, and Mexico. A new, independent empire would be formed with Burr as its ruler.

Several versions of the invasion plot were in circulation.

It was said that the western states would break away and join the new empire—or that Burr's purpose was to establish a new agricultural community on lands near Monroe, Louisiana—or that the British and American navies would lend their support—or that the city of New Orleans would be seized and money plundered from its banks to finance an invasion of Vera Cruz—or that the United States Army would be participating. The country was in a state of high alarm, and many people were anticipating a war with Spain and an invasion of Spanish territories.

GENERAL ANDREW JACKSON hosted a public dinner for Aaron Burr on September 26, 1806 in Nashville. Burr told the guests that Spanish soldiers had invaded American soil east of the Sabine River, and that a war with Spain was imminent. Jackson issued a proclamation for the Tennessee Militia to be ready for duty, and wrote to President Jefferson that Tennessee would be supplying three regiments.

Meanwhile, Burr's fellow conspirator, General Wilkinson was in the process of stopping the impending war with Spain over the Sabine River boundary issues. On September 27th, Spanish commander Lieutenant Colonel Simon de Herrara evacuated his troops from east of the Sabine River, and retreated to the west bank, effectively removing all cause for war. Shortly after this, a messenger arrived from Aaron Burr, bringing a letter in cipher code for Wilkinson detailing plans for the invasion. The General took no action until October 20th when he wrote to President Jefferson disclosing a plot to invade Vera Cruz by a powerful group of unnamed individuals, who would reach New Orleans in December. The General had decided to betray Aaron Burr—that his own future would be better served as an informer. On November 5th, he signed a "Neutral Ground Agreement" with Herrara establishing a neutral border zone area.

HUNDREDS OF VOLUNTEERS were traveling in small groups to join the expedition. They were to rendezvous

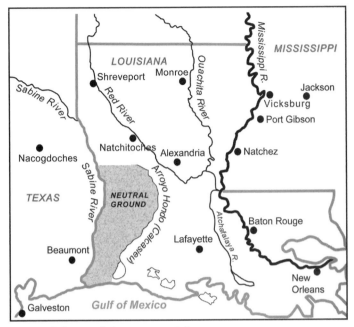

Neutral Ground Agreement Map

The Neutral Ground Agreement was signed between General James Wilkinson and Lieutenant Colonel Simon de Herrara on November 5, 1806. It established the "Sabine Free State" or a "Neutral Strip"—an area that was off limits to the soldiers of both countries, and was not open to settlement. The agreement was not ratified by either government, but endured until the Adams-Onis Treaty established the Sabine River as the boundary line between the two countries in 1821.

The western boundary was the Sabine River and the eastern boundary was the Hondo ("Deep River")—today's Calcasieu River. The southern boundary was the Gulf of Mexico. The area was about 55 miles at its widest and about 110 miles in length. It was an area of wetlands and bayous in the south and pine forests in the north.

The Neutral Strip became a haven for outlaws, fugitive slaves, mixed race people, and filibuster expeditions. The local inhabitants were the few remaining Attakapas Indians. The Lafitte Brothers kept African slave camps for the slave trade here. Their pirate headquarters were on nearby Galveston Island.

at the Red River south of Natchez, Mississippi. Boats were being built up and down the Ohio River. Altogether, there were probably 1,500–2,000 men on the move, planning to join the expedition. Many believed the expedition was secretly supported by the administration. They were being told their final destination was Mexico, but that they would first rendezvous at the Bastrop lands between the Red and Oauchita Rivers.

In early December of 1806, a group of men were assembling on Blennerhassett Island, the home of a wealthy Irish aristocrat, in the middle of the Ohio River near Parkersburg, West Virginia. Fifteen gun boats for the expedition, "ample enough for 500 men," were being built at nearby Marietta, Ohio. However, a messenger from Jefferson informed the Ohio governor of Burr's plans, and on December 9th, local militia seized the boats and a keelboat for provisions. Harmon Blennerhassett and the other conspirators hurriedly left the island the next day.

The events on the island would later form the basis of the federal case against Aaron Burr and his trial for treason in Richmond, Virginia. Burr was not present on the island because he had been undergoing two grand jury investigations in Kentucky. The grand juries were attempting to investigate charges that Burr was planning an invasion of Mexico, but due to lack of witnesses who were willing to testify, he was not indicted.

JEFFERSON ISSUED A PROCLAMATION on November 27th, finally responding to the crisis and warning the country that:

> "sundry persons—are conspiring and confederating together to begin—a military expedition or enterprise against the dominions of Spain."

The President instructed all participants in the expedition to withdraw from the enterprise without delay. Jefferson had been waiting for as long as possible to respond to the conspiracy—he wanted Burr to commit an overt act, so that a charge of treason could be proved against him. The October 20th message from General Wilkinson warning him of the conspiracy forced his hand. He ended up charging an unnamed group of individuals with preparing a filibustering expedition—a lesser offense, but still unlawful. (A filibuster is a unauthorized military expedition into a foreign country to support or start a revolution.)

Blennerhassett and about 30 companions were joined by recruits from the Louisville area as they traveled down river to meet Burr and his Tennessee recruits at the mouth of the Cumberland River. The flotilla consisted of ten boats with a total crew of about 60 men. They were carrying agricultural implements and concealed weapons. Three boats with ammunition had been stopped at Louisville by the authorities.

When the boats reached Fort Massac on the Ohio River, Burr told the fort commander, Daniel Bissell, that he now knew that General Wilkinson had made an agreement with the Spanish commander establishing the "Neutral Ground" area. He had just come from his second visit to Nashville, where his reception from Andrew Jackson had been much cooler.

BURR STILL THOUGH THE CONSPIRACY to seize New Orleans was in place. The plot was that the Mexican Association of New Orleans would turn over the city to Burr in a *coup d'etat*. Burr's stepson, John B. Prevost, was Judge of the Superior Court of New Orleans Territory. Prevost, and other wealthy and influential men, were leaders of a 300 member association whose purpose was to foster a war for Mexican independence. Many American residents in New Orleans were eager to see a revolution begin. On September 23, 1806, the *New Orleans Gazette*, the only English language newspaper, urged:

> "Gallant Louisianians! Now is the time to distinguish yourselves. . . Should the generous efforts of our Government to establish a free, independent republican empire in Mexico be successful, how fortunate, how enviable would

be the situation in New Orleans! The deposit at once of the countless treasures of the South, and the inexhaustible fertility of the Western States, we would soon rival and outshine the most opulent cities of the world."

Historian Thomas Abernethy, author of *The Burr Conspiracy*, says that Burr believed that Wilkinson had arranged for a truce on the Sabine because of orders from the President, but that Burr still expected Wilkinson to arrange for the city's secession.

Burr stopped at Fort Pickering on the Chickasaw Bluffs (now Memphis, Tennessee), where three years later Meriwether Lewis would spend some of the last days of his life. Burr spent a day persuading the only officer at the fort, Lieutenant Jacob Jackson, to resign his commission and return home to Virginia to raise a company to join his expedition. Burr was trying to fill the manpower loss caused by the evacuation of Blennerhassett Island before all the recruits arrived.

On January 10th, 1807, Burr in an advance boat with 12 men, arrived at Bayou Pierre north of Natchez (near Port Gibson, Mississippi). His friend showed him a newspaper featuring the cipher code letter to Wilkinson. He learned that Wilkinson had betrayed him, of the President's proclamation, and that an order for his arrest had been issued by the Governor of Mississippi Territory. The next day he surrendered.

NEW ORLEANS WAS IN A PANIC. General Wilkinson had arrived in the city on November 27th, announcing that Burr was on his way to attack the city with 2,000 men. By the time of Burr's arrest, the General had spent six weeks reinforcing New Orleans' two forts and demanding that Governor William Claiborne and the Orleans Territorial Legislature give him special powers. Denied his request for martial law, he proceeded to do what he wanted to do anyway—he rounded up five fellow conspirators who had arrived in New Orleans, imprisoned them, and shipped them out of the area to Richmond,

Virginia—where they were released due to lack of evidence. The General was in an awkward position. He was trying to prevent what he knew was a real possibility—that Burr's volunteers would be arriving to seize New Orleans—although members of the Mexican Association were denying the existence of any such plan. If Burr had seized control of New Orleans, it was anticipated that an army of 7,000-10,000 men would assemble there to invade Mexico in the spring.

WHAT WERE THE MOTIVES of Burr, Wilkinson and Jefferson in the conspiracy? Why did the President place General Wilkinson and Burr's family members in positions of power in the new territories? Why did Wilkinson betray Burr? Why didn't the war with Spain happen?

Thomas Jefferson must have been anticipating a war with Spain in March, 1805 when he appointed Wilkinson the first Governor of Louisiana Territory; Burr's brother-in-law, Joseph Browne, the first Territorial Secretary of Louisiana; and Burr's stepson, John B. Prevost, the highest ranking Judge in Orleans Territory. Before his appointment Wilkinson had delivered a set of maps of Texas and Mexico to the War Department. Wilkinson continued as Commanding General of the U. S. Army while serving as Governor of Louisiana, reflecting Jefferson's concern for the security of the borderlands area.

During 1804-06, after leaving the Vice-Presidency, Burr had been deep in negotiations with British agents, French exiles, and the Spanish minister, plotting the invasion of Mexico. The British negotiations had come to nothing due to the fall from power of Lord Melville and the death of Sir William Pitt in January, 1806.

In the summer of 1806, Burr was meeting with General Jean Victor Moreau, one of Napoleon's top generals living in American exile; and the Spanish minister to America, the Marquis de Casa Yrujo. Burr's chief of staff for his invasion plans was a French refugee, Colonel Julien De Pestre, who had served in both the French and British armies. De Pestre accompanied Burr on his travels, and stayed loyal to him through his trial for treason, refusing to testify against him.

James Madison, who was serving as Jefferson's Secretary of State, suggested that Yrujo was allied with the French party of Spain, and that this was behind Burr's conspiracy. This is the most likely story—that the final conspiracy plan involved working with French agents to liberate Mexico from Spanish rule. Did Jefferson know that Burr was conspiring with foreign governments? Senator William Plummer (Federalist–New Hampshire) wrote in his journal on January 17, 1807 that he had dined with Jefferson and the President had told him:

> ". . . he did not believe either France, Great Britain, or Spain was connected with Burr in this project, but he tho't the marquiss de Yrujo was—that he had advanced large sums of money to Mr. Burr—and his associates. But he believed Yrujo was duped by Burr. That last winter [1805-06] there was scarse a single night, but that at a very late hour, those two men met & held private conversations. I have since ascertained the fact."

WILKINSON WAS THE PIVOT POINT, and a war with Spain over the Sabine River boundary issue would be the decisive moment. Spanish troops crossed the river in March of 1806. They crossed the river to provoke a war with the United States. Who wanted the war? —Mexican revolutionaries, including army officers, working with French agents, who were relying on the promise of support from the filibustering expedition led by Aaron Burr. What did they hope to achieve? A new country, led by Aaron Burr, which would benefit the commercial interests of New Orleans and others.

General Wilkinson had taken his time responding to the border invasion. On May 16th, orders had been issued for him to proceed to the Sabine "with as little delay as possible," but he didn't head south with his troops until August. He reached

Natchez, Mississippi, 150 miles east of the Sabine River, on September 7th.

Wilkinson spent the summer months organizing two expeditions—the mysterious one with his business partner John McClellan that wound up in the Northwest; and the famous Zebulon Pike Expedition to the Southwest. His own son, James B. Wilkinson, accompanied the Pike Expedition part of the way—leaving before Pike and his companions were captured by the Spanish. Before Wilkinson left St. Louis he wrote a friend that he did not anticipate a war with Spain over the Sabine River.

When the General finally arrived at the Sabine on October 22nd, he was not entirely certain as to whether it would be war or peace. The day before he had sent Thomas A. Smith (the older brother of John Smith T.) off to Jefferson with a message hidden in his boot, which the General hoped would provide cover for himself. Historian Thomas Abernethy remarked about this message:

> "... he said he was enclosing a paper which had fallen into his hands. The louder the Brigadier talked of his honor, the faster President Jefferson should have counted his spoons, for the document enclosed was obviously written by Wilkinson himself."

In any event, General Wilkinson and Lieutenant Colonel Herrara—on their own authority—signed the "Neutral Ground Agreement" on November 5, 1806, thus avoiding war. Herrara was disobeying orders, but Wilkinson was anticipating the orders of Jefferson to avoid war.

Abernethy stated that Herrara had the courage to defy orders from his superiors, who would have been ruined if he had disclosed their complicity in the plot to revolutionize Mexico with French support. Herrara, who had an English wife, had visited the United States and met George Washington, whom he admired greatly. Abernethy also noted that William Simmons, the War Department accountant, reported that Wilkinson received $16,883.12 in October-November, 1806 and January, 1807 in unaccounted for funds.

LIEUTENTANT ZEBULON PIKE and his men were captured by Mexican troops that winter. After Pike's capture, he became a guest under house arrest in Herrara's home in San Antonio. Pike's diary entry for June 13, 1807 noted a conversation between Herrara, who was also Governor of Nuevo Leon Province; Colonel Manuel Cordero, Governor of the Province of Texas, and himself. Herrara told them that after he made his report about the Neutral Ground Agreement that—

> "Until an answer was received... I experienced the most unhappy period of my life, conscious that I had served my country faithfully, at the same time that I had violated every principle of military duty. At length the answer arrived, and what was it, but the thanks of the viceroy and the commandant-general for having pointedly disobeyed their orders, with assurances that they would represent his services in exalted terms to the king [of Spain]."

Pike and his men returned to the United States under military escort two weeks later, on July 1st.

TWO OTHER POSSIBLE CONSPIRACIES preceded the famous filibuster expedition of 1806, and both involve other famous episodes in American history—the Burr-Hamilton duel of 1804, and the famous close election in 1801 between Burr and Jefferson for the presidency of the United States.

In 1801, the election of the third president of the United States hung in balance that winter. Due to a tie vote in the electoral college between Thomas Jefferson and Aaron Burr, the House of Representatives became responsibile for choosing who would become president. The second highest vote getter would become the Vice-President under laws existing at that time. It took a week of balloting, and finally on the 36th ballot, Jefferson was declared the winner on February 17, 1801.

IF BURR HAD WON THE ELECTION OF 1800 would an invasion of Spanish territories have taken place? It is quite possible, and that an invasion would have used the troops stationed at Cantonment Wilkinsonville near Cairo, Illinois and the junction of the Ohio and Mississippi Rivers. On January 5, 1801 about 700 soldiers arrived at Wilkinsonville. Approximately 1,000-1,500 men were stationed there during its peak occupancy between March and August, 1801.

Six or seven of these soldiers later joined the Lewis and Clark Expedition: Sergeant Patrick Gass; Privates Thomas Proctor Howard, Hugh McNeal, John B. Thompson, Joseph Whitehouse, Richard Windsor, and perhaps Silas Goodrich. A cantonment is a military camp without fortifed walls. In recent years the site has been the subject of archeological digs and research conducted by Southern Illinois University.

The contractor at the cantonment, John R. Williams— who later became the first Mayor of Detroit—wrote about the possibility of the cantonment being used as a staging ground for an invasion of Spanish territory in an 1845 letter:

> "Mr. Jefferson having been elected President of the U. S. The policy of the Government changed instead wresting the posts on the west bank of the Mississippi by force of Arms as was previously contemplated—They were eventually obtained by peaceable & Successful negociation."

In March, 1802 the U. S. Army numbered about 3,500 soldiers, so the troops stationed at Cantonment Wilkinsonville represented between 28-42% of the total strength of the army. The troops served a definite military purpose during a very unstable time in the Mississippi Valley, regardless of any plans to invade Texas. Napoleon was intending to take back the Mississippi Valley and Louisiana in 1801-02, but over 50,000 French soldiers died of yellow fever while they were fighting the slave rebellion in San Domingo. It was their deaths which persuaded Napoleon to sell Louisiana to the United States in 1803; in 1804 San Domingo gained its independence and became known as Haiti.

THE PHILIP NOLAN EXPEDITION TO TEXAS was most likely a filibuster unit tied to invasion plans from Cantonment Wilkinsonville. Nolan was a young Irishman who had lived in Wilkinson's household as a teenager. He made several long trips into Texas, to catch wild horses, and was famous for his strength and daring. He also made maps during these trips—and it was his maps that Wilkinson delivered to the War Department in the winter of 1804-05.

In December, 1801, Nolan led a filibuster of 25 men into Texas where they built a stronghold of small forts and mustang corrals in the Hill Country of Texas (near Blum, Texas south of Dallas). On March 21st, 1801 Nolan was killed by Spanish soldiers. It was two weeks after the inauguration of President Jefferson. Nolan was the only man killed, though others were jailed and some escaped. One of the men who escaped, Robert Ashley, later helped Aaron Burr in his attempt to escape capture by Wilkinson's men in 1807.

ONE MORE INDICATION of an early Burr-Wilkinson Conspiracy is a statement by J. H. Daviess, the District Attorney in Kentucky who instigated the grand jury investigations of Aaron Burr in 1806. He was a staunch Federalist, who attempted several times to warn President Jefferson of the Burr-Wilkinson Conspiracy. In gathering evidence to confirm his suspicions he met with General Wilkinson. Daviess wrote in his book, *A View of the President's Conduct Concerning the Conspiracy of 1806*, published in 1807, that the General was showing him some maps of New Mexico when—

"... after some conversation about it, tapping it with his finger, told me in a very low and very significant tone and manner, that 'had Burr been president, we would have had all this country before now.'"

THE BURR-HAMILTON DUEL may have been connected to the same type of conspiracy plans. Historian Thomas Fleming in his book, *Duel: Alexander Hamilton, Aaron Burr and the Future of America*, provided some convincing evidence that General Wilkinson was considering both Alexander Hamilton and Aaron Burr as potential partners for him in a new invasion plan for Mexico. The two men were bitter enemies, and Fleming speculates that Burr killed Hamilton to prevent his taking his place with Wilkinson in the scheme which became known as the Burr-Wilkinson Conspiracy of 1806.

The duel occurred on July 11, 1804 while Burr was still serving as the Vice President of the United States. Hamilton had been Secretary of the Treasury under George Washington, and had served as de facto commander of the army under Washington in 1798-01 during the Quasi-War with France. Hamilton and Wilkinson had made the plans for Cantonment Wilkinsonville together.

On May 23, 1804, less than two months before the Burr-Hamilton duel, General Wilkinson had sent Aaron Burr a very confidential note:

"To save time of which I need much and have little, I propose to take a bed with you this night, if it may be done without observation or attention—Answer me and if in the affirmative I will be with [you] at 30 after the 8th hour."

The subject of their meeting may have been the same as that which Wilkinson had written about in a letter to Alexander Hamilton on March 26th. Wilkinson invited Hamilton to come to New Orleans, adding that:

> "I would give a Spanish Province for an In-
> terview with you. My topographical of the S.
> West is now compleat. The infernal designs of
> France are obvious to me, & the destinies of
> Spain are in the Hands of the U. S."

During the Quasi-War with France, which was an undeclared war fought entirely at sea in 1798-01, Hamilton had been eager to make a pre-emptive strike against the Spanish territories of the two Floridas and Texas in the event of an expanded war with France. When John Adams negotiated a peace truce with France in September, 1800, it ended their plans.

THERE WERE MANY SUCH PLANS during these years of the early republic. The first presidents skillfully negotiated the survival of the American Republic in a time of the Napoleonic world wars between the European powers. France and Great Britain wanted to regain their former control of the Mississippi Valley, and Spain wanted to hold onto its power as long as possible.

There were many attempts to fragment the United States and establish separate governments. But of all the early plotters Aaron Burr and James Wilkinson posed the greatest threats. Aaron Burr—because he was connected on a high level with leaders around the world and was capable of starting a new government—was probably the greater threat.

The Spanish Empire was in the process of breaking up, and its colonies in the New World were seen as prizes to be taken. Great Britain and France were both interested in fostering revolutions in the colonies. If Jefferson didn't keep Burr and Wilkinson busy, others might. And, as always, changing politics and fortunes of war shifted everyone's plans.

Neither Burr nor Wilkinson was ever viewed as "trustworthy" by government leaders. But they both had an uncanny ability to land on their feet despite whatever threatened their survival. Jefferson had decided to remove Wilkinson from his command of the U. S. Army, and had already removed him from his post as Governor of Louisiana Territory in the last months of 1806, when the Lewis and Clark Expedition was returning home. The General had been alerted by a Senator friend that he would lose his military appointment in the next session of Congress. It was undoubtedly a deciding factor in his decision to betray Aaron Burr.

Jefferson believed that the Spanish territories would fall into the hands of the United States without war. He was determined to stop Burr's plans to establish a rival empire in the southwest. He believed that the two Floridas and Texas could be acquired by negotiation and purchase rather than war.

WHEN BURR SURRENDERED at Bayou Pierre on January 11, 1807 he chose to surrender in Mississippi Territory rather than Orleans Territory where Wilkinson held power. Wilkinson wanted to try Burr in a military court. Instead, Burr's trial was conducted in a civil court at the small territorial capital of Washington, Mississippi a few miles north of Natchez. He and his men were entertained at dinners and balls by the local residents, and many of his followers settled in the area.

On February 4th, a grand jury packed with Federalists absolved him of all charges. Local residents were satisfied that Burr's only aim was to invade Spanish territories, not to cause a break up of the western states. But after the trial was over, Burr was still held on bond, despite the fact he wasn't indicted.

Wilkinson sent six men armed with pistols and dirks to seize him. They had no warrants or criminal charges in their orders. Burr, fearing for his life, forfeited his $5,000 bond and disappeared into hiding the day after his hearing. A $2,000 reward was offered for his capture. The Governor of Mississippi Territory announced he was a fugitive from justice, and the former Vice President of the United States was now on the run.

Burr was captured on February 18th in the company of

Robert Ashley near Mobile, Alabama. They were on their way to Pensacola, Florida. Spanish officials from Pensacola had visited Burr while he was in jail in Washington, Mississippi. Burr was put under arrest at Fort Stoddert (30 miles north of Mobile), and Major Ashley once again escaped from capture. An attack on Mobile and Pensacola, supported by local revolutionaries was undoubtedly being planned, until the commander of the fort decided to send his famous prisoner on his way.

On March 5, 1807, Aaron Burr was taken from Fort Stoddert under military escort to Richmond, Virginia where he would stand trial for treason.

Back East—1807

UPON THEIR RETURN TO ST LOUIS, Lewis's role as the true commander of the expedition now became apparent—he was responsible for the financial reports; discharging and paying the expedition members; delivering the artifacts they had collected to the President; bringing the Mandan Chief and his entourage to Washington; and publishing the account of their journey. William Clark, on the other hand, was anticipating spending time with his family in Louisville, and going to Fincastle, Virginia to woo his young sweetheart Julia Hancock.

Immediately after reaching St. Louis, on September 23, 1806, Lewis sent off a lengthy and detailed report to Jefferson describing the geography and fur trade potential of the country they had explored. He provided a copy of the report for Clark to send to his brother Jonathan in Louisville. It was expected that the report would be published in the newspapers, and that Clark's letter would become the first notice of the safe return of the expedition and what they had found.

For the next month they stayed in St. Louis awaiting the arrival of Pierre Chouteau and a delegation of Osage Chiefs who were going to travel east with them; attending to paperwork; and enjoying the hospitality of their friends. They also heard a lot of disturbing news about government affairs in St. Louis.

The wealthy French residents of St. Louis had petitioned President Jefferson to appoint Aaron Burr's brother-in-law, Joseph Browne, the new Governor of Louisiana Territory. Browne, the Territorial Secretary, became the Acting Governor after Wilkinson left on his long-delayed departure for the Sabine River on August 16th. The petition, submitted by Auguste Chouteau on July 15th, praised General Wilkinson in the most extravagant language, the petitioners stating that:

" their warm approbation, their unshaken confidence, and their firm attachment have been often expressed [regarding Wilkinson]. . . the virtues of his heart, equalled only by the excellence of his Judgement, his unvarying and steady defense of the cause of Justice and truth, his unwearied assiduity in public service, and the crowd of envious and busy detractors, who have only served to illustrate the purity of his character. . . his purposed departure from this Territory throws a gloom over their prospects, and causes the same emotions as when a child is about to be deprived of the presence of a beloved father. . ."

More than likely the General wrote it himself for the petitioners' signatures, as it has that "Wilkinsonian" style of expression. If Wilkinson wasn't going to return to St. Louis, then the petitioners wanted Joseph Browne to be named the new Governor—whose "integrity of principles" eminently qualified him for the office.

However, Judge John B. C. Lucas, one of three members of the board of land commissioners, Will Carr, the federal land agent, and Silas Bent, the newly arrived federal land surveyor, were all writing very different letters to Washington—and, based on their reports, it was determined that a new administration was needed in Louisiana Territory.

Judge Lucas complained that his two fellow land commissioners were meeting at irregular times and places without him and were not keeping proper records. Both men, James Donaldson and Clement Biddle Penrose, were loyal supporters of Wilkinson; in addition, Penrose was Wilkinson's nephew. Lucas was refusing to confirm large land claims which greatly exceeded the legal limit of the 800 arpents granted to settlers under Spanish law.

Under Spanish rule, very few completed land titles had been established, as the process was long and difficult. Then there was the two year period from 1801-1803 when France had secretly owned Louisiana. In the old days, local residents hadn't much cared about legal niceties. Most French villagers had three kinds of land: residential lots in town, grazing land for their animals, and agricultural lots in the common fields. They simply agreed among themselves about working claims in the lead mine district. With the advent of American land speculators, settlers, and the land claims commission, there was a great rush to acquire titles. The process was exceedingly slow and aggravating for both large and small land claimants.

Judge Lucas, a friend of Albert Gallatin, the Secretary of the Treasury, doggedly insisted on following the letter of the law. Will Carr, the federal agent for the lead mine district—who was a friend of Meriwether Lewis's—supported Judge Lucas in his opposition to the large land claimants. The new land surveyor, Silas Bent (father of the famous Bent Brothers in the southwestern fur trade), reported missing and altered land records to his superiors in Washington.

By January, 1807—after Lewis had reached Washington—President Jefferson had had enough. He wrote to Albert Gallatin that he "had never seen such a perversion of duty as by Donaldson & Penrose" and fired Donaldson, who was also the Registrar of Land Titles. Before they had left St. Louis, Judge Rufus Easton had asked Lewis and Clark to inspect the land records and inform the administration about the "innumerable alterations and forgeries!" Since territories were administered by the federal government, both land titles and the soon to be enacted mineral leasing rights for the lead mine district were subject to congressional politics and approval.

LEWIS AND CLARK LEFT FOR WASHINGTON in late October. The group traveling together was a large one, consisting of Lewis and his dog Seaman; Clark and his slave York; Chief Big White and his wife and son; the Chief's interpreter Rene Jessaume and his wife and two children; two members of the expedition, Sgt. John Ordway and Private Francis

Labiche, who came along to help out; and Indian Agent Pierre Chouteau escorting a delegation of six chiefs from the Arkansas band of the Osage. Peter Provenchere was also most likely in the group.

The group would split up in Kentucky. Chouteau took the Osage Chiefs to Washington via the Ohio River, heading north. Big White and his group, accompanied by Ordway and Labiche, remained with Meriwether Lewis.

Lewis and Clark enjoyed the hospitality of the extended Clark family in Louisville. On November 8th, a dinner party was held at Locust Grove, the home of Clark's sister Lucy and her husband William Croghan. Now a National Historic Landmark, Locust Grove became the home of their brother General George Rogers Clark during the last years of his life. William Clark remained in Louisville until December 15th, but Lewis and his group traveled south on the Wilderness Road through Kentucky to the Cumberland Gap, the historic gateway of the Allegheny Mountains.

AFTER PASSING THROUGH THE GAP, Lewis, at the request of local citizens in Fincastle, made a survey of the latitude of the boundary line between the states of Virginia and North Carolina. The line, known as the Walker Line, lay a couple of miles east of the Gap. He reported on November 23rd that the boundary was "nine miles and 1,077 yards North of its proper position," giving the state of Virginia those extra miles—a nice present to his home state.

Upon arriving at his mother's house in Charlottesville, Lewis found a letter waiting for him from the President urging him to pay a visit to nearby Monticello with Big White and the others even though Jefferson was in Washington. Jefferson was preparing a "kind of an Indian Hall" at Monticello, displaying artifacts from the Mandans and other Indian tribes and he wanted Lewis and Big White to see it. By December 28th, Lewis and his party had reached Washington.

Clark would arrive in Washington about two weeks later,

missing a party held in their honor on January 14th. Clark spent the holidays at Fincastle, where another party had been held on January 8th. He was courting Julia Hancock and obtained her family's consent that they would be married one year later, in January, 1808. Julia, who was born November 21, 1791, had just celebrated her 15th birthday; Clark was 36 years old—a not uncommon arrangement in those days.

BACK IN ST. LOUIS, JOHN SMITH T. was preparing to go down river with 12,000 pounds of lead to join the Aaron Burr conspiracy. Lead was used to make bullets, a vital necessity for any invasion of Mexico. Colonel De Pestre, Burr's chief of staff, had come to St. Louis in October, offering commissions in the new army. A disgusted Auguste Chouteau threw the commission in the fire when it was offered to him.

John Smith T. (the "T" stood for Tennessee); Joseph Browne's son-in-law, Robert Westcott; Dr. Andrew Steele, and the Sheriff of Ste. Genevieve, Henry Dodge, set out to join Burr with their cargo of lead, but upon reaching New Madrid, they learned about the President's proclamation of November 27th declaring Burr's expedition illegal, and they abandoned their plans. When they got back to Ste. Genevieve, Judge Otho Shrader—a friend of Meriwether Lewis's—had Smith T. and Dodge arrested on charges of treason. After Dodge was arrested, he beat up nine of the grand jury members, and Smith T. threatened to kill Shrader if he tried to arrest him—ending the matter of arrest for both men.

Smith T. was a relative of General Wilkinson. His mother's name was Lucy Wilkinson Smith; the family came from Essex County, Virginia near Wilkinson's birthplace in Calvert County, Maryland. Smith T. was infamous as a killer; he was reputed to have killed 15-20 men in duels. He was a small man, who usually dressed in heavily fringed and decorated buckskin shirts and doeskin pants. He always carried four pistols, one dirk (a dagger), and a rifle called "Hark from the Tombs." Wilkinson appointed Smith T. a Judge of the Court of Common Pleas in

Ste. Genevieve, where he heard his cases fully armed.

John F. Darby, the Mayor of St. Louis in 1835, said of John Smith T. that he was:

> "as polished and courteous a gentleman as ever lived in the state of Missouri, and as mild mannered a man as ever put a bullet in a human body."

Smith T. was a major land speculator in the southeastern United States. He had participated in the Yazoo land frauds, owning the northern half of the state of Alabama among other large land holdings. He moved to Missouri to speculate in the lead mine district, purchasing a wild card "floating claim" to 10,000 arpents, giving him the right to claim about 13 square miles of land wherever he wanted. He would send in armed men to illegally seize working claims, and employ lawyers to contest these claims in court.

He was up against Moses Austin (the father of Stephen Austin, the founder of Texas). Austin was a lead mine operator from Virginia, who introduced a new smelting technique, a reverberatory furnace, to the lead mine district south of St. Louis. Austin proposed paying taxes on minerals dug from the land, and providing smelting services to the government. Captain Amos Stoddard had estimated the value of the lead mine district as being able to pay off the fifteen million debt for the purchase of Louisiana within a few years. It was the richest known deposit of lead ore in the world, and was reserved as public land under the new American government.

John Smith T., however, wanted to use the lead for bullets for an invasion of Mexico. If the invasion had proceeded as planned, many volunteers would have come from the St. Louis area. Both Moses Austin and John Smith T. employed private armies and lawyers to defend their land claims in the lead district's "Mineral Wars."

MERIWETHER LEWIS WAS APPOINTED the new Governor of Louisiana Territory on March 3, 1807. William

Clark received appointments as Agent of Indian Affairs for Louisiana and Brigadier General of the Territorial Militia. On the same day, Congress passed the Lead and Salt Leasing Act of 1807, placing both the lead and salt petre mines under 3 year leasing provisions. (Saltpetre is used in making gun powder.)

Lewis had to remain on the east coast, finishing up government paperwork and making arrangements for the publication of the expedition journals. He wrote to William Clark on March 13th, sending Clark's commission as Brigadier General to him at Fincastle in care of Robert Frazer, a member of the expedition. Frederick Bates, who had been appointed the new Territorial Secretary, would serve as Acting Governor until Lewis arrived in St. Louis. Both Clark and Bates arrived in St. Louis in late April. Lewis wrote that Clark and Bates should:

> ". . . take such measures in relation to the territory as will be best calculated to destroy the influence and wily machinations of the adherents of Col. Burr. It is my wish that every person who holds an appointment of profit or honor in that territory and against whom sufficient proof of the infection of Burrism can be adduced, should be immediately dismissed from office, without partiality favor or affection, as I can never make any terms with traitors. Mr. Robert Waistcoat, son in law to Secretary Brown, Col. John T. Smith and Mr. Dodge sherif of the district St Genvieve are high implicated and there is good reason for believing that Mr. Brown himself might be sensured without injustice."

LEWIS WAS IN PHILADELPHIA from April to July, visiting with old friends, meeting girls, and reporting about their travels and discoveries to the mentors who four years earlier had helped prepare him for the expedition. He engaged a publisher and issued an advertising prospectus for the journals. He attended the monthly meetings of the American

Philosophical Society; arranged for the plant specimens to be described and sketched; and gave bird specimens to his friend Alexander Wilson to paint.

Lewis probably came to Philadelphia accompanied by Pierre Chouteau and the Osage Indians, and Ordway, Labiche, Provenchere, and Big White's party, because the French artist Charles St. Memin sketched profiles of Lewis, Big White and his wife, Yellow Corn, and an Osage warrior with the aid of his physiognotrace. (Two of the portraits are seen on pp. 267-68.) The Indians were on their way back home, stopping at several cities en route.

Lewis sat for his famous portrait by Charles Willson Peale—the one that matches the portrait of William Clark, whose portrait was painted by Peale in 1810 (p. 282). Peale had a museum on the second floor of Independence Hall, where he displayed the artifacts collected by Lewis and Clark, and where the little prairie dog and magpie bird captured by Lewis and Clark were living. Jefferson had sent them to Peale, writing that the burrowing squirrel was a "most harmless and tame creature."

While Lewis was in Philadelphia, Peale was busy mounting and sketching the animal specimens they had collected. Later that year he created a life size wax figure of Captain Lewis to display in his museum; it was dressed in a fringed buckskin outfit, and wore the tippet or shoulder cape decorated with 140 ermine skins given to Lewis by Sacagawea's brother, Cameahwait, the Chief of the Shoshone. Lewis called it the most elegant Indian clothing he had ever seen. (See portrait, p. 269.) Springtime in Philadelphia must have been delightful, offering a few months of pleasure and intellectual companionship before Lewis returned to Washington in July.

MEANWHILE, BURRITES IN ST. LOUIS were not happy with the change of government. Robert Frazer, a member of the expedition, who had been supplying information about the Burrites in St. Louis, wrote to President Jefferson from Henderson County, Kentucky on April 16, 1807:

> "At Breckenridge court house I was informed of a number of inquiries that some of the party (dispatched to overtake & wrest from me my papers) had been making relative to my business at Washington. . . I also learned from a gentleman of high respectability, directly from St. Louis that Colo. John Smith (T) will not suffer himself to be taken by the civil authority; but has threatened and reviled me with the harshest and most bitter epithets.
>
> From this man's character as a desperado & from the servility of a vile and desperate junto of which he is the head, I really think I am in no small danger of assassination, or some other means of taking me off.
>
> I delivered the commission with which I was charged to Genl. Clark at Fincastle. He could not travel as fast as I did and therefore advised me to proceed as quick as possible. Whatever may be the fate I shall meet with, I have the [. . .] consolation to that I have been [. . .] true to my country. And whatever may be the temptation I trust I shall perish sooner than prove otherwise."

Frazer went on to write that his friends told him to ride for his "personal safety" by way of Vincennes.

Frederick Bates, the Acting Governor, wrote to Jefferson on May 6th that Colonel John Smith T. "had been removed from all his offices civil and military" and other known Burrites had also left office. However, he believed Ste. Genevieve Sheriff Henry Dodge to be "young and innocent." Dodge went on to become the first Territorial Governor of Wisconsin in 1836, justifying Bates's faith in him.

RETURNING THE MANDAN DELEGATION to their homes in North Dakota was Clark's first priority. Originally it was intended that Ensign Nathaniel Pryor and 14 soldiers would escort the Mandan group, together with a group of 32 traders led by Auguste Pierre Chouteau, Pierre's son, back to the Knife River Villages. Then 15 Sioux warriors turned up in St. Louis with trader Pierre Dorion, and it was decided to add the Sioux and Dorion's trading group, and an additional military escort, to the return expedition. Big White thought it would be helpful to travel together. Altogether there were between 102 and 108 people, including 32 Indians—18 men, 8 women, and 6 children. Three former members of the Corps of Discovery were part of the expedition: Ensign Nathaniel Pryor, George Shannon and, most likely, Joseph Field.

On September 9th, they met with unexpected trouble when they arrived at the picketed Arikara earth lodge villages, guarding both sides of the Missouri River in South Dakota. They learned the Arikara were at war with the Mandans, and were still upset their chief had died while visiting Washington the year before. They were traditional middle men on the Upper Missouri, trading their crops with Indians who hunted.

Manuel Lisa and his trading group, including other former members of the Corps of Discovery, had passed the Arikara Villages a few weeks earlier. The Arikara and their Sioux allies had looted them of half their trade goods, and determined to kill them on their return. Lisa told them that Pryor's trading party would be along to supply them with more goods.

The Arikara were going to allow Pryor's boat carrying the Indians and soldiers to continue on, but they wanted the boat with trade goods to stay. Twenty one year old Auguste Chouteau was not willing to part with his goods on unfavorable terms—he offered to trade only half of them, and refused to give any presents. A council was attempted and the two interpreters were on shore when a battle began.

There were 650 Arikara and Sioux warriors—all armed with guns—when shots were fired. The battle continued for about an hour, with fighting on both sides of the river. Chouteau lost 4 men—one was still alive, but mortally wounded. He had six more wounded. Pryor had three wounded, including George Shannon, who eventually lost his leg due to this encounter and who would wear a wooden peg leg for the rest of his life. The expedition retreated to St. Louis, and it would be two years before they tried again to return the Mandan delegation to their villages. Nathaniel Pryor ended his report to Clark with the observation that:

> "A force of less than 400 men ought not to attempt such an enterprize. And surely it is possible that even one thousand men might fail in the attempt."

Two years later Meriwether Lewis as Governor would be judged harshly by the bureaucrats in Washington, because they didn't understand, or care about, the difficulties in returning the Chief to his home.

AARON BURR'S TRIAL FOR TREASON was held in the Virginia State House in Richmond, Virginia—in the same Hall of Delegates where Meriwether Lewis's bust would be placed in 2008. The trial began on May 22, 1807, presided over by the Chief Justice of the United States John Marshall.

General Wilkinson finally arrived after a long delay; and on June 15th, behind closed doors, a grand jury began questioning him and 47 other witnesses regarding the General's relationship with Aaron Burr. The General talked for four days himself. No record was kept of their testimonies. But by a vote of 9 to 7, Wilkinson escaped indictment for not reporting knowledge of a treasonous plot ("misprision of treason").

The jury based its decision on the fact that the overt act of treason was supposed to have been committed on Blennerhassett's Island, and that General Wilkinson had not been present. The foreman of the grand jury, Congressman John Randolph of Roanoke, Virginia, who detested Wilkinson, wrote to a friend :

> "The mammoth of iniquity has escaped...

Wilkinson is the only man I ever saw who is from the bark to the very core a villain. The proof is unquestionable; but, my good friend, I cannot enter upon it here. Suffice it to say that I have seen it, and that it is not susceptible of misconstruction."

The problem was that if Wilkinson was indicted, he would be viewed as bearing the greatest responsibility for the plot because of the widespread suspicion that he was a pensioner of Spain. Wilkinson's indictment not only would discredit Jefferson's administration, it would also shift the blame from Burr. Above all else, Jefferson wanted to permanently destroy Burr's dreams of establishing a new empire.

Major James Bruff had come from St. Louis in March to warn the Secretary of War General Henry Dearborn about Wilkinson being a pensioner of Spain and an accomplice of Burr. The Secretary told the Major that although the General had recently lost favor with the administration, his energetic actions in New Orleans had restored him to favor. He added:

"that after the actual bustle was over there might perhaps be an inquiry, but meanwhile, Wilkinson must and would be supported."

This, in fact, did happen. Wilkinson underwent a military court of inquiry in 1808, two congressional hearings in 1810, and two military courts martial in 1811 and 1815. However, he was cleared in all of these investigations.

The grand jury did present bills of treason and high misdemeanor against Aaron Burr, Harmon Blennerhassett, and four others. The trial would begin on August 3rd. Meriwether Lewis arrived back in Washington on July 15th, and attended the trial as an observer for President Jefferson, though neither he nor the President left any paper trail. The jury was seated on August 17th.

The Constitution of the United States states that:

"no person shall be convicted of treason unless on the

testimony of two witnesses to the same overt act, or on confession in open court."

The Chief Justice ruled on the last day of August that no testimony regarding Burr's conduct elsewhere, or afterwards, could be admitted as evidence. The case was dependent upon two witnesses testifying they had witnessed an overt act by Burr within the jurisdiction of the court hearing the case, that is, in the state of Virginia. (At this time, Blennerhassett Island in West Virginia was still a part of Virginia.) The jury delivered a verdict of "not guilty" on September 1st.

President Jefferson demanded that the testimony of the trial, which had not been recorded, be put in writing in order to submit it to Congress; and that no witness would be paid or allowed to leave until their testimony was taken. So the Burr trial now switched to the charge of high misdemeanor and continued until October 19th with testimonies being recorded. If Aaron Burr couldn't be convicted of treason, then Jefferson wanted to impeach John Marshall. However, once it became apparent that Wilkinson's involvement would ruin any chance of impeachment, the matter was dropped and all further charges were not pursued.

Burr's reputation was thoroughly ruined—at least in terms of running for public office. He left the country, and for four years tried unsuccessfully to persuade the British government and then the French government to back his plans for an invasion of Mexico. He returned to New York and continued his practice of law until his death in 1836. Other plans for an invasion and the revolutionizing of Mexico went on without him.

Meriwether Lewis most likely spent his spare time during the three month trial writing a very long report entitled:

"Observations and reflections on the present and future state of Upper Louisiana, in relation to the government of the Indian nations inhabiting that country, and the trade and intercourse with the same."

It was a detailed and thoughtful analysis of the relationships of the Indian tribes with Spanish and British traders, and what Lewis would recommend as the new Governor of Louisiana Territory and Superintendent of Indian Affairs.

PERSONAL MATTERS OCCUPIED LEWIS over the next few months. He was at the family home in Albemarle County by November 3rd, where he wrote a letter to his friend Mahlon Dickerson in Philadelphia, asking him to loan some money for living expenses to Lewis's young stepbrother, John H. Marks, who was going to Philadelphia to study medicine. Lewis was paying his tuition, and would repay the additional money needed. He gossiped about his "little affair" with an unidentified young woman which had not worked out, and said,

> "What may be my next adventure god knows, but on this I am determined to get a wife."

Soon he was off to St. Louis, accompanied by his younger brother, Reuben Lewis, his new valet, John Pernier, and Seaman the dog, his ever faithful companion. William Clark had alerted his friend to a potential matrimonial prospect, 16 year old Letitia Baldridge, who lived in Fincastle. The Lewis brothers both thought she was lovely, but Letitia fled to her beau in Richmond, whom she married six months later.

The Lewis brothers stopped over in eastern Kentucky to look after various land holdings owned by their family which took several weeks to investigate. Finally, they arrived in St. Louis in early March, 1808.

St. Louis, 1808–09

LEWIS FOUND A NEWSPAPER PUBLISHER named Joseph Charless in Louisville, Kentucky who was willing to relocate his printing business to St. Louis. An announcement was published in the Louisville newspaper—

> "Those who wish to subscribe to the *Missouri Gazette* are respectively informed that a subscription book is open at this Office. A capable Editor is employed, and a number of Gentlemen have volunteered to devote their leasure hours in writing on such subjects as will enrich its columns. Essays on Indian antiquity, Mines, Minerals, and an acount of the Fur-Trade, with Topographical scetches will be diligently sought after."

Grace Lewis Miller, who devoted much of her life to the study of Meriwether Lewis, argues persuasively that Lewis purchased the printing press and type with his own money before leaving the east coast, knowing there was a great need for a territorial newspaper and for printing the territorial laws. Lewis received double pay for his two and a half years on the expedition, and apparently became a silent partner in the printing business with Joseph Charless. The Ramage printing press from Philadelphia arrived in St. Louis in the same boat bringing newlyweds William and Julia Clark.

Charless and his assistant must have come with the press, because the first issue of the *Missouri Gazette* was printed on July 12, 1808. Lewis advanced Charless $225; loaning him $100, and giving him $125 in subscription fees he had collected from the Chouteau brothers and others. On July 22nd he advanced him another $500 to buy paper to print the territorial laws, and Charless returned to Louisville to obtain the paper and relocate his family.

WILLIAM CLARK had left the territory in August of 1807, and spent several weeks collecting over 300 mammoth and other fossil bones at Big Bone Lick in Kentucky for Jefferson. He was gone for almost a year before returning to St. Louis with his new bride on July 2, 1808.

They settled into one of the nicest homes in St. Louis, rented by Meriwether Lewis, who offered to share it with them. Located at Main and Spruce Streets, the four room house was too small; even if it did have wall paper and oil paint on the walls. Soon after they arrived, Lewis moved into bachelor quarters next door. The Clarks had brought William's 18 year old niece Ann to keep Julia company, but Ann went back to Kentucky in the fall. Sixteen year old Julia was pregnant with their first child, a boy who would be named Meriwether Lewis Clark when he was born on January 10, 1809.

Clark's slave York came to St. Louis against his will, leaving his wife and family behind in Louisville. The Clarks brought nine or more slaves west, including a brother, sister, and nephew of York's. They were all unhappy about leaving Louisville, and Clark hired most of them out to work for others. He complained about their bad attitudes and wrote to his brother that he was whipping them. That fall, at Lewis's urging, he agreed to hire York out in the Louisville area. Clark ultimately gave York his freedom and set him up in the hauling business. In 1832, Clark reported to the author Washington Irving that York had died of cholera in Tennessee.

THE TERRITORIAL CAPITAL'S population at that time was between 1200 and 1400 residents. In the next few years American style homes of brick, stone, and frame houses began to replace the old Creole style homes, which had vertical log post construction and whitewashed interiors. The grounds of the St. Louis Gateway Arch along the Mississippi River waterfront encompass much of the area of the old French village of St. Louis. Town politics were dominated by the Chouteaus, whose family had founded St. Louis in 1763, and by the other

French families in the fur trade.

THE ST. LOUIS MASONIC LODGE was established by Meriwether Lewis. He became its First Master in November, 1808. The members met in the town billiard parlor at Second and Walnut Streets. Lewis had joined the Masons as a young army officer in 1797. The book *Territorial Masonry* states that:

> "St. Louis, in 1808, was not the most fertile field which might be have been found in which to locate a lodge of Freemasons, and, but for the influence of the Governor of the Territory, it might never have been organized. In Meriwether Lewis, fresh from his conquest of the West, Freemasonry found an active exemplar."

> . . . "The family at his home he stayed told that their guest committed suicide, which for a time was generally accepted. But developments of a later date lead us to believe that he was foully murdered in the expectancy of securing money."

TERRITORIAL SECRETARY FREDERICK BATES was Meriwether Lewis's enemy almost from the start of their relationship. Bates was a younger brother of Tarleton Bates, a friend of Lewis's who had been killed in a duel in 1806. Lewis had suggested the 30 year old Bates for the job. Bates had been a merchant in the Detroit area before coming to St. Louis.

Frederick Bates—who had arrived in St. Louis in April, 1807—served as the Acting Governor and the Superintendent of Indian Affairs until Lewis's arrival in March, 1808. He also assumed Clark's responsibilities as Indian Agent when Clark left the territory in August, 1807. In addition, President Jefferson appointed Bates to fill the positions of the fired James Donaldson as Recorder of Land Deeds, and as one of the three members of the Land Claims Commission.

Bates had gotten used to wielding almost all the power in the territory during that first year, and he found it difficult to acknowledge Meriwether Lewis's authority. Later—when Lewis accused him of wanting to take his job—Bates wrote to his brother Richard on July 14, 1809:

"Gov. Lewis leaves this in a few days for Phila. Washingn &c. He has fallen from the Public esteem & almost into the public contempt. He is well aware of my increasing popularity. . . . and has for some time feared that I was at the head of a Party whose object it would be to denounce him to the President and procure his dismission. . .

I made him sensible that it would be the extreme of folly for me to aspire above my present standing; that in point of *Honor*, my present offices were nearly equal to the government and greatly superior in *emolument* [salary]

. . .How unfortunate for this man that he has resigned his commission in the army: His habits are altogether military & he can never I think succeed in any other profession.

In a subsequent letter to his brother, on November 9th, Frederick described his relationship with the Governor:

"I bore in silence the supercilious air of the Governor for a long time; until last summer he took it in his head to disavow certain statements which I had made. . .

Sometime after this, there was a ball in St. Louis, I attended early, and was seated in conversation with some Gentlemen when the Governor entered. He drew his chair close to mine—There was a pause in the conversation—I availed myself of it—arose and walked to the opposite side of the room. The dances were now commencing.—He also rose—evidently in passion, retired in an adjacent room and sent a servant for General Clark, who refused to ask me out as he foresaw that a Battle must have been the consequence of our meeting.

He complained to the General that I had treated him with contempt & insult in the Ball-Room and that he could not suffer it to pass. He knew my resolution not to speak to him except on business and he ought not to have thrust himself in my way."

He ends his letter with the lament:

"Richard, this is a strange world, in which we live! I had thought that my habits were pacific; yet I have had acrimonious differences with almost every person with whom I have been associated in public business. I have called myself to a very rigid account on this head, and before God, I cannot acknowledge that I have been blamable in any one instance. My passions blind me I suppose."

LEWIS WAS INVESTING IN LAND, like everyone else who came to Louisiana Territory. As Governor he was required by law to own at least 1,000 acres and to reside in the territory. Within five months of the date of his arrival on March 8, 1808, he had purchased 17 tracts of land. They were all choice properties, totalling about 5,700 acres and purchased for about $6,000.

He was expecting to bring his widowed mother Lucy Marks out to St. Louis to live; and perhaps his sister Jane and her family. His brother Reuben was already living there. He had selected a 1,000 acre site for their mother's residence on the western edge of town.

Lewis bought a great Indian mound near the riverfront, approximately 12 feet high, and 120 x 130 feet wide on its flat top. It was one of the most important mounds in a group of thirty mounds, located north of today's Martin Luther King Memorial bridge. St. Louis was once called the "Mound City" because of the dozens of mounds that dotted its landscape. Lewis may have bought the great mound in the hopes of preserving it; but eventually, like the others, it was levelled.

Today, across the river in Illinois, the great Cahokia Mounds are a World Heritage Site.

THE MISSOURI GAZETTE occupied much of Lewis's attention, as he served as its sole editor during the months that Charless was back in Louisville. The July 26th issue featured news of the war in Europe, and news received by the "last mail" of events in Paris, Boston, Baltimore, Norfolk, Philadelphia and Europe. News of local Indian and territorial matters were featured on the remaining two pages along with a few ads.

When Charless returned to St. Louis in late November, he published a notice warning people not to do business with his assistant—he had run off with unpaid debts of $600 and $200 in goods—stating he had swindled his customers out of money for newspaper subscriptions, horses and watches. He provided the following description of him:

> "This hopeful *Sprig* is about 24 years old. . .he shuffles as he walks, has a shallow [sic] complexion . . . is cross eyed and very near sighted . . . plainly stamped *The Villain*. . ."

Newspapers and the free press were cornerstones of good government and the Enlightenment philosophy which advocated reason, knowledge and independent judgment. Lewis was determined to have a newspaper operating in the territory when he took on the job of Governor. At that time it was the common practice to publish articles using a psuedonym, rather than your own name. As President Jefferson's private secretary, he had written articles for the *National Intelligencer* newspaper in Washington. There were about sixty issues of the weekly newspaper published during Lewis's time in the territory. Though he never received any credit in print, he continued to serve as its editor and as a contributor.

For one week in September, 1808 there was no paper published due to the "sudden and severe illness of the editor." Lewis was undoubtedly ill with malaria. Malaria causes fevers and severe flu-like symptoms. It will become a chronic disease if the person continues to live in an area where malaria is endemic, due to reinfection by moquito bites. Lewis was periodically incapacitated by malarial attacks.

THE *LAWS OF THE TERRITORY OF LOUISIANA* were printed in May, 1809 with the new press. In July, 1808, Lewis had advanced $500 to buy paper for printing 250 copies of the book in English, and 100 in French. For this and other expenses, Governor Lewis made six drafts on Secretary of State Robert Smith. Altogether, Lewis had advanced $1,517.95 of his own money for the books. But when he submitted the drafts for payment to Washington, they were refused and returned to him.

SECRETARY OF STATE ROBERT SMITH refused to pay for printing the *Territorial Laws* on the grounds that Lewis had not received prior approval for the expenditures. There was politics involved—and certainly a desire to force Lewis out of his Governorship. Smith's brother, Maryland Senator Samuel Smith, was President pro Tem of the U. S. Senate during 1805-1809. The brothers were shipping merchants from Baltimore and longtime friends of Aaron Burr's.

They were leaders of a group of Washington insiders called the "Invisibles," who intrigued and worked against President James Madison and his Secretary of the Treasury Albert Gallatin. The President had selected his cabinet members based on geography and party unity, rather than their affinity with him.

THE "INVISIBLES" undoubtedly included another cabinet member—the Secretary of War William Eustis from Massachusetts, who was a very close personal friend of Aaron Burr's. Eustis also refused to honor a draft on the War Department from Lewis—a bill for $940 for the return of the Mandan Chief Big White in 1809. The refusal of payment for these bills is what sent Meriwether Lewis on his final journey to Washington in September and October, 1809.

WHERE WAS AARON BURR during this time? He was over in England trying to persuade His Majesty's government that he was really a British citizen because he was born in New Jersey while it was still a British colony. He was also trying to persuade them to finance his plans for invading the two Floridas and Mexico. In November, 1808 the British government declared him to be "forever an alien." He was expelled from Great Britain in April, 1809, and travelled to Sweden, Denmark and Germany.

By March of 1810, Burr was in Paris submitting plans to Napoleon's government for invading the Bahamas, the two Floridas and New Mexico. If that didn't suit them, he offered the alternatives of taking Canada and Nova Scotia. His base of operations for these projects was to be Pensacola, Florida.

Burr's proposals were rejected by Napoleon—and then it was more than a year before he was finally able to obtain a passport to return to the United States. Traveling under an assumed name, Burr returned to New York City in June of 1812, where he resumed his old law practice.

PRESIDENT MADISON was faced with internal opposition from northeastern leaders, who resented both the Louisiana Purchase and the disproportionate representation of slave holding states in the House of Representatives —achieved by counting every slave as 3/5 of a person, whose owners acquired their votes. They were considering breaking away from the union and establishing a Northern Confederacy based on shipping and mercantile interests. The "Invisibles" were members of his own Republican Party. Robert Smith was intending to run for the presidency in 1812, and was undercutting Madison and Gallatin in every way that he and his powerful brother could devise. His disloyalty was well known. Robert Smith was dismissed as Secretary of State on April 1st. He was replaced by James Monroe.

THE RETURN OF THE MANDAN CHIEF was of

primary importance in maintaining good relationships with the Mandan-Hidatsa Indians. Their villages were the largest trading center on the northern plains. Originally numbering about 20,000– 25,000 persons in the 1700's, their numbers had been reduced by small pox epidemics to about 3,000—still more than twice the size of the population of St. Louis.

Nathaniel Pryor, the leader of the unsuccessful expedition to return the chief in 1807, had warned that a much larger force was needed to deliver Chief Sheheke (Big White), his interpreter Rene Jessaume, and their wives and children back to their villages on the Knife River in North Dakota. Pryor's expedition had numbered about 80 armed men; 4 men had been killed and 9 wounded in the fight at the Arikara Villages. Pryor recommended that a force of 400-1,000 men was needed to successfully pass the Arikara Villages on the Missouri River.

THE ST. LOUIS MISSOURI FUR COMPANY was organized in 1809. After Manuel Lisa had returned from his expedition to Montana with $7,000 worth of beaver skins, members of the St. Louis establishment invested and became partners with him. William Clark was the agent for the company in St. Louis, and Lewis's brother Reuben was a partner. The Chouteaus and others were also partners.

The government paid the new company $7,000 to escort the Mandan party back to their home. The Missouri Fur Company sent 13 keelboats and barges carrying over 400 men up river. About 160 of them were militia under the direction of Pierre Chouteau. When they arrived at the Arikara Villages the militia escorted the boat flotilla, marching alongside the boats on both sides of the river. Chouteau was an old and respected Indian trader, and he knew what he was doing. After Chouteau and members of the militia had successfully managed the return of the delegation, they returned to St. Louis.

SACAGAWEA, four year old Pomp, and her husband Toussaint Charbonneau came back with them. As William

Clark had promised them, he set them up on a small farm in the Florissant village next to St. Charles. Sacagawea and her husband returned to the Mandan-Hidatsa villages in 1811, leaving six year old Pompey behind in the care of William Clark.

Sacagawea had another child, a girl named Lisette, in 1812. Later, after Sacagawea's death at Fort Manuel (near today's Kenel, South Dakota) in December, 1812, Manuel Lisa and the men of the Missouri Fur Company brought the little baby down to St. Louis. She was most likely accompanied by Toussaint Charbonneau's other Shoshone wife, Otter Woman, who also had a young baby girl. They were evacuating all Missouri Fur Company posts on the western frontier, due to the start of the War of 1812.

On August 11, 1813 guardianship papers were filed in the St. Louis courts, and William Clark arranged to adopt both Pompey and Lisette.

MERIWETHER LEWIS "ADOPTED" the Jessaumes' thirteen year old son, Toussaint, who wanted to remain in St. Louis and attend school when his family went back home. On May 13, 1809 Lewis signed a five year indenture contract with his father, agreeing to pay for the education and care of his son and "to render him a useful member of society" at his own expense. He had known young Toussaint since his family joined the expedition at the Mandan villages. It must have been fun for Seaman, the Newfoundland dog, to have a boy to play with. What happened to Toussaint after Lewis's death is not known.

AS COMMANDER OF THE MILITIA, it was Lewis's responsibility to defend American residents of the territory against Indian attacks. The British were providing weapons to Indians, who were attacking settlers throughout the sparsely settled frontier. The 1810 census listed 20,845 residents in what would soon become known as Missouri Territory (today's states of Missouri and Arkansas). During 1808, Lewis called out the militia and arranged for two forts to be built. The forts were also government trading houses—Fort Osage was located near present day Kansas City, Missouri, and Fort Madison, on the Des Moines River.

AS SUPERINTENDENT OF INDIAN AFFAIRS, Lewis spent much of his time dealing with Indian matters. He and William Clark, who served as Indian Agent, shared the responsibility of dealing with the Indians and the federal government. The most significant accomplishment of Lewis's administration was the Treaty with the Osage Indians, who dominated the area of present day Missouri, Kansas and Arkansas. They ceded over 80,000 square miles of land to the United States in 1808-09. William Clark was in charge of building Fort Osage and presiding over the first treaty making with the Osages at Fire Prairie. This treaty was rejected by the main body of the Osages, and Lewis negotiated a second treaty with the aid of Pierre Chouteau, their long time Indian Agent. This treaty was not satisfactory until the consent of the Arkansas band of the Osage was obtained. The last official act of Lewis before leaving the territory on September 4th, 1809 was to complete negotiations with the Arkansas band.

LEWIS WROTE A LETTER ON HIS 35TH BIRTH-DAY, August 18th, to Secretary of War William Eustis in reply to a letter he had received from him that had refused to authorize the additional sum of $940 to return the Mandan Chief:

> "Yours of the 15th July is now before me, the feelings it excites are truly painful... I have never received a penny of public Money, but have merely given the Draft to the person who has rendered the public service, or furnished articles for public use, which have been invariably applied to the purposes expressed in my Letters of advice.
> ...I shall leave the Territory in the most perfect state of Tranquility, which I believe, it has ever experienced...
> I shall take with me my papers, which I trust when ex-

amined, will prove my firm and steady attachment to my Country, as well as the Exertions I have made to support and further its interests in this Quarter.

... Be assured Sir, that my Country can never make 'A Burr' of me—she may reduce me to poverty; but she can never sever my Attachment from her.

... Those protested Bills from the Departments of War and Treasury, have effectively sunk my Credit; brought in all my private debts, amounting to about $4,000, which has compelled me, in order to do justice to my Creditors, to deposit with them the landed property which I had purchased in this Country as Security.

... Some weeks after making the Contract with the Misoury-Fur-Company, for taking the Mandane Chief to his Village, I received information through the Sous and Mahas that the Chyenne had joined the Arikaras and were determined to arrest all Boats which might ascend the River. I conceived it necessary, in order to meet the additional Force, and to insure the success of the Expedition conveying the Mandane Chief, to make the further advance [$940 in goods] with a view, that should it become necessary to engage an auxiliary Force among the friendly Nations through which they would pass, that Mr. Chouteau, the Commanding Officer, might be enabled to acquire such aid by means of these supplies."

... I have reason to believe that sundry of my letters have been lost, as there remain several important Subjects on which I have not yet received an Answer."

Lewis was so sick with malaria at this time that the letter was written in the handwriting of his friend, Jeremiah Connor, the Sheriff of St. Louis. It was signed and a postscript added by him. The postscript says that if Eustis went ahead with his plans to remove Chouteau as Indian Agent for the Osage there would be war with that nation.

Eustis had rejected his draft of $940 to cover the additional expenses of returning the Mandan Chief. Together with the rejection of the drafts to pay for printing the *Territorial Laws*—reimbursing Lewis for the $1,517.95 he had already spent—the total was $2,457.95. His annual salary as Governor was $2,000.

The next few days were spent in arranging for three friends, William Clark, Will Carr and Alexander Stewart, to have power of attorney to take care of his real estate property. He would lose some of his property at least, if he could not persuade the government to honor its obligations.

On the 27th of August, Lewis wrote a very thoughtful and long letter to the President regarding the administration of law and the jurisdiction of the courts involving Indians. He included the various court opinions that troubled him. This letter was written in the handwriting of Frederick Bates.

On the 1st of September, Pierre Chouteau's son wrote a long letter to Eustis, defending his father's role as Agent to the Osages. Auguste Pierre was responding to the news that Eustis wanted to dismiss his father as Indian Agent.

On the 2nd of September, Lewis wrote to Auguste Pierre asking him to furnish trade goods by 2 o'clock that afternoon so that Lewis could deliver the goods to the "chiefs and warriors of the Great Ozages of the River Arkanses." They had signed the land cession treaty on the 31st of August; the same treaty that had been signed by the Great and Little Osage bands the previous year. He had delayed his departure from St. Louis until the treaty was signed—ending his 18 months in the territory with a significant accomplishment .

WHEN LEWIS DEPARTED FROM ST. LOUIS with only his servant John Pernier and Seaman to accompany him on the 4th of September, he was leaving the territory in the "most perfect state of tranquility" it had ever been, but he had enemies both in St. Louis and Washington who wanted him out of office. He was also still suffering from malarial attacks.

He was expecting to be back in the territory by December where he had Toussaint Jessaume to look after; the prospect of relocating their mother to St. Louis in the Spring; and the journals to get ready for publication.

The Last Days

L EWIS MADE OUT HIS WILL IN NEW MADRID, Missouri, near the junction of the Mississippi and Ohio Rivers. He was ill with malarial fevers, and was carried on shore in a litter to recuperate in the town. While he was there, he made out a Will in a small minute book, a pocket size book in which he recorded all of his important financial transactions. The Will left everything to his mother. It was signed, dated and witnessed on September 11th. By September 28th the *Missouri Gazette* wrote:

> "A report prevailed here last week that his Excellency Governor Lewis was much indisposed at New Madrid. We were informed yesterday by a person direct from that place, that he seen him off in good health for New Orleans, on his way to the Federal City.

Lewis was again carried off the boat in a litter when they reached Fort Pickering at the Chickasaw Bluffs (today's Memphis, Tennessee) on September 15th. There, the Commander of the Fort, Captain Gilbert Russell, nursed him back to "perfect health within about six days." The Captain denied Lewis the use of liquor, only permitting him "claret and a little white wine" and said that Lewis told him he would "never drink any more spirits or use snuff again." This drinking had to be quite an exceptional matter for him—his worst enemy, Frederick Bates, never once said that Lewis had any kind of drinking or drug problem, or suffered from depression, and he would have been the first to make an accusation if any of this were true.

Malaria causes chills and fevers; it has been among the leading causes of sickness and death throughout human history. It is caused by the bite of an infected mosquito. St. Louis, New Orleans and Washington, D. C. all had high incidences of malaria due to their climates.

Dr. David Peck, the author of *Or Perish in the Attempt,* says that all the members of the Lewis and Clark Expedition probably had malaria; and that they would have been protected in varying degrees by their immune systems. It was so prevalent it wasn't discussed. In 1832 Dr. John Sappington of Arrow Rock, Missouri began making and advertising "Anti-Fever Pills" made out of pure quinine, which was the first truly effective remedy for malarial fevers.

Captain Russell wrote to President Jefferson about Lewis's stay at the fort. He said that after Lewis recovered his health, Lewis waited around for another 6-8 days because he hoped that he and Russell could travel together to Washington. The Captain had requested permission from General Wilkinson to go to Washington and was waiting for an answer. He had the "same problem" with Eustis that Lewis had—that is, he was personally responsible for drafts he had made on the government that were refused payment. (See # 10, pp. 246-47.)

William Clark had also encountered stiff resistance from Eustis for his estimated expenses as Indian Agent, and it appeared likely his budget would be severely cut. He was informed that decisions he had made to hire people were not authorized. He too was going to Washington to discuss matters with the Secretary of War. Clark, however, was traveling with Julia and their ten month old son by way of Louisville and Fincastle in order to visit their families.

THE DAY AFTER ARRIVING AT THE FORT, Lewis wrote a letter to President Madison, saying he had changed his travel plans, due to "fear of the original papers of the voyage" falling into the hands of the British, and that he would be travelling overland through Tennessee and Virginia.

Lewis was certainly aware of the situation on the Gulf Coast—2,000 soldiers were stationed in New Orleans in 1809 under the command of General Wilkinson to protect against British incursions into Florida. A week later, in a letter to his friend Amos Stoddard (whom he mistakenly believed was at

Fort Adams, south of Natchez Mississippi) Lewis said that
"indisposition" prevented his travel down to New Orleans and
he was going to travel by way of the Natchez Trace.

It was most likely that he wanted to avoid meeting General
Wilkinson. He may have assumed that Wilkinson was moving
up river with his troops in September to Fort Adams, but in
fact he was still in New Orleans. The General was also indis-
posed and suffering from illness. Lewis could not have avoided
seeing Wilkinson at Fort Adams; but in New Orleans, one of
the largest cities in the U. S., he could have avoided him.

JAMES NEELLY, Indian Agent to the Chickasaw Indians
showed up at Fort Pickering on September 18th, three days after Lewis's arrival. Neelly was brand new to the job of Indian
Agent, having received his appointment from Eustis on August
9th. The Chickasaw Nation Agency was located about 100
miles to the south, near today's Tupelo, Mississippi.

General Wilkinson controlled the appointment of Indian Agents. He was the Commanding General of the United
States Army; and Indian Affairs were under the jurisdiction of
the military. The General had been associated with the Natchez Trace area for years. The Trace was a 500 mile old Indian trail running from Natchez to Nashville. In 1801-03 the
General had used troops from Cantonment Wilkinsonville to
make the Trace into a federal military road, and he had negotiated the treaties with the Chickasaw, Choctaw and Creek
Nations, through whose lands it passed.

Agent Neelly was behaving very strangely—unless it is assumed that he was acting under orders from Wilkinson. He
stayed at the fort for ten days, until finally—when it was learned
that General Wilkinson refused to give permission to Captain
Russell to travel to Washington—Neelly got the job of escorting Meriwether Lewis to Nashville. Captain Russell later wrote
to President Jefferson, saying that if he had sent his own man
with Lewis—rather than Neelly escorting him—Lewis would
still be alive. (See # 12, pp. 248-49.)

Further evidence of Neelly's strange behavior is found in a newspaper announcement in the Nashville *Democatic-Clarion* on October 20th, 1809. The paid announcement, addressed to "Travellers and Others," is signed by James Neelly and dated "Chickasaw Agency, October 3d, 1809." In other words, it was composed at the Agency during the time when Neelly was en route to Nashville with Lewis. Neelly and Lewis, who left the fort on September 29th, traveled 100 miles south to the Agency before heading north to Nashville on the Natchez Trace. (See map on p. 276.)

Neelly needed to do some damage control regarding the matter of a local thief who had stolen a pair of saddlebags in September from a traveler who stopped at an inn run by James Colbert. The Colberts were a wealthy, mixed-blood family who were tribal leaders of the Chickasaw Nation for many years. Apparently the theft of the saddlebags had become a subject of speculation and gossip.

Neelly paid to have an announcement placed in the Nashville, Natchez and New Orleans newspapers. The announcement was signed by Neelly and eight others. It testified to the fact that James Colbert was an honest man, and that

> ". . . no blame is, or ought to be attached to the character of Colbert or his family—let malicious characters report what they may."

The announcement named the thief and said that he was now in confinement for the crime. Neelly—instead of taking the thief to the Nashville jail—paid Jeremiah K. Love $90 to take him to Nashville. What was in the saddlebags is not known, nor is anything else known about the affair, except that Neelly cared enough about being at Fort Pickering from September 18th–29th to pay someone else to do his job.

On October 18th in Nashville, Neelly wrote to Secretary Eustis asking to be reimbursed for the $90 he had paid to Jeremiah Love for transporting the prisoner. Eustis denied his request. It was the same day that Neelly wrote to President Jefferson with the news of Lewis's death.

Captain Russell charged in his letter to President Jefferson that Neelly had Lewis's pistols and other items in his possession. (Only his horse and rifle were eventually recovered from Mrs. Neelly by Lewis's stepbrother John Marks.) Neelly also claimed to have lent the Governor money, which Russell says was not true—Neelly had no money when he left the fort. Lewis before his death had more than a $100 in cash, and a check from Russell for $99.58. After his death, neither the money nor the check was found. Lewis's gold watch and the pistols were never recovered from Neelly. (See #12 pp. 248-49).

BEFORE LEAVING THE FORT, on September 27th, Lewis had borrowed $379.58 from Captain Russell (equal to more than $2,000 in today's money). He got a check for $99.58 from Russell which he could cash at a bank, and two horses worth $280. He noted the transaction in his minute book.

The next day, Lewis took the precaution of making a signed agreement with Russell regarding the care and delivery of the two trunks of Captain House that he was transporting for him, and two trunks of his own, plus a case and a package. (See # 11, p. 247-48).

Benjamin Wilkinson took Captain House's trunks to New Orleans on September 29th. It turns out that the General's nephew was at the fort, and that he left the fort on the same day that Lewis and Neelly left for the Chickasaw Agency. Wilkinson is known to have died on board ship in February, 1810 en route to Baltimore. The cause of his death is unknown.

LEWIS'S TWO TRUNKS, the case, and package were to go back to Will Carr, his friend in St. Louis—

"unless otherwise instructed by M. L. by letter from Nashville."

Lewis emphasized that only Jean-Pierre Cabanne, a wealthy St. Louis fur trader, should be entrusted with them:

"M. Lewis would thank Capt. R. to be particular to whom he confides these trunks &c, a Mr. Cabboni of St. Louis may be expected to pass this place in the course of the next month, to him they may be safely confided."

At some unknown date, a messenger arrived at the fort, with a verbal message—supposedly from Lewis—asking Captain Russell to hold the trunks. It seems obvious that someone wanted to examine their contents. After Lewis's death, Jefferson wrote to Madison that he had written to Captain Russell requesting Lewis's private property at the fort be sent to him.

Lewis's minute book notes:

"Also left with Capt. Russell two trunks one containing papers &c a case for liquor and a package of blankets sheets and coverlid to be sent to William C Carr of St. Louis for me—unless I shall otherwise direct."

It appears that Lewis might have been following through on his pledge not to drink liquor.

AS THEY SET OFF ON THEIR JOURNEY, Lewis was accompanied by John Pernier, his personal servant, a free mulatto who had worked for President Jefferson in the White House, and by Seaman, his Newfoundland dog. According to Captain Russell, he heard reports that Lewis was drinking heavily as he traveled, with the liquor being supplied by James Neelly. However, this may have been a story told to deceive Russell. It is interesting to note that Neelly himself never made this charge in his letter to Jefferson, and it would have been an obvious supporting argument for suicide.

Lewis had a lot on his mind. He must have feared assassination. He was carrying important documents. He may have decided to leave the most incriminating evidence behind in the trunk with his other papers at Fort Pickering. The kind with information that would destroy the careers or plots of his enemies. The trunks of papers were to go back to Will Carr, the federal land agent in St. Louis, if Lewis didn't send a letter from Nashville.

The implication seems to be that *if* Lewis arrived safely in Nashville *and* sent a letter to Captain Russell, *then* the trunks with the papers could be sent to Nashville. Otherwise Russell should be particularly careful to send them only in the care of Jean-Pierre Cabanne to Will Carr.

After his death, the papers and possessions that Lewis was carrying with him were neatly categorized and sorted out in Nashville. They were entrusted to the care of Thomas Freeman to take to Isaac Cole, who had served as private secretary to both Presidents Jefferson and Madison. Thomas Freeman was a long time associate and employee of General Wilkinson. When the papers reached Isaac Cole they were so "badly assorted" that Cole could not make any sense of their organization. (See #s 5 & 6, pp. 236-39.)

THE NATCHEZ TRACE was notorious for robbers and crooks in these early days. It was a well-traveled path, where people banded together in groups for protection against thieves and murderers. The temptation for criminals was that many travelers were carrying large sums of money. They had floated down the Mississippi on flatboats, sold their goods, or earned their pay as boatmen, and were traveling back north on foot and by horseback. The average day's travel was 25 miles. There were "stands" or traveler's inns every 15-20 miles or so. It took three weeks to travel from Natchez to Nashville.

Slaves were being taken down the Trace in chains to be sold at auction in Natchez to work in the cotton fields. It was also Indian Country, where the tribes controlled who operated the stands. George Colbert, James's brother, ran a ferry across the Tennessee River and became a very wealthy man. It was a very rough place, and travelers went heavily armed. It was not an empty road. Many people would have seen Governor Lewis on the Trace. In fact one gentleman even got an advertising prospectus for Lewis's journal from him.

ON THE LAST DAY OF LEWIS'S LIFE, October 10th, Neelly claimed that two horses had run away the night before, and he had gone off in search of them. He said that he advised Lewis, Pernier, and a servant of Neelly's to go on ahead to Grinder's Stand, a traveler's inn and tavern on the edge of the Chickasaw Nation land. This may come close to the truth—that the horses were missing and that Lewis, the two servants, and the dog went on ahead without him to Grinder's Stand.

THE REST IS A MYSTERY. We know that Mrs. Grinder had a infant, a 9 year old daughter, and two or three young hired help with her. We know it was claimed that her husband, Robert Grinder, and their sons were away that night. What happened at Grinder's Stand—according to the three versions told by Mrs. Grinder—may be read in the documents section of this book. (See #4, p. 234; #14, p. 251, and #18, p. 260).

John Guice, the editor of a recent book, *By His Own Hand? The Mysterious Death of Meriwether Lewis,* has established that the night of October 10-11, 1809 was the night after a new moon. Therefore, the accounts of seeing anything during that night are not believable. We know Lewis most likely died of a bullet wound during the night. That is all that can be said with certainty about the manner of his death.

James Neelly arrived during the day of October 11th. It is reported that Lewis's body was found on the Natchez Trace at sunrise by the local mail carrier, Robert M. Smith. He contacted his friend, Robert M. Cooper.

Cooper, a blacksmith, built a special coffin for Lewis because Lewis was a tall man, six feet or more. The log coffin was made from splitting a large chestnut oak tree, and Cooper forged large, long square nails for it. The iron nails were used to identify Lewis's gravesite when the gravesite monument was erected in 1848. When the grave was opened and the nails identified, it is reported that Robert M. Smith's son—

"on seeing the skull with the hole in it reminded those

present of his father's story of the great hole in Lewis's head."

A coroner's inquest was held at this time, according to local tradition; but coroner's inquests for this time period in Maury County went unrecorded. It is said that Robert Grinder was accused of Lewis's murder—and though all six jury members believed he was guilty, they were afraid to convict him.

And it was reported that Seaman—Lewis's Newfoundland dog that had traveled from Pittsburgh to the Pacific Ocean and back with him— died of grief on his master's grave. (See #17, p. 259.)

John Pernier carried the news of Lewis's death to Lewis's mother, and to Presidents Jefferson and Madison. It was reported that Pernier committed suicide in May of 1810 while trying to collect his back pay of $240 from the Lewis estate. (See #13, pp. 249-51.)

James Neelly disappeared for a while, turning up in Nashville on October 18th. It was a two day trip from Grinder's Stand to Nashville, and it could be made in one day. But Neelly took seven days to report the news of Lewis's death.

WHO COMMITTED THE MURDER? It may have been Robert Grinder. In 1814 he bought a 100 acre farm for $250 on the Duck River near Centerville, Tennessee. ("Grinder's Switch," a railroad switching track just outside of Centerville, was named for the Grinder family. It later became famous for being the fictional home town of Grand Ole Opry star, Cousin Minnie Pearl.)

The local tradition in the Hohenwald area is that Grinder committed the murder. Whether or not it was Grinder, or whether or not he had accomplices—the questions really are—who paid for the killing, and what were their motives? Throughout this account, I have attempted to present the case for murder. The documents section also contains materials that have shaped the suicide story for many years, and they are available for you to form your own opinion.

If an exhumation of the remains of Meriwether Lewis takes place, then there may be conclusive evidence found that he was murdered. And there may not. In any event, in the last chapter, possible motives for his assassination are presented.

Motives for the Assassination

Who benefits? is always the question when trying to solve an assassination murder mystery. Another question is, what is the evidence? In this case, we have evidence that there was an orchestrated plot to plant false evidence concerning Meriwether Lewis's mental state and the circumstances of his death at Grinder's Stand on the Natchez Trace. The false evidence reveals the existence of a much larger conspiracy.

JAMES WILKINSON AND JOHN SMITH T.—in this author's opinion—benefitted and were the masterminds behind the conspiracy to assassinate Lewis. In this final chapter, I will provide the evidence that leads me to this conclusion.

Their general motive for killing him was that Meriwether Lewis could jeopardize their plans for an invasion of Mexico in 1810. The invasion plan was a replay of the Burr-Wilkinson Conspiracy of 1806, and the goal was the same—the fabulous wealth of the silver mines of Mexico. Another motive must have been control of the lead mines south of St. Louis. Lead was another source of great wealth—and of military power, because bullets were made from lead in that era.

RECORDS OF THE LAND CLAIMS BOARD in St. Louis played an important role in the assassination. Smith T. had very large land claims in the lead mine district south of St. Louis, worth hundreds of thousands of dollars. Smith T. had been waging a private war in the lead district for years against Moses Austin (the father of Stephen Austin, the founder of Texas) for control of profitable mines. He also manufactured bullets and employed two slaves full time in making guns. Their guns were considered the best in the West.

During Wilkinson's tenure as the first Governor of Louisiana Territory in 1805-06, he had been notoriously involved in fraudulent land claims. Both Wilkinson and Smith T. probably feared exposure of their corrupt land dealings.

LEWIS WAS CARRYING PAPERS to Washington that they wanted to obtain. There are two rather direct proofs of this. The first is that the neatly bundled papers that were given to Thomas Freeman to carry to Virginia after Lewis's death were so badly mixed up when they arrived in Virginia that no sense could be made of them in regards to their original inventory. Thomas Freeman was a long time associate and employee of General Wilkinson. (See #5 and #6, pp. 236-39.)

The second is that Lewis wrote a very carefully worded memorandum for Captain Russell about the two trunks of papers he left at the fort. (See #11, pp. 247-48.) They were either to go to St. Louis in the care of Jean-Pierre Cabanne; or—if Lewis sent a written request from Nashville—they were to be sent to Nashville. Regretfully, this may indicate that Lewis didn't know if he was going to be alive to make it to Nashville. If he did, then he would write. Otherwise Cabanne was to take the trunks back to St. Louis and give them to Will Carr, the federal land agent.

Russell wrote in his first letter (#10, pp. 246-47) that he was going to follow the instructions of someone who showed up at the fort after Lewis left—someone who told him that Lewis said to hold the trunks at the fort. In other words, don't send them back to St. Louis. They must have wanted to examine the papers in the trunks and to destroy whatever incriminating evidence the papers contained. (Jefferson later requested these trunks be sent to him.)

Russell also noted on the memorandum that Benjamin Wilkinson, the General's nephew, left the fort on the same day as Lewis, September 29th, taking Captain James House's trunks to New Orleans by boat. Lewis had originally intended to take a ship out of New Orleans and was taking House's trunks as a favor to him. House was traveling by an overland route to Baltimore. Benjamin Wilkinson was also traveling to Baltimore, but by ship. He died on board ship, in February, 1810, of an unknown cause.

FALSE STORIES WERE NOW BEING TOLD. There were several people involved in the conspiracy in the region. Someone showed up at the fort and said hold the trunks. This was probably the same person who told Captain Russell that Lewis was drinking heavily as he travelled with James Neely, the Indian Agent. The drinking heavily story lays the ground work for the death by suicide story. It was part of the conspiracy plot. (See #12, pp. 248-49.)

The stories of derangement and attempted suicides were launched in Nashville, even before Meriwether Lewis had left the fort. Captain House wrote a letter to his friend Frederick Bates, on September 28th, reporting an alarming rumor. He had seen Major Amos Stoddard in Nashville—

> "I arrived here two days ago on my way to Maryland— Yesterday Majr Stoddard of the Army arrived here from Fort Adams, and informs me that in his passage through the Indian nation, in the vicinity of Chicka-saw Bluffs he saw a person, immediately from the Bluffs who informed him, that Governor Lewis had arrived there (sometime previous to his leaving it) in a State of mental derangement—that he had made several attempts to put an end to his own existence, which the patroon [boat leader] had prevented, and that Cap Russell, the commanding officer at the Bluffs had taken him into his own quarters where he was obliged to keep a strict watch over him to prevent his committing violence on himself and had caused his boat to be un-loaded at the ferry to be secured in his stores."

The Major met this person as he traveled from Chickasaw Bluffs, the site of Fort Pickering on the Mississippi River, to Nashville. The encounter probably took place about five days earlier, around September 23nd. By then Lewis had recovered his health, but he was waiting another week at the fort for

Captain Russell to receive permission from General Wilkinson to travel with him. This permission was denied. The person whom Major Stoddard met, who had come immediately from the fort, was probably the same person who told Captain Russell to hold the trunks. He was never identified.

The false stories of derangement and attempted suicides are entirely contradictd by the two letters that Russell, the commander of the fort, wrote to Thomas Jefferson. (See #10. pp. 246-47 and #12, pp. 248-49.) The letter of Captain House to Frederick Bates is the only statement with false evidence to appear before the death of Lewis. Secretary Bates, of course, spread the news in St. Louis. He wrote to his brother Richard on November 9th, about the reaction to these rumors in St. Louis:

> "You have heard no doubt, of the premature and tragical death of Gov: Lewis. Indeed I had no personal regard for him and a great deal of political contempt; Yet I cannot but lament, that after all his toils and dangers that he should die in *such a manner*.
>
> At the *first, in Washington*, he made to me so many friendly assurances, that I then imagine our mutual friendship would plant itself on rocky foundations. But a very short acquaintance with the man was sufficient to undeceive me. He had been spoiled by the elegant praises of Mitchell & Barlow, and overwhelmed by so many flattering caresses of the *high & mighty* that, like an overgrown baby, he began to think that everybody about the House must regulate their conduct by his caprices. . . .
>
> I should not speak of these things now, but for the purposes of explaining what followed. Gov. Lewis, on his way to Washington became *insane*. On the arrival of this unhappy news and before we heard of his death, an Honble. Gentleman of this place, a Colleague of mine at the Land Board [Clement Biddle Penrose], commenced a regular and systematic traduction of

my character—He asserted in several respectable companies that the mental derangement of the Governor ought not to be imputed to his political miscarriages; but rather to the *barbarous conduct of the Secretary* [Frederick Bates]."

Clement Biddle Penrose, a nephew of General Wilkinson's wife, was one of the three original members of the Land Claims Board. He was obviously more than a little upset with Frederick Bates.

Frederick Bates now held almost all the governmental power in the territory—Territorial Secretary, Acting Governor and Superintendent of Indian Affairs, and Recorder of Land Titles. He was also one of three members of the Land Claims Board, having been appointed to fill the position of the commissioner whom Jefferson had fired.

WAS BATES IN ON THE PLOT to assassinate Lewis? He was conspiring with Lewis's enemies on land claims issues, but it is doubtful he was a conspirator in the assassination plot. He ended a letter of July 14th, 1809 to his brother by bragging:

"A circumstance, besides has lately transpired, as much *for* me, as *against* my Colleagues, and I really feel so triumphant on the occasion that I cannot forbear mentioning it to you. The People had appointed a committee of correspondence on the subject of their claims to Lands depending before the commissioners . . . the gentlemen addressed themselves to certain members of the Senate who replied that 'the opinions of Mr. B. if in favour, would have great weight in inducing government to grant the Petition. . . . It places me however in the most dangerous & delicate of all imaginable situations, to conduct myself in which with prudence & exempt from imputation will require all the wariness & circumspection of which I am master."

"THE MOST DANGEROUS & DELICATE of all imaginable situations" referred to an effort led by Smith. T. to get rid of the most honest member of the Land Board, Judge John B. C. Lucas. At the same time that Governor Lewis was preparing to go to Washington, his nemesis John Smith T. was also preparing to go to Washington. Smith T. was bringing a formal protest from a citizen's committee asking Congress to not reappoint Judge Lucas as Territorial Judge and Land Board Commissioner. Judge Lucas was an old friend and ally of Albert Gallatin, the Secretary of the Treasury.

LEAD MINE OPERATOR MOSES AUSTIN, Smith T.'s greatest rival, wrote to Bates on August 27th with a warning. He reported having a conversation with "one of the members of the Grand Committee" (the Citizens Committee headed by John Smith T.). This person told Austin that drafting the Memorial to Congress was being postponed until they had an opportunity to examine the Commissioner's books and—

> "... to take such extracts as would answer the intentions of the party. They are to be taken from time to time and in such a way as not to give alarm to the Comrs. it was also hinted that if the extracts could not be obtained in any other way, a friend in court would furnish them. I will not say who this friend is, but the board you know, has three members. and a clerk. . . How far the board of Comsrs. are bound to suffer a mutilated Statement to be taken from the books is not for me to say. . . the drawing of the memorial is suspended until Octb 2 next. . . I felt it a duty incumbent on me to apprize both yourself and Judge Lucas of the plans preparing to stab your reputation with the Government."

The letter was torn in a place that obscures the name of the person they wanted to remove in addition to Lucas. But Judge Lucas was "more particularly pointed out." The other name would have been Clement Penrose—since there were only three commissioners, and Bates was the third one.

This warning from Moses Austin must have referred to the "most dangerous & delicate" situation Frederick Bates found himself in—Bates was "the friend in court" who would remove the records if necessary. Austin ends the letter with a P. S. that Thomas Riddicks, the clerk, is not to be doubted.

In effect, Austin was warning Bates that he had informed Judge Lucas of the planned attempts to alter or destroy the records, and that Bates had better not try to do it. Austin implored Bates to keep silent, as:

> "I need not tell you how much I have suffered by this same party. . . as you value my safety and the peace of my family [the page is torn]

Austin was referring to the real possibility that John Smith T. would try to kill him if he knew he had written this letter. John Smith T. had already killed 15-20 men in duels.

JUDGE LUCAS wrote to Secretary of War Eustis sometime in December, 1809. It was received on January 11, 1810. The letter explained the history of the Board of Land Commissioners and the reason why he had enemies.

First of all, before the board even started meeting in December, 1805, General Wilkinson, the first Governor of Louisiana Territory, had been meeting with area residents for three months teaching them how to "enter their claims."

> ". . . everyone got a lecon from him agreably to their respective cases—as to the best way to get the most possible from the united States . . . he lamented and sympathized very much with the fate of Land Claimants. . . whether this extraordinary conduct on the part of James Wilkinson was the result of a desire of a vain, popular applause, or of a deep laid scheme to secure on his side the phisical strength of the Territory, for some future important occasion is a thing foreing to the subject of this Letter."

Judge Lucas refused to go along with the other two board members when these claimants appeared before the board.

"It was my peculiar Misfortune to entertain opinions Much less favorable to the land Claimants."

President Jefferson, however, supported Judge Lucas's opinions, and a "Board of Revisions" was ordered. The Board of Revisions (the new name of the Land Board) had just finished taking oral testimony and confirming land titles under 800 arpents (678 acres) in December, 1809. Finally, after four years, all ordinary land holders had their titles legally sorted out and confirmed by the board.

THE CITIZENS' COMMITTEE was formed in response to the next stage of the Board of Revisions work—the matter of the large land claimants, with Smith T. being the obvious problem.

Bates stated that when Lewis arrived in Louisiana Territory he immediately "assumed the whole management" of the lead mine business. One thousand square miles of the lead district has been reserved as public land by Congress. New claims could be leased for a period of three years. Both Austin and Smith T. had acquired old Spanish land claim titles. Smith T. had a "floating claim" where he took over any productive mines that he wanted with the use of armed men and lawsuits.

After Lewis's death, the inventory of his possessions that was supposed to be carried to Virginia and Washington, D. C. included a bundle of papers "relative to the mines" for President James Madison. It is doubtful that these papers reached the President. (See #4 and #5, pp. 236-39.)

JOHN SMITH T. represented the Citizens Committee in Washington. In January, 1810 he brought a formal protest, or "remonstrance," to Congress stating that Judge Lucas should not be reappointed as a Judge of the General Court— and should be removed as Commissioner of Land Titles when his term as Judge expired in March, 1810. It would be "a great public calamity" if he continued in office. Smith T. also brought a petition signed by hundreds of residents asking that the Louisiana territorial status be upgraded to the 2nd grade, so they would be allowed to elect representatives to the territorial legislature rather than have federal appointees.

CONGRESS, however, decided to reappoint Judge Lucas in March and left the territorial status of Louisiana unchanged. The death of Meriwether Lewis undoubtedly influenced the decision to remain with the status quo.

REUBEN SMITH, John Smith T.'s younger brother, set off on a "trade mission" to Sante Fe in the winter of 1809-10. Smith's group left from Ste. Genevieve on November 20th, less than three weeks after news of Lewis's death reached St. Louis. Smith was accompanied by John McLanahan, James Patterson, interpreter Manuel Blanco, and three slaves.

It was a most unusual time of year to start on a 500-600 miles journey to Sante Fe. Traveling without the required passports, they were captured and arrested by Spanish officials in February, 1810. The three traders were taken to Chihuahua, Mexico where they were put to work in chains in the silver mines of Chihauhau.

McLanahan was a former sheriff of St. Louis and Patterson was from Giles County, Tennessee, the county south of Maury County, where Meriwether Lewis met his death. The three of them were ransomed by John Smith T. in 1812. Within months, all three were participating in a new filibuster. Along with Wilkinson's son, Joseph B. Wilkinson, they joined the Gutierrez-Magee Expedition to liberate Mexico in September of 1812.

In November, 1809 the *Missouri Gazette* changed its name to the *Louisiana Gazette*. The name change occurred in the very next issue after the announcement of Governor Lewis's death—providing evidence of Lewis's role as a silent partner in the *Missouri Gazette*. In the same month, the newly-named

Louisiana Gazette announced the departure of Reuben Smith's group "to open a commercial intercourse with the upper provinces of Mexico."

Then in 1811 the *Louisiana Gazette* responded indignantly to a story in the national *Philadelphia Gazette*. The Philadelphia article on August 14, 1810 contained some inaccuracies—

> "Three Americans, and a Spaniard called Blanco, spies or emissaries of Bonaparte, have been arrested at Chihuagua . . . that these persons had arrived at Upper Louisiana from Baltimore and were going to the town of Sante Fe. . . . there were found in their possession a paper written in English and a letter from the curate of Ste. Genevieve in France also thirteen fire arms, six cutlasses, three axes and five flasks of powder."

Joseph Charless quoted this story in the *Louisiana Gazette* issue of March 14, 1811 and noted:

> " * Mark the pretended ignorance of these bloodhounds, they knew these gentlemen were from St. Genevieve in the Territory of Louisiana, they well knew the character of the worthy pastor (Rev. Mr. Maxwell), whose letters of credence they bore."

Mud slinging was going back and forth.

FATHER MIGUEL HIDALGO, an educated and liberal Mexican priest, rang the bell of liberty at his church in Dolores on September 16, 1810, starting an armed conflict between Mexican nationalists and their Spanish rulers. September 16th is still celebrated as Mexican Independence Day, or *El Grito de Dolores* ("Cry of Dolores"). Dolores is located in central Mexico in the state of Guanajuato, the site of the some of richest silver mines in Mexico. The revolution started by Father Hildalgo failed, but Mexico would finally gain its independence in 1821.

THE GUTIERREZ-MAGEE EXPEDITION established "The First Republic of Texas" in 1813, flying an emerald green flag. Augustus Magee, a protege of General Wilkinson, was a young former U. S. Army Lieutenant and West Point graduate. Col. Bernardo Gutierrez, who participated in a revolt at San Antonio, had traveled to Washington seeking support for the revolution against the royalists.

Secretary of State James Monroe wrote to the Governor of Tennessee on September 3, 1812 about an "illegal enterprise" of armed citizens "assembling in Giles County for the purpose of joining the Mexican revolutionists" under the leadership of Augustus Magee. That month Magee and his party of 300 men crossed the Sabine River into Texas. This venture would also fail. Magee would be dead by February 6, 1813, dying while he and his men were under seige at the Presidio La Bahia (fort on the bay) in Goliad, Texas.

GENERAL WILKINSON IN 1809 was in a lot of trouble. An army of 2,000 soldiers had been ordered to New Orleans to defend against possible incursions by the British into Florida or the French into Texas. The General had been busy acting as a special envoy of President Madison, visiting Spanish officials in West Florida and Cuba while en route to New Orleans. When he finally arrived in New Orleans, he found many of the troops were sick and dying.

Disregarding direct orders from Secretary of War William Eustis to move the troops up to the relatively healthy climate of Natchez, Mississippi, General Wilkinson selected land on the eastern edge of New Orleans. It was called "Terre aux Boefs," and would become as infamous in its day as the same site was during Hurricane Katrina in 2005—that is, as a place of suffering and death. It was three feet under sea level normally.

Finally, in September, 1809 the General followed orders and began moving the troops up river. Military historian James Ripley Jacobs states in his biography of James Wilkinson, *Tarnished Warrior,* that over a one year period, from February, 1809 to January, 1810 "losses [by death and desertion] aggregated about 1,000 men out of about 2,036 men."

Not only was the General struggling to cope with this catostrophe, he was also facing the most serious personal attacks against him during his long and contentious career. The richest man in New Orleans, his former friend Daniel Clark, published a book in 1809 entitled *Proofs of the Corruption of Gen. James Wilkinson and of his Connexion with Aaron Burr*. Excerpts were published in newspapers around the country.

Wilkinson responded in 1811: *Burr's Conspiracy Exposed; and General Wilkinson Vindicated Against the Slanders of His Enemies*. In it, he provides a great deal of information and sworn testimony—that, in fact, is very damaging to his own defense. He talks about what was happening that fall of 1809 in New Orleans. Daniel Clark had published his book, and the General had learned that the accountant for the War Department, William Simmons, was "ransacking the war department" for evidence to be used against him in the next session of Congress. In addition, the editor of the *Louisiana Gazette & New Orleans Advertiser*, James Sterrett, was told that Jefferson had turned against Wilkinson, and he would be gotten out of the service.

As if this weren't bad enough, Wilkinson's old friend John Adair, the Senator from Kentucky—whom the General had arrested in New Orleans during the Burr Conspiracy in 1806 and shipped out of New Orleans to Richmond—pressed charges on grounds of false imprisonment against him. A warrant was issued for the General's arrest in Washington County, Mississippi, on October 9, 1809. This was two days before Lewis's death. It is not known whether the General went to jail. He posted $7,000 bond on October 25th. It is rather suspicious that the General reports this matter and includes the documents in his own book. The records themselves have long been missing.

In November, 1809 the General was removed from his command and ordered to report to Washington for congressional investigations. Two investigations were held in 1810 without results—one on the deaths at Terre aux Boeufs, and the other on charges that he was in the pay of Spain. The investigations were turned over to a military court in 1811. A court martial cleared him of all charges, and he returned to service. During the War of 1812, he was in command of a planned attack on Montreal; and he again faced a court martial in 1815 in regards to his failure on the northern frontier. And again he was cleared. He retired from the service and wrote a three volume set of his Memoirs. The General moved to Mexico City in 1822, where he spent the last three years of his life distributing bibles for the American Bible Society and advising the new Mexican nationalist governments.

WILKINSON COMPOSED THE FORGED RUS-SELL STATEMENT during his first court martial at Frederick Town, Maryland in November, 1811. Forensic documents examiner Gerald Richards has provided an analysis of the handwriting of the Russell statement, and a 12 page court brief signed with the name of James Wilkinson that was written around the same time preparing for his defense. (See Appendix for this analysis.) Richards's examination shows that neither document was written by either Russell or Wilkinson, but instead both were written in the handwriting of a third person—probably a clerk.

Major Russell was present at the court martial on November 26, 1811, the date of the so-called statement. Jonathan Williams's trial notes indicated that Russell testified very briefly about an unrelated matter. Does this mean that Russell had a change of heart and wrote a statement almost two years later that contradicts everything he wrote in his letters to Jefferson? No, for the statement is written in the unmistakable, overblown, hyperbolic style of General James Wilkinson. A deeply offensive passage comes at the end of statement, where Lewis's last words are supposedly reported—

> "he lay down and died with the declaration to the Boy that he had killed himself to deprive his enemies of the pleasure and honour of doing it."

Wilkinson had been a master of intrigue and forged documents since his earliest days in the army when he participated in the Conway Cabal against George Washington. Historians agree that he created forged documents which ended the career of his rival, General George Rogers Clark, William Clark's older brother. Aaron Burr feared that he would be assassinated by Wilkinson's agents, and Wilkinson admittedly used altered documents against Burr. He was a master of the paper trail.

What is interesting is that in 1811, when he was immersed in justifying his own conduct, he thought it would be prudent to get a new statement that could be passed off as coming from Captain Russell. He was right. It lay unseen in the files of his old friend Jonathan Williams for almost two hundred years before Donald Jackson published it in his *Letters of the Lewis and Clark Expedition* in 1962. When it was published, without the accompanying letters written by Captain Russell to President Jefferson, it was accepted as being written by Russell, and as a confirmation of Lewis's suicide. (Though author Vardis Fisher questioned its authenticity in his book, *Suicide or Murder? The Strange Death of Governor Meriwether Lewis.*)

Then, at the 1996 Coroner's Inquest, the two document examiners both testified that the statement was neither written nor signed by either Gilbert C. Russell or Jonathan Williams, who witnessed it. Williams was serving as one of the judges at the Court Martial of Wilkinson. If it was in truth a copy of an official statement, it should have noted by the copyist that it was a copy. In addition, if it was a real copy, the signature would have been correctly signed Gilbert C. Russell. Instead, since it was manufactured by Wilkinson, the signature was written as Gilbert Russell. Altogether, it is a fake document, meant to confuse and conceal Wilkinson's role in the assassination of Meriwether Lewis.

In preparing the documents for this book it became apparent that William Clark had also received forged letters from "Captain Russell." They have never been found. But again, it was the mark of a master intriguer to have thought to throw William Clark off the track of suspecting murder. Clark had received a letter from Lewis indicating how unhappy he was with the situation he was in, but that letter has never been found. A man can be excused for writing to his best friend about his troubles. The other letters that Clark received immediately after Lewis's death are what persuaded him to accept the suicide story.

IN CONCLUDING THIS CHAPTER discussing the possible motives for Lewis's assassination, it is clear that Lewis was in the midst of a nest of intriguers, the old "Burrites" in St. Louis, who resented his attempts to bring order out of chaos. The two events surrounding Lewis's departure—John Smith T. going to Washington on behalf of the large land claimants, and his brother Reuben Smith's departure for Sante Fe—are reasons for his assassination. Lewis was bringing incriminating evidence to Washington which could derail their plans. Wilkinson was undoubtedly involved—both in what they wanted concealed and in the assassination itself.

Did they benefit by the assassination? Wilkinson kept his job, despite two congressional hearings and two court martials; Smith T. became one of the wealthiest men in Missouri; Reuben Smith became a merchant and mine operator in the lead mine district; and Frederick Bates continued in office, eventually becoming the second Governor of the State of Missouri.

Lewis's estate wound up paying for the publication of the *Territorial Laws*, as the $1,517.95 he had advanced for its publication was never repaid—and Frederick Bates received the credit for publishing them.

Pierre Chouteau reimbursed Lewis's estate for the $940 in trade goods Lewis had advanced for his expedition to return the Mandan Chief. The arrangement always was that Chouteau would keep the goods if they weren't needed. The issue was that the government should pay for them if they were needed. Lewis's estate paid all of his debts; and when it was finally settled in February, 1815, the remaining assets totalled $9.43 and 1/2 cents.

WILLIAM CLARK was asked to take the job of Governor of Louisiana Territory after Lewis's death, but he refused. In 1813, he agreed to became Governor of the new Missouri Territory and Superintendent of Indian Affairs—both vitally important positions on the western frontier during the War of 1812. When Missouri acquired statehood in 1821, Clark lost his bid for governor, but he continued serving as Superintendent of Indian Affairs until his death in 1838.

Clark arranged for Nicholas Biddle in Philadelphia to edit the expedition journals for publication. Expedition member George Shannon, who had lost his leg in the Arikara attack on the Pryor Expedition, helped him. The journals were finally published in 1814.

RATHER THAN DWELLING ON MERIWETHER LEWIS'S DEATH on the Natchez Trace, his hasty burial in a lonely grave, and Seaman choosing to die with his master, I prefer to keep an image in mind of a happier time. I imagine Lewis taking a hike in St. Louis with 13 year old Toussaint and Seaman on a lovely day in early summer to climb the great Indian mound overlooking the Mississippi River, and enjoying the view.

Appendix A: Document Examination

DOCUMENT EXAMINATION
by Gerald B. Richards, Richards' Forensic Services
December, 2008

The statement (letter) dated November 26, 1811, (referred to as the 11/26/1811 letter) signed Gilbert Russell and J. Williams and the October 31, 1811 letter (referred to as the 10/31/1811 letter) signed J. A. Wilkinson were compared to determine if they were, or were not, written by the same writer. In addition, they were compared with the known writing of Russell and Wilkinson, respectively, to determine if either individual wrote one or both letters.

Writing can only be compared to other comparable writing, i.e. upper case "A"s can only be compared to other upper case "A"s, and lower case "d"s can only be compared to other lower case "d"s. This can make the comparison extremely difficult if there are two relatively large bodies of writing that are similar in style and letter design, but composed of different letter combinations and words, such as in the case of these letters. The 11/26/1811 Russell letter is four pages long, and the 10/31/1811 Wilkinson letter is twelve pages long. To assist in determining which letter combinations and words are the same between the two documents, and inter-comparing that writing, a computer program was employed. This program has been used by Forensic Document Examiners for a number of years and is called "Write-On 2", Document Comparison Software, by Pikaso Software Inc., 528 River Road, Ottawa, Ontario, Canada, K1V 1E9, 613-859-6544, www.pikaso.com . To give an example, there are a total of 920 unique words in the two documents, there are 258 "the"s; 159 "of"s; 115 "and"s; and only 1 "weather"; "whose"; "wild"; and "washington"; etc. The program allows the examiner to determine what these common words and letter combinations are and then to see the actual written words on the computer screen.

Based on this examination it was determined that the 11/26/1811 Russell letter and the 10/31/1811 Wilkinson letter were both written by the same writer. It was further determined that it is highly probable that neither Gilbert Russell or J. A. Wilkinson wrote either the 11/26/1811 Russell letter or the 10/31/1811 Wilkinson letter. It is most likely that both of the questioned letters are "fair copies" of the original letters or drafts written by a third individual.

Appendix B: Department of Interior Letter

The following letter reversed the decision of the National Park Service rejecting the original application to exhume Meriwether Lewis. It is the latest and unreversed official statement on the subject which is being implemented at this time.

United States Department of the Interior
OFFICE OF THE SECRETARY
WASHINGTON DC 20240

BY FACSIMILE AND U.S. MAIL   JAN 11 2008
Mr. Steven P. Quarles, Esq.
Ms. Ann Klee, Esq.
Crowell & Moring
1 OO 1 Pennsylvania Avenue, NW
Washington, D.C. 20004-2595

Re: Application to Exhume the Remains of Meriwether Lewis

Dear Mr. Quarles:
Thank you for taking the time to meet with the National Park Service (NPS) and the Department of the Interior to discuss your clents' application for permission to exhume the remains of Mr. Meriwether Lewis from the grounds of the Meriwether Lewis National Monument. As you know, the regional director for the southeast region of the NPS denied your clients' application on the basis that the proposed action would conflict with NPS policy. You have asked my office for a review of this decision.

We have thoroughly and independently reviewed your clients' application under the Archeological Resources Protection Act (ARPA), associated provisions of the Code of Federal Regulations, and applicable provisions of the NPS Management Policies (2006) ("Management Policies"). We have analyzed your clients' plans for performing the exhumation in a minimally intrusive manner, their qualifications for research and study, and the historical values that would be served by the proposed exhumation of the remains. Additionally, we note with special consideration that Mr. Lewis's descendants overwhelmingly support the proposed exhumation.

Based on the material presented to us, the unique circumstances of the death of Meriwether Lewis, and the desires of the Lewis family, we believe that the applicants have presented compelling arguments and documentation that the proposed exhumation of Mr. Lewis may provide the public and the Lewis family with new and important information about his past. For these reasons we find that the applicants have demonstrated that the proposed exhumation of Mr. Lewis' mains for this purpose is appropriate and in the public interest.

As you may know, the final issuance of the requested permit will be subject to compliance with the National Environmental Policy Act. To facilitate the timely completion of this process, please make arrangements to meet with NPS staff at your nearest convenience to discuss, among other things: (1) the time and duration of the exhumation and study; (2) plans to access the park unit during the proposed activity; (3) anticipated disposition of an retrieved artifacts; (4) the scope of the environmental assessment and the costs thereof; and (5) the nature of your destructive analysis and expectations for the reburial ceremony. As background information, the NPS will provide the applicants, within 10 working days of this letter: (1) a copy of all documentation concerning the NPS reconstruction of the Meriwether Lewis National Monument in 2000-2001; and (2) a draft permit which will include substantially all conditions that the applicants must meet for final permit to issue.

Thank you again for your courtesy in this matter. In the event you have any concerns which require the immediate attention of this office, please feel free to call us at ███████████.

Sincerely,

Lyle Laverty (signed)
Assistant Secretary of the Interior
Fish and Wildlife and Parks

cc: Mary Bomar, Director of the National Park Service

Notes for
"The Case for Murder"
by Kira Gale

For further information and updates see:
www.deathofMeriwetherLewis.com
contact: kira@lewisandclarktravel.com

Returning Home in the Summer of 1806 (pp. 285-297)

Doctrine of Discovery (page 285)
See Robert J. Miller's *Native America, Discovered and Conquered: Thomas Jefferson, Lewis & Clark, and Manifest Destiny.* Jefferson's instructions to follow the Missouri River to its headwaters and take latitude and longitude readings at all important river junctions were based on the Doctrine of Discovery. The extent of the Louisiana Purchase would be revealed by the furthest extent of the Missouri River drainage system.

Blackfeet Indians (pages 286-289)
See *The Blackfeet: Raiders on the Northwestern Plains* by John C. Ewers (University of Oklahoma Press, 1958). Ewers quotes *New Light on the Early History of the Greater Northwest*, Volume 2, for the involvement of British traders, pages 539-40. He cites artist Alfred Jacob Miller as estimating in 1837 that 40-50 trappers were killed each season. See *The West of Alfred Jacob Miller*, p. 147 (University of Oklahoma, 1951/68). To read the journal entries for Lewis's encounter with the Blackfeet, see www.lewisandclarkroadtrips.com under the Historic Campsites tab for links to both the print and online journals. T*he Definitive Journals of Lewis & Clark: Over the Rockies to St. Louis*, edited by Gary Moulton (University of Nebraska Press, volume 8 of the Nebraska Edition, 1993) contains Lewis's entries for July 26-28, 1806 on pp. 127-139.

Welsh Indians/Mandan Indians (pages 291-292)
See *Footprints of the Welsh Indians: Settlers in North America before 1492* by William L. Traxel (Algora Publishing, 2004). *The Legend of Prince Madoc and the White Indians* by Dana Olson is available through the Falls of the Ohio Interpretive Center. Self-published in 1987, it contains much interesting information. The description of Big White as 6 feet ten inches tall appears in *Persimmon Hill: A Narrative of Old St. Louis and the Far West* by William Clark Kennerly as told to Elizabeth Russell, p. 18 (University of

Oklahoma Press, 1948). See also *Sheheke: Mandan Indian Diplomat: The Story of White Coyote, Thomas Jefferson, and Lewis and Clark* by Tracy Potter (Far Country Press, Fort Mandan Press 2003).

Spanish Expeditions and Lewis & Clark (pages 293-294)

See *Flood Tide of Empire: Spain and the Pacific Northwest, 1543-1819* by Warren L. Cook, pp. 446-83 (Yale University Press, 1973). Other information is found in *The Expeditions of Zebulon Pike*, Vol. II, pp. 409-422 regarding Pike's visit to the Pawnee village.

John McClellan Expedition (pages 295-296)

Gary Moulton discusses the McClellan Expedition and the probable death of Lewis and Clark members in a footnote on page 364, *Lewis and Clark Journals: Over the Rockies to St. Louis*. See also *The Nez Perce Indians and the Opening of the Northwest* by Alvin Josephy, Jr. pp. 36-39 (University of Nebraska Press, 1965). Regarding the trade goods, see *Tarnished Warrior: Major General James Wilkinson* by James Ripley Jacobs, p. 219 (MacMillan Co, 1938) and *Pedro Vial and the Roads to Santa Fe* by Noel M. Loomis and Abraham P. Nasatir, p. 238 (University of Oklahoma Press, 1967).

The Burr-Wilkinson Conspiracy (pp. 298–314)

The Burr-Wilkinson Conspiracy
Various topics are found in *The Burr Conspiracy* by Thomas Perkins Abernethy (Oxford University Press, 1954), the primary reference source. See:
  Andrew Jackson and Burr, pp. 71, 110-112
  Herrara's withdrawal from Sabine, pp. 146-47, 156-157
  Number of volunteers anticipated, pp. 102-107, 115, 148, 150-151
  Burr's flotilla, pp. 113, 204-209
  Fort Massac, pp.113-114
  Fort Pickering, pp.115-117
  Coup d'etat, New Orleans, pp. 165-171
  Mexican Association, pp. 25, 29, 30, 105,166-167, 272
  General Moreau, pp. 57-58, 92, 161
  James Madison and French party Spanish conspiracy, p. 306
  Plummer's Jefferson quote, pp. 197-198
  Pike-Wilkinson expedition, pp. 119, 156-157, 252
  Wilkinson's fake document for Jefferson p. 151-152
  War Department funds unaccounted for, p. 163
  Burr's escape and capture, pp. 218-226.

Herrara's Decision to Disobey Orders (pp. 307-308)
See Abernathy's *The Burr Conspiracy*, pages 155-157 and *The Expeditions of Zebulon Pike*, edited by Elliott Coues, volume II, pp. 702-04 (Dover Publications, 1987).

Burr-Hamilton Duel and Wilkinson (pp. 311-312)
See *Duel: Alexander Hamilton, Aaron Burr and the Future of America* by Thomas Fleming (Basic Books, Perseus Book Group, 1999)pp. 50-51 and 269-270. For Wilkinson's letter of March 16, 1804 to Hamilton see Volume 26, p. 217-218, *The Papers of Alexander Hamilton*, edited by Harold Syrett (Columbia University Press, 1979).

Cantonment Wilkinsonville (pp. 309-311)
"Searching for Cantonment Wilkinsonville" by Mark J. Wagner, a 22 page account of Professor Wagner's archeological and historical investigations, is posted on www.shawneecc.edu; www.southernmostillinoishistory.net also has many interesting links for the Cantonment and the Burr-Wilkinson Conspiracy. See also an article, "Cantonment Wilkinsonville" by Norman W. Caldwell, in *Mid-America, An Historical Review*, 1949, vol 1: no. 1, pp. 3-29. *The Search for Cantonment Wilkinsonville*, a DVD by Richard Kuenneke (2005), is available for purchase at www.clickonhistory.com. *Mr. Jefferson's Army: Political and Social Reform of the Military Establish-*

ment, 1801-1809 by Theodore J. Crackel, p. 44 (New York University, 1987) supplied the numbers for the army strength in 1802. See also Kira Gale's blog on the www.deathofmeriwetherlewis.com website.

Hamilton and the Quasi War with France (page 311-313)
See *The Quasi-War: The Politics and Diplomacy of the Undeclared War with France, 1797-1801* by Alexander De Conde, pp. 116-119 and 170-171 (Charles Scribner's Sons, 1966).

Philip Nolan's Filbuster (p. 310-311)
See "Philip Nolan's Entry into Texas in 1800" by Noel M. Loomis in *The Spanish in the Mississippi Valley, 1764-1804* edited by John Francis McDermott, pp. 120-132 (University of Illinois Press, 1974). Also, *Philip Nolan and Texas: Expeditions to the Unknown Land, 1791-1801* by Maurine T. Wilson and Jack Jackson (Texian Press, 1987).

If Burr Had Won the Election (pp. 309-311)
The letter by John R. Williams is found in T*he Expeditions of Zebulon Pike*, edited by Elliott Coues, Vol. I, pp. xxiii–xxx (Dover Publications. 1987). The remark by J. D. Daveiss is found in "View of a President's Conduct Concerning the Conspiracy of 1806," p. 89, *Quarterly Publication of the Historical and Philosophical Society of Ohio*, Vol XII, Nos. 2 & 3, 1917. (Also available online at www.archive.org)

Online Resources

Many texts are available online regarding Wilkinson, Burr and Blennerhassett, the conspiracy and the trial . See www.archive.org and Google Books. Both sites allow the texts to be browsed by keywords.

Burr's Conspiracy Exposed and General Wilkinson Vindicated Against the Slanders of His Enemies on that Important Occasion by James Wilkinson, pp. 90-99 (1811, Google Book Search). *Proofs of the Corruption of Gen. James Wilkinson* by Daniel Clark (1809, Google Book Search). *Memoirs of My Own Times* by General James Wilkinson, Vol II (1816, Google Book Search). *Three Years Among the Indians and Mexicans* by Thomas James,(1846 unabridged edition Google Book Search). For all subjects, *The Handbook of Texas* Online at www.tshaonline.org is an excellent source. Google Book Search is available at http://books.google.com.

The Thomas Jefferson Papers and James Madison Papers and many other historical documents and images are available online at the Library of Congress American Memory website. See www.memory.loc.gov to browse the collection of texts and images, which can be downloaded .

Back East (pp. 315–328)

Territorial Politics (pp. 315-17)
Territorial Papers, Louisiana–Missouri Territory, compiled and edited by Clarence Edwin Carter, Vol. XIII (1803-06) and Vol. XIV (1806-14) published by the U. S. Gov't. Printing Office.

Auguste Chouteau July 15, 1806 to President, Vol. XIII, pp. 550-555

John B.C. Lucas Aug 5, 1806 to Sec. of Treasury, Vol. XIII, pp. 559-67

Will Carr, November 14, 1805 to Sec. of Treasury, Vol. XIII, pp.273-74

Will Carr September 1, 1806 to Sec. of Treasury, Vol. XIV, pp. 6-7

Samuel Smith September 16, 1806 to President, Vol. XIV, p. 8

Silas Bent to Jared Mansfield, October 5, 1806 Vol. XIV, pp. 13-14

Will Carr November 22, 1806 to Sec. of Treasnury, Vol. XIV, pp. 38-39

Rufus Easton December 1, 1806 to President, Vol XIV, pp. 43-46

President January 4, 1807 to Sec. of Treasury, Vol. XIV, pp. 57-58

Lewis's Boundary Line Survey (p. 318)
Lewis's letter to Colonel Arthur Campbell, dated Wallings, November 23, 1806 certifying the survey of the boundary line. Grace Lewis Miller Archives, Jefferson National Expansion Memorial.

Letters Regarding Travel (pp. 317-18)
Clark's letter to his brother, September 24, 1806, stating Lewis would travel with the Indians to Washington—*Dear Brother: Letters of William Clark to Jonathan Clark*, edited by James Holmberg (Yale University Press, 2002). The President's letter to Lewis, Oct. 26, 1806 with invitation to visit Monticello—*Letters of the Lewis and Clark Expedition,* edited by Donald Jackson, Vol. II, pp. 350-351 (University of Illinois Press, 2nd edition, 1978)

Smith T. and Lead for the Burr Conspiracy (pp. 319-21)
The information about the 12,000 pounds of lead comes from the Harry Burke papers, "Moses Austen and the Lead for Aaron Burr," an undated typescript, at the Missouri History Museum. The immense value of the land is discussed in Will Carr's letter of Nov. 14, 1805 in *Territorial Papers.* See also:

"Burr-Wilkinson Intrigue in St. Louis" by Clarence E. Carter, *Bulletin* of the Missouri Historical Society, Vol. X, No 4, Part 1, pp. 447-465 *Personal Recollections of John F. Darby*, pp. 58-65 (Hawthorne Publishing Co., 1880, reprint circa 1978). *Frontier Swashbuckler: The Life and Legend of John Smith T.* by Dick Steward, pp. 71-85 (University of Missouri Press, 2000). *Lead King: Moses Austin* by James Alexander Gardner, pp. 111-121 (Sunrise Publishing Co., 1980). *Moses Austin: His Life* by David Gracy II, pp. 94-118 (Trinity University Press, 1987). *Opening*

the Ozarks: *A Historical Geography of Missouri's Ste. Genevieve District,*
1760-1830 by Walter A. Schroeder, pp. 136-145 (University of Missouri
Press, 2002). *The Genesis of Missouri: From Wilderness Outpost to Statehood* by William Foley, pp. 180-181 (Univ. of Missouri Press, 1989)

Lewis in Philadelphia (pp. 321-22)
A History of the Lewis and Clark Journals by Paul Cutright, pp. 40-49 (University of Oklahoma Press, 1976). Selected Papers of Charles Willson Peale
and His Family: Volume 2, Part 2, *Charles Willson Peale: The Artist as Museum Keeper, 1791-1810* edited by Lillian B. Miller, pp. 1012, 1018, 1027,
1037, 1053, 1056-57 (Yale University Press, 1988). *Lewis and Clark Across
the Divide* by Carolyn Gilman pp. 69,121, 139, 340-43, 357, 368, 370-71,
377 (Smithsonian Press, 2003)

Burrism in St Louis (pp. 322-323)
Robert Fraser to Jefferson, document # 266, pp. 409-410, *Letters of the
Lewis and Clark Expedition,* edited by Donald Jackson (University of Il-
linois Press, 2nd edition, 1978). Frederick Bates to Jefferson, pp. 120-21,
Territorial Papers, Vol. XIV.

Attempted Return of Mandan Delegation in 1807 (pp. 323-325)
William Clark to Sec. of War, pp. 126-7, *Territorial Papers,* Vol. XIV
Nathaniel Pryor to William Clark, pp. 432-38, *Letters of Lewis and Clark
Expedition,* edited by Donald Jackson *Sheheke, Mandan Indian Diplomat*
by Tracy Potter, pp. 137-47 (Far Country Press, Fort Mandan Press, 2003).

Aaron Burr Treason Trial (pp. 325-328)
The Debates and Proceedings in the Congress of the United States (also known
as the Annals of Congress) are now available on Google Books. The testimony of the Aaron Burr Trial can be found by doing a keyword search. It
was entered into the record of the Tenth Congress, 1st session. *History of
the United States of America During the Administrations of Thomas Jefferson*
by Henry Adams, pp. 907-29 (Library of America, 1986). Thomas Danisi,
biographer of Meriwether Lewis, located a letter from Wilkinson to President Jefferson, dated September 15, 1807 that places Lewis at the trial. See
Library of Congress American Memory website for Jefferson papers.

Lewis's Report on Indian Affairs (pp. 327-328)
The report is document #443, "Observations and Reflections of Lewis," pp.
696-719, in the *Letters of the Lewis and Clark Expedition,* edited by Donald
Jackson (University of Illinois Press, 2nd edition, 1978).

Personal Affairs (p. 328)
The Lewis brothers visit to Fincastle is discussed in *The Visits of Lewis &
Clark to Fincastle, Virginia* by Gene Crotty, pp. 54-56 (History Museum
and Historical Society of Western Virginia, 2003).

St. Louis, 1808-09 (pp. 329-342)

The Missouri Gazette (pp. 329, 334-335)
Grace Lewis Miller's master's thesis from the University of Texas in 1948 is at the Jefferson National Expansion Memorial Archives, "His Excellency Meriwether Lewis and the First Publication West of the Mississippi River." See p.p. 66-69 for discussion of the printing press; pp. 91-96 for discussion of finances; and page 77 for the "sudden illness." *Wilderness Journey: The Life of William Clark* by William E. Foley (University of Missouri Press, 2004) See pp. 166-69. *Joseph Charless: Printer in the Western Country* by David Kaser, pp. 58-76 (University of Pennsylvania Press, 1963).

William and Julia Clark (pp. 329-330)
"The First House of Governor Lewis in Louisiana Territory" by Grace Lewis Miller in *William & Mary Quarterly*, pp 357-68. *Dear Brother: Letters of William Clark to Jonathan Clark*, edited by James Holmberg (Yale University Press, 2002). See pp. 126-26 for Big Bone Lick; pp. 141, 158, 164, 200-05, 212 for York. *Lion of the Valley: St. Louis, Missouri* by James Neal Primm (Prouett Publishing Co, 1981) See pp. 80-92 for life in early St. Louis.

Territorial Masonry (p. 331)
Territorial Masonry: The Story of Freemasonry and the Louisiana Purchase, 1804-21 by Ray Vaughan Denslow (Missouri Lodge of Research, 1990) See pp. 84-96 for "The Lodge of Meriwether Lewis."

Frederick Bates (pp. 331-333)
The Life and Papers of Frederick Bates edited by Thomas Maitland Marshall (Missouri Historical Society, St. Louis, two volumes, 1926) Frederick Bates to Richard Bates, July 14, 1809, pp. 67-73, Vol. II. Frederick Bates to Richard Bates, November 9, 1809, pp. 108-112, Vol. II *Suicide or Murder? The Strange Death of Meriwether Lewis* by Vardis Fisher pp. 87-88 for letter of Captain House (Swallow Press, 1962)

Land Investments (pp. 333-334)
"The Landed Estate of Meriwether Lewis in Louisiana Territory" (1970) and "Life as Governor Until Death," Part III of notes for an unpublished biography by Grace Lewis Miller (Grace Lewis Miller Archives, Jefferson National Expansion Memorial).

The Smith Brothers and the "Invisibles" (pp. 335-336)
James Madison: A Biography by Ralph Ketcham, pp. 481-91 (University of Virginia Press, 1990) *Albert Gallatin: Jeffersonian Financier and Diplomat* by Raymond Walters, Jr., pp. 223-36 (MacMillan Company, 1957)

Burr in Europe (p. 336)
Political Correspondence and Public Papers of Aaron Burr, edited by Mary-Jo Kline, pp. 1040-46, 1047-49, 1116-119.

The Return of the Mandans (pp. 336-338)
Sheheke Mandan Indian Diplomat: The Story of White Coyote, Thomas Jefferson, and Lewis and Clark by Tracy Potter, p. 60 for population; and pp. 147-72 for exile in St. Louis and return. The Toussaint Jessaume Indenture papers are in the Lewis & Clark Collection, Missouri History Museum

Treaty with the Osages (pp. 339-341)
The Imperial Osages: Spanish-Indian Diplomacy in the Mississippi Valley by Gilbert C. Din and Abraham P. Nasatir, pp. 357-84. (University of Oklahoma Press, 1983) *William Clark: Indian Diplomat* by Jay H. Buckley, pp. 65-88 (University of Oklahoma Press, 2008)

Correspondence (pp. 339-341)
The letters to and from the Secretary of War and the President are included in *The Territorial Papers of the United States,* compiled and edited by Clarence E. Carter, pp.285-86 289-97, 312-319. The letter from Lewis to Chouteau is found in the Grace Lewis Miller Archives, 1809 correspondence. Thomas Danisi identified the handwriting of Jeremiah Connor. See *Meriwether Lewis* by Thomas C. Danisi and John C. Jackson, pp. 282. n. 38, 293, 335 (Prometheus Books, 2009).

Online Resources

Interactive Map of Old St. Louis Online

Bob Moore, the NPS historian at Jefferson National Expansion Memorial has created an interactive map of the old riverfront. The website is: http://www.nps.gov/jeff/historyculture/people.htm There are other interesting materials on this site, including papers presented at Lewis and Clark Sympoisums held at the Arch in 2001-2004.

Finding Aids to St Louis Archival Collections
Grace Lewis Miller Archives, Jefferson National Expansion Memorial are located in the Old Court House in St. Louis.
http://www.nps.gov/jeff/historyculture/grace-lewis-miller-papers.htm

Missouri History Museum Library and Research Center
http://www.mohistory.org/lrc-home

www.deathofMeriwetherLewis.com for the latest updates.

The Last Days (pp. 343-52)

Meriwether Lewis's Will (p. 343)

The will was recorded at the Albemarle County Court house, which has a copy. The original, a torn page, is at the Unversity of Virginia Archives in the Lewis-Marks Collection. A copy is on file at the Missouri History Museum in St. Louis.

Malaria (p. 343-344)

Or Perish in the Attempt: Wilderness Medicine in the Lewis & Clark Expedition by David J. Peck, M.D. , p. 49, pp. 294-95. (Far Country Press, 2002) *Lion of the Valley: St. Louis, Missouri* by James Neal Primm, p. 359 (Pruett Publishing Company, 1981)

James Neely and the Newspaper Ad (pp. 345-47)

The Jefferson Conspiracies: A President's Role in the Assassination of Meriwether Lewis by David Leon Chandler, pp. 287-298 (William Morrow and Company, 1994) *Suicide or Murder?: The Strange Death of Governor Meriwether Lewis* by Vardis Fisher, pp. 127-38 (Swallow Press, 1962) *Democratic-Clarion newspaper*, October 20, 1809 (Tennessee State Library and Archives). Letters Received by the Secretary of War, Record Group 107, M-221, rolls 27 and 39 for Neely's correspondence.

Benjamin Wilkinson (p. 347)

Annals of St. Louis in its Territorial Days from 1804 to 1821 by Frederic Billon, p. 269 (Arno Press & The New York Times, 1971)

Lewis's Trunks at the Fort (pp. 347-349)

The Thomas Jefferson Papers, American Memory, Library of Congress website. Do a search for Jefferson to Madison, November 26, 1809.

Lewis's Last Night and Burial (p. 350-352)

By His Own Hand? The Mysterious Death of Meriwether Lewis, edited by John D. W. Guice, p. 94 (University of Oklahoma Press, 2006) *Lewis and Clark: Partners in Discovery* by John Bakeless, pp. 419-422 (William Morrow & Company, 1947) Bakeless's classic biography contains the information about Grinder's farm. *Colonel Robert Melville Cooper and the Meriwether Lewis Death Story* is available on the Alabama Genealogy website. www.algen.us Do a search for "death of Meriwether Lewis." It is under "Davidson County Newpaper Articles." Or else do a general web search for the above title. It was originally printed in a family history. *Tragedy at Grinder's Stand: The Death of Meriwether Lewis,* a Master's thesis by Martin Cooper Avery, Middle Tennessee State University, 1978 has information about the coroner's inquest and its jury and events surrounding his death.

Motives for Assassination (pp. 353–368)

Land Claims and John Smith T. (pp. 353-354)
Duels and the Roots of Violence in Missouri by Dick Steward, pp. 24-30 (University of Missouri Press, 2000). *Frontier Swashbuckler: The Life and Legend of John Smith T.* by Dick Steward, pp. 88-97 (University of Missouri Press, 2000). *Territorial Papers of the United States, Vol. XIV, Louisiana-Missouri Territory, 1806-1814* compiled and edited by Clarence E. Carter, pp. 365-368 (Government Printing Office, 1949).

Captain James House's Letter (pp. 354-57)
Suicide or Murder?: The Strange Death of Governor Meriwether Lewis by Vardis Fisher, pp. 87, 236 (Swallow Press, 1962). Frederick Bates Collection, Missouri History Museum.

Frederick Bates's Letters (pp. 356-359)
The Life and Papers of Frederick Bates edited by Thomas Maitland Marshall, Vol II, pp. 67-73, 77-79, 108-112 (Missouri Historical Society, St Louis 1926).

Citizen's Committee (pp. 360-361)
Territorial Papers of the United States, Vol. XIV, Louisiana-Missouri Territory, 1806-1814 compiled and edited by Clarence E. Carter, pp. 334-42, 353-374 (Government Printing Office, 1949).

Reuben Smith's Expedition to Sante Fe and the Guttierez-Magee Filibuster Expedition (pp. 361-363)
Frontier Swashbuckler: The Life and Legend of John Smith T. by Dick Steward, pp. 97-110 (University of Missouri Press, 2000). "Reuben Smith" by W. A. Goff in *The Mountain Men and the Fur Trade of the Far West,* Vol. 7, edited by Le Roy R. Hafen, pp. 261-279 (Arthur H. Clark Company, 1969). *Personal Recollections of John F. Darby: Mayor of St. Louis, 1835* by John F. Darby, p. 63 (Hawthorn Publishing Company, reprint of 1880 edition, nd). *Pedro Vial and the Roads to Sante Fe* by Noel M. Loomis and Abraham P. Nasatir, pp. 250-51 (University of Oklahoma Press, 1967). *The Sword Was Their Passport: A History of American Filibustering in the Mexican Revolution* by Harris Gaylord Warren, pp 23-26 (Kennikat Press, 1943/1972). *Green Flag Over Texas: A Story of the Last Years of Spain in Texas* by Julia Kathryn Garrett, pp. 24-25 (Cordova Press, 1939, reprint UMI Books on Demand, 2008). *Three Years Among the Indians and Mexicans* by Thomas James, unabridged edition with Appendices, pp. 286-92 (J. B. Lippincott, 1962).

General James Wilkinson (pp. 363-367)
Tarnished Warrior: Major-General James Wilkinson by James Ripley Jacobs, pp. 246-274 (MacMillan Company, 1938). *The Beginnings of the U. S. Army, 1783-1812* by James Ripley Jacobs, pp. 342-355 (Princeton University Press, 1949). *Proofs of the Corruption of Gen. James Wilkinson and of His Connexion with Aaron Burr: A Full Refutation of His Slanderous Allegations in Relation to the Character of the Principal Witness Against Him* by Daniel Clark (University Press of the Pacific, 2005).

Lewis's Estate (p. 365)
The estate settlement, filed on February 8, 1815 by Edward Hempstead is on file at the Missouri History Museum. Lewis's estate paying for the Territorial Laws is found in Grace Lewis Miller's thesis, pp. 84-85, "His Excellency Meriwether Lewis and the First Publication West of the Mississippi River" in the Grace Lewis Miller Archives at the Jefferson National Expansion Memorial in St. Louis.

Online Resources

The Library of Congress American Memory website has an abundance of historical materials, including the Thomas Jefferson Papers, with the original letters available for download. www.memory.loc.gov

The Library and Research Center of the Missouri History Museum is another source of materials, with many of their archives itemized on line.

Grace Lewis Miller Archives, Jefferson National Expansion Memorial are located in the Old Court House in St. Louis. The finding aid, compiled by Ruth Frick is available for download.
http://www.nps.gov/jeff/historyculture/grace-lewis-miller-papers.htm

The Texas State History Online website has many excellent articles.
http://www.tshaonline.org

Tennessee State Library and Archives
http://www.tennessee.gov/tsla/

www.deathofmeriwetherlewis.com for the latest updates.

Bibliography

Abernethy, Thomas Perkins. *The Burr Conspiracy*. New York: Oxford University Press, 1954.

Ambrose, Stephen E. *Undaunted Courage: Meriwether Lewis, Thomas Jefferson and the Opening of the American West*. New York: Simon & Schuster, 1996.

Armstrong, Thom M. *Politics, Diplomacy and Intrigue in the Early Republic: The Cabinet Career of Robert Smith 1801-1811*. Dubuque, Iowa: Kendall/Hunt Publishing Company, 1991.

Bakeless, John. *Lewis and Clark: Partners in Discovery*. Lundberg Press, 2007.

Bass, Dr. Bill and Jon Jefferson. *Beyond the Body Farm: A Legendary Bone Detective Explores Murders, Mysteries, and the Revolution in Forensic Science*. New York: William Morrow, 2007.

Bates, Frederick. *The Life and Papers of Frederick Bates*. Edited by Thomas Maitland Marshall. 2 vol. St. Louis: Missouri Historical Society,1926.

Bernier, Olivier. *The World in 1800*. New York: John Wiley & Sons, 2000.

Brown, Gordon S. *Toussaint's Clause: The Founding Fathers and the Haitian Revolution*. Jackson: University Press of Mississippi, 2005.

Buckley, Jay H. *William Clark: Indian Diplomat*. Norman: University of Oklahoma Press, 2008.

Burr, Aaron. *Political Correspondence and Public Papers of Aaron Burr*. Edited by Mary-Jo Kline. 2 volumes. Princeton: Yale University Press, 1983.

Cantwell, Robert. *Alexander Wilson: Naturalist and Pioneer, A Biography*. Philadelphia: J. B. Lippincott Company, 1961.

Carter, Clarence E.. editor. *The Territorial Papers of the United States*. 28 volumes. GPO, 1934-1962.
   Volume XIII, Louisiana-Missouri Territory, 1803-1806
   Volume XIV, Lousiana-Missouri Territory, 1806-1814
—— "The Burr-Wilkinson Intrigue in St. Louis." Missouri Historical Society *Bulletin* 10 (July, 1954): 447-64.

Casswell, Frank A. *Merchant Congressman in the Young Republic: Samuel Smith of Maryland 1752-1839*. Madison: Univ. of Wisconsin, 1971.

Chandler, David Leon. *The Jefferson Conspiracies: A President's Role in the Assassination of Meriwether Lewis*. New York: William Morrow and Company, 1994.

Chuinard, Eldon G., M.D. *Only One Man Died: The Medical Aspects of the Lewis & Clark Expedition*. Fairfield, Wash: Ye Galleon Press, 1979.

Clark, Daniel. *Proofs of the Corruption of Gen. James Wilkinson and of His Connexion with Aaron Burr: A Full Refutation of His Slanderous Allegations in Relation to the Character of the Principal Witness Against Him.*

Bibliography

Honolulu, Hawaii: University Press of the Pacific, 2005.

Clark, Thomas D. and John D. W. Guice. *Frontiers in Conflict: The Old Southwest 1795-1830.* Albuquerque: Univ of New Mexico Press, 1989.

Clark, William. *Dear Brother: Letters of William Clark to Jonathan Clark.* Edited and with an introduction by James J. Holmberg. New Haven: Yale University Press, 2002.

Coates, Robert M. *The Outlaw Years.* Foreword by John D. W. Guice, Lincoln: University of Nebraska Press, 1986 (1930).

Colby, Susan M. *Sacagawea's Child: The Life and Times of Jean-Baptiste (Pomp) Charbonneau.* Spokane, Wash: Arthur H. Clark Co., 2005.

Colter-Frick, L. R. *Courageous Colter and Companions.* Self-published, 1997.

Cook, Warren L. *Flood Tide of Empire: Spain and the Pacific Northwest, 1543-1819.* New Haven: Yale University Press, 1973.

Côté, Richard N. *Theodosia Burr Alston: Portrait of a Prodigy.* Mount Pleasant, North Carolina: Corinthian Books, 2003.

Coues, Elliot, editor. *The Expeditions of Zebulon Montgomery Pike.* 2 vol. New York: Dover Publications, 1986.

Cox, Isaac Joslin. *The West Florida Controversy, 1798-1813.* Reprint. Johns Hopkins Press, 1918.

Crackel, Theodore J. *Mr. Jefferson's Army: Political and Social Reform of the Military Establishment, 1801-1809.* New York: New York University Press, 1987.

Daniels, Jonathan. *The Devil's Backbone: The Story of the Natchez Trace.* New York: McGraw Hill Book Company, 1962.

Danisi, Thomas & John C. Jackson, *Meriwether Lewis.* Amhert, New York: Prometheus Books, 2009.

Darby, John F. *Personal Recollections of John F. Darby, Mayor of St. Louis, 1835.* Reprint. Hawthorn Publishing Company, original date, 1880.

De Conde, Alexander. *The Quasi-War: The Politics and Diplomacy of the Undeclared War with France, 1797-1801.* New York: Charles Scribner's Sons, 1966.

Denig, Edwin Thompson. *Five Indian Tribes of the Upper Missouri: Sioux, Arickaras, Assiniboines, Crees, Crows.* Edited and with an introduction by John C. Ewers. Norman: University of Oklahoma Press, 1961.

Dillon, Richard. *Meriwether Lewis: A Biography.* Lafayette, California: Great West Books, 2003.

Douglas, Walter B. *Manuel Lisa.* Edited and annotated by Abraham P. Nasatir. New York: Argosy-Antiquarian, Ltd., 1964.

Ewers, John C. *The Blackfeet: Raiders on the Northwestern Plains.* Norman: University of Oklahoma Press, 1958.

Fehrenbach, T. R. *Fire & Blood: A History of Mexico.* New York: Da Capo Press edition, 1995. First published, 1973.

Bibliography

Fisher, Vardis. *Suicide or Murder? The Strange Death of Governor Meriwether Lewis.* Athens, Ohio: Swallow Press, 1962.

Foley, William E. *The Genesis of Missouri: From Wilderness Outpost to Statehood.* Columbia: University of Missouri Press, 1989.

——*Wilderness Journey: The Life of William Clark.* Columbia: University of Missouri Press, 2004.

Fleming, Thomas. *Duel: Alexander Hamilton, Aaron Burr and the Future of America.* Basic Books, Perseus Books Group, 1999.

Friedenberg, Daniel M. *Life, Liberty and the Pursuit of Land: The Plunder of Early America.* Buffalo, New York: Prometheus Books, 1992.

Gale, Kira. *Lewis and Clark Road Trips: Exploring the Trail Across America.* Omaha, Nebraska: River Junction Press LLC, 2006.

Gardner, James A. *Lead King: Moses Austin.* St. Louis: Sunrise, 1980

Garrett, Julia Kathryn. *Green Flag Over Texas.* Reprint. Cordova Press, 1939.

Gaspar, David Barry and David Patrick Geggus, editors. *A Turbulent Time: The French Revolution and the Greater Caribbean.* Bloomington: Indiana University Press, 1997.

Gibson, Arrell. *The Chickasaws.* Norman: Univ. of Oklahoma Press, 1971.

Gilman, Carolyn. *Lewis and Clark Across the Divide.* Smithsonian Books/ Missouri Historical Society, 2003.

Gracy, David B. II. *Moses Austin: His Life.* Trinity University Press, 1987.

Guice, John D. W., editor. *By His Own Hand? The Mysterious Death of Meriwether Lewis.* Norman: Oklahoma University Press, 2006.

Hallcox, Jarrett and Amy Welch. *Bodies We've Buried: Inside the National Forensic Academy, the World's Top CSI Training School.* Foreword by Dr. Bill Bass. New York: Berkley Books, 2006.

Hay, Thomas Robson and M. R. Werner. *The Admirable Trumpeter: A Biography of General James Wilkinson.* Doubleday, Doran & Co., 1941.

Hunter, Clark. *The Life and Letters of Alexander Wilson.* Philadelphia: American Philosophical Society, 1983.

Isenberg, Nancy. *Fallen Founder: The Life of Aaron Burr.* New York: Viking Press, 2007.

Jacobs, James Ripley. *Tarnished Warrior: Major-General James Wilkinson.* New York: MacMillan Company, 1938.

——*The Beginnings of the U. S. Army, 1783-1812.* Princeton, New Jersey: Princeton University Press, 1947.

Jackson, Donald. *Letters of the Lewis and Clark Expedition.* 2nd edition. 2 vol. Champaign: University of Illinois Press, 1978.

Jackson, John C. *The Piikani Blackfeet: A Culture Under Siege.* Missoula, Montana: Mountain Press Publishing Company, 2000.

James, Thomas. *Three Years Among the Indians and Mexicans.* Reprint. University of Nebraska Press, 1984.

Bibliography

Jones, Landon Y. Jones. *William Clark and the Shaping of the West.* New York: Hill and Wang, 2004.

Kaser, David. *Joseph Charless: Printer in the Western Country.* Philadelphia: University of Pennsylvania Press, 1963.

Ketcham, Ralph. *James Madison: A Biography.* Charlottesville: University of Virginia Press, 1990.

Linklater, Andro. *The Fabric of America: How Our Borders and Boundaries Shaped the Country and Forged Our National Identity.* New York: Walker and Company, 2007.

Loomis, Noel M. and Abraham P. Nasatir. *Pedro Vial and the Roads to Sante Fe.* Norman: University of Oklahoma Press, 1967.

Luttig, John C. *Journal of a Fur-Trading Expedition on the Upper Missouri 1812-1813.* Preface and notes by Abraham P. Nasatir. New York: Argosy-Antiquarian Ltd., 1964.

Mathews, Catharine VanCortlandt. *Andrew Ellicott: His Life and Letters.* Alexander, North Carlina: WorldComm, 2001.

McCaleb, Walter Flavius. *The Aaron Burr Conspiracy.* Honolulu, Hawaii: University Press of the Pacific, 2006.

McDermott, John Francis, editor. *The Spanish in the Mississippi Valley 1762-1804.* Champaign: University of Illinois Press, 1974.

Meyer, Roy W. *The Village Indians of the Upper Missouri.* Lincoln: University of Nebraska Press, 1971.

Miller, Grace Lewis. *Finding Aid to the Grace Lewis Miller Papers.* Compiled by Ruth Frick. National Park Service, 1999.

—— "His Excellency Meriwether Lewis and the First Publications West of the Mississippi River." Master's Thesis, University of Texas, 1948.

—— "The First Home of Governor Lewis in Louisiana Territory." Missouri Historical Society *Bulletin*, XIV (July, 1958), pp. 357-368)

—— "Financial Records: 'Expedition to the Pacific Ocean.'" Missouri Historical Society *Bulletin*, X (July, 1954), pp. 465-489.

Miller, Robert J. *Native America, Discovered and Conquered: Thomas Jefferson, Lewis & Clark, and Manifest Destiny.* Westport, Conn: Praeger, 2006.

Montgomery, M. R. *Jefferson and the Gun-Men: How the West Was Almost Lost.* New York: Crown Publishers, 2000.

Morris, Larry E. *The Fate of the Corps: What Became of the Lewis & Clark Explorers After the Expedition.* New Haven: Yale University Press, 2004.

Moulton, Gary, editor. *The Lewis and Clark Journals.* Lincoln: University of Nebraska Press, 1983-2001.

Oglesby, Richard E. *Manuel Lisa and the Opening of the Missouri Fur Trade.* Norman: University of Oklahoma Press, 1963.

Olson, Dana. *The Legend of Prince Madoc and the White Indians.* Jeffer-

Bibliography

sonville, Indiana: Olson Enterprises, 1987.

Owsley, Frank Lawrence, Jr. and Gene A. Smith. *Filibusters and Expansionists: Jefferson Manifest Destiny, 1800-1821*. Tuscaloosa: University of Alabama Press, 1997.

Peck, David J., D. O. *Or Perish in the Attempt: Wilderness Medicine in the Lewis and Clark Expedition*. Far Country Press, 2002.

Potter, Tracy. *Sheheke, Mandan Indian Diplomat: The Story of White Coyote, Thomas Jefferson, and Lewis & Clark*. Far Country Press, 2003.

Pratt, Julius W. *Expansionists of 1812*. Gloucester, MA: Peter Smith, 1957.

Richardson, Edgar P. & Brooke Hindle, Lillian B. Miller. *Charles Willson Peale and His World*. New York: Harry N. Abrams, 1982.

Schroeder, Walter A. *Opening the Ozarks: A Historical Geography of Missouri's Ste. Genevieve District 1760-1830*. Columbia: University of Missouri Press, 2002.

Shreve, Royal Ornan. *The Finished Scoundrel: General James Wilkinson, sometime Commander-in-Chief of the Army of the United States, who made intrigue a trade and treason a profession*. Indianapolis: Bobbs-Merrill Company, 1933.

Starrs, James E. with Katherine Ramsland. *A Voice for the Dead: A Forensic Investigator's Pursuit of the Truth in the Grave*. New York: Berkeley Books, 2005.

——*Meriwether Lewis: His Death and His Monument, An Historical and Pictorial Portfolio*. Self-published, 1997.

Steward, Dick. *Frontier Swashbuckler: The Life & Legend of John Smith T.* Columbia: University of Missouri Press, 2000.

——*Duels and the Roots of Violence in Missouri*. Columbia: University of Missouri, 2000.

Sublette, Ned. *The World That Made New Orleans: From Spanish Silver to Congo Square*. Chicago: Lawrence Hill Press, 2008.

Traxel, William L. *Footprints of the Welsh Indians: Settlers in North America Before 1492*. New York: Algora Publishing, 2004.

Walters, Raymond Jr. *Albert Gallatin: Jeffersonian Financier and Diplomat*. New York: MacMillan Company, 1957.

Warren, Harris Gaylord. *The Sword Was Their Passport: A History of American Filibustering in the Mexican Revolution*. Port Washington, New York: Kennikat Press, 1972 (1943 reprint).

Weber, David J. *The Spanish Frontier in North America*. New Haven: Yale University Press, 1992.

Wilkinson, General James. *Memoirs of My Own Times*. 3 volumes. Reprint. Philadelphia, 1816.

Wilson, Maurine T. and Jack Jackson. *Philip Nolan and Texas: Expeditions to the Unknown Land, 1791-1801*. Waco: Texian Press, 1987.

Index